AND

RUS

CW00349133

VAKIA

NGARY

RUMANIA

OSLAVIA

Black Sea

BULGARIA

Albania

GREECE

TURKEY

Athens

CYPRUS

CRETE

'Bomb Alley'

Mersa Matruh

El Alámein

Alexandria

Port Said

Tobruk

Benghazi

Suez

Cairo

BYA

EGYPT

MALTA HISTORIC AIRCAFT
PRESERVATION GROUP
161, SPITFIRE MEMORIAL
CRAFT VILLAGE TA'QALI
EXP NO 1402-1835
14:23   04-12-2006
                              9210
DEPT. 7   5.000 F

SUBTOTAL   5.000 F

TOTAL   5.000
  TL ITEMS   1
        ✓✓ AA 01002868

AGAINST ALL ODDS

RAAF pilots in the Battle for Malta 1942

LEX McAULAY

HUTCHINSON AUSTRALIA

Century Hutchinson Australia Pty Ltd
20 Alfred Street, Milsons Point, New South Wales 2061

Sydney Melbourne London
Auckland Johannesburg
and agencies throughout the world

First published 1989

National Library of Australia
Cataloguing-in-Publication Data

McAulay, Lex, 1939-
  Against all odds.

  ISBN 0 09 169570 8.

  1. Australia. Royal Australian Air Force. 2. World
  War, 1939-1945—Aerial operations, British.
  3. World War, 1939-1945—Campaigns—Malta.
  4. Air pilots, Military—Australia. I. Title.

940.54'4994

Typeset by Midland Typesetters, Maryborough, Victoria
Printed in Singapore
Production by Vantage Graphics, Sydney

Contents

Introduction

Malta has been of crucial importance to the future of Western Europe on more than one occasion. In 1565 it withstood a siege by the Turks, who were then trying to bring Europe into the fold of Islam. From 1940 to 1942 it withstood the concentrated might of the Italian Regia Aeronautica and the German Luftwaffe, and was instrumental in disrupting supplies to the Axis forces in North Africa. Without these attacks on shipping from Malta, Rommel would have been well enough supplied and equipped to have reached the Suez Canal and changed the course of the war.

The small band of Australian fighter pilots who flew and fought in RAF squadrons over Malta in the months of 1942, when that island was one of the most important defenders of the future of Western democracy, has received little acknowledgement of their exploits. They flew in what was the most intense and prolonged period of operations experienced by RAAF fighter pilots during the Second World War.

Always outnumbered, to all intents and purposes marooned on a small island hundreds of miles from friendly forces, on starvation diets, and sometimes ill, the RAF squadrons flew in defence of a tiny stronghold of the British Commonwealth which many military and political minds thought should have been surrendered at the beginning of hostilities.

There has been a flood of books about the Second World War, and the air war over Europe has been well documented in official histories, non-fiction books, novels, film and TV. But, apart from brief references in the official histories, and a few articles in wartime newspapers, little is known of the RAAF pilots who were sent to Malta.

Recently, there has been a number of books about the battles for Malta, and these deal with the entire campaign or the part

1

played by various units in it. It is not my intention to over-emphasise the part played by the RAAF pilots in 1942, but merely to present, in one book, the Australian contribution to the defence of Malta.

The wartime squadrons of the RAF were probably unique in the history of warfare for the way in which men and women of many nationalities worked together through years of hardship, defeat and triumph, despite the loss of many friends, to achieve victory over a common foe. I am sure that the members of the RAAF portrayed in this book would not want their actions presented as being superior to those of their fellows of other Allied Air Forces, and it is not my intention to do so.

My simple wish is that through these pages the part played in a decisive campaign by young Australian volunteers may be better known to their countrymen and friends.

In that spirit, the book is dedicated to all those volunteers for the RAAF 1939-45.

*   *   *

This book is also dedicated to my wife, Josephine, for her continued patience as this writing project and others contribute to the controlled disorder in my study.

1

First Storm

Malta—June 1940 to March 1942

On 10 June 1940, the day the German forces crossed the Seine, and Mussolini declared war on France and the British Commonwealth, the island of Malta seemed to be an easy conquest for the Italian forces. Malta produced only about one-third of its food requirements; there were no stocks of food; fourteen obsolescent coastal guns; an airfield with a few bi-plane fighters but no modern aircraft; a first-class harbour but no modern defences; no spare parts or adequate reserve of fuel; no modern construction or rock-drilling equipment; few of the technicians necessary in modern war; long distances to friendly bases at Gibraltar or Alexandria. But the Italian Air Force, the Regia Aeronautica, had bases in Sicily, only one hundred kilometres to the north, and recently had been singing its own praises after the campaigns in Abyssinia and the Spanish Civil War.

British naval and military strength on Malta consisted of seven submarines, twelve motor-torpedo-boats and their supply ships, plus four weak infantry battalions with some anti-aircraft units. There was no air force as such, but an *ad hoc* arrangement, later to go into legend, had been created with RAF pilots from various places on Malta and Royal Navy bi-planes.

Before September 1939, it had been decided that the island was indefensible in modern war, and so no preparations had been made to hold it against the Italians. For their own part, the Italians had completed plans in 1938 for the invasion and occupation of Malta. However, Admiral Cunningham, the Royal Navy commander, had long urged a more positive view, and when Winston Churchill replaced the ineffectual Neville Chamberlain

3

as Prime Minister after the German blitzkrieg smashed across Belgium, Cunningham had a ready ear in London.

With the almost incredible spirit of defiance which has typified the British in adversity, it was decided that Malta would not surrender, but would resist, and be used as a base for reconnaissance against the Italian fleet and merchant ships, and for attacks against them. However, little attacking could be done at first. More importantly, Malta was to serve as a radio interception point close to southern Europe and the Balkans. This aspect alone was worth British and Commonwealth blood and materials in great measure.

Malta measures seventeen miles (27 km) by nine miles (14.5 km), and in 1940 had a population of 280 000, with another 25 000 on the sister island of Gozo. Space for airfields and dispersals was a problem. There were three locations for airfields, and during the coming battles, two more would be constructed. The airfields which existed were Hal Far, a grass strip near the RAF base at Kalafrana, Takali, which was built on an ancient lake bed between Valletta and Rabat, and Luqa.

Hal Far and Takali were subject to deterioration and closure due to wet weather, but Luqa had been built on harder, rockier ground, and had been opened only in June 1939. Work was done on all these airfields to extend and improve them, as well as to provide protection for the aircraft which used them. Lack of machinery meant hundreds of thousands of manhours had to be spent during the coming months and years to achieve a suitable standard at these airfields.

The Luqa-Hal Far road was used as a taxiway, along which were numerous pens and revetments for the aircraft. Two grass strips were completed by February 1942, each 1200 metres long, the whole being called Safi Strip.

The air commander was Air Commodore F. H. Maynard, who realised early in 1940 that promises to send fighter squadrons to Malta could not be kept. Fortunately, one radar set had arrived and was operating by March 1939. The more serious problem of fighter defence was partially resolved in a way that has passed into legend. Eight Sea Gladiators, the Naval version of the Gloster Gladiator fighter, were found in crates in the base at Kalafrana, left behind when the aircraft carrier HMS *Glorious* sailed for the Norwegian campaign.

Four of these fighters were issued to the RAF in April, and

after some inter-Service haggling, were retained for use in the defence of Malta. It will be noted that this was before Italy declared war. A fighter defence plan was in operation, however lacking in materials, before hostilities began.

On 11 June the first of what was to be 3340 air raid alarms during the next three years sounded, as ten Savoia-Marchetti SM79 bombers attacked Valletta and Hal Far, but did little damage.

The raids continued, and for eighteen days the Gladiators, flown by seven pilots gathered from a variety of posts on the establishment of the RAF on Malta, fought over the island. The ground-crews performed brilliantly, swapping parts from one aircraft to make another flyable, modifying them to get that extra few miles an hour of speed, or a faster climb, or better firepower. Against them were two hundred enemy.

Somewhere, possibly in a public relations office, was born the legend of the three stalwart defenders, 'Faith', 'Hope' and 'Charity'. However, pilots who flew the Gladiators could not recall using the names, and from incomplete records it seems that there may have been as many as ten Gladiators available.[1]

Four Hurricanes en route to the Middle East landed on Malta and Air Commodore Maynard persuaded the Air Ministry that his need was greater, so the modern fighters remained. However, enemy pressure increased and the handful of RAF machines was always hard-pressed. More Hurricanes were flown in, taking off from the aircraft carrier HMS *Argus*, which made several sorties in the Mediterranean to do so. Later these were combined with the Gladiators to form 261 Squadron.

In September 1940, the Italians attacked from Libya into Egypt, beginning 33 months of combat which surged back and forth along the North African coastline, turning the Mediterranean into an arena. British convoys got through to Malta in September, October and November of 1940. The small bomber force of two squadrons of Maryland and Wellington bombers, with the navy, achieved little destruction among the Axis ships and in the second half of the year less than three per cent of enemy shipping was sunk.

In December, the Luftwaffe moved into Sicily, and General Geisler's X Fliegerkorps decisively altered the situation. In January, intense battles were fought over the Operation Excess convoy pushing through to supply Malta. The aircraft carrier HMS *Illustrious* was badly damaged by the experienced Stuka crews of II/St. G. 2 led by Major Walter Enneccerus, and I/St. G. 1, led by Hauptman Paul-Werner Hozzel. Six direct hits had been scored. The ship only survived through a feat of arms, repair work and seamanship to reach Egypt, and then the USA, for repair work lasting a year.

As a result of this hammering, the Navy requested strong fighter protection from Malta for any future convoys, but RAF head-quarters in Egypt did little to reinforce the island.

In May 1941 the Germans withdrew, in preparation for the Russian campaign. Maynard was replaced by Air Vice-Marshal Hugh Lloyd, and the Regia Aeronautica remained as his sole enemy. Hurricanes were now more numerous and better able to cope with the Italian aircraft. After some reinforcement flights, and amalgamation with existing units, there were three Hurricane squadrons on the island by the end of June 1941: 126, 185 and 249 Squadrons. Blenheim light bombers began to attack shipping, and Malta began to assert a more definite domination of the central Mediterranean. In March, only about 10 per cent of Axis convoys were lost to air attack, but by November 1941 the loss rate was about 80 per cent. On the other hand, two British convoys had arrived at Malta, one on 27 July and one on 28 September. Supplies would be adequate until March 1942.

However, the German offensive in Russia was being halted by the winter conditions, and planning began for the 1942 operations. The Germans intended to push south into the Caucasus and capture the oil supplies there. Also, the Axis forces in the Mediterranean would gain final victory, but it was realised that Malta would have to be occupied and an invasion was intended for the middle of the year.

Hitler was angered at the continual destruction of convoys carrying supplies to the Axis forces in North Africa, and ordered Generalfeldmarschall Albert Kesselring to take his Luftflotte II from Russia to Italy, to crush Malta in preparation for invasion.

By now, Australians had begun to arrive after completing their training, and in November one of the RAAF pilots who was to become well-known at the time flew in with 242 Squadron. This was J. L. 'Tony' Boyd, a 21-year-old from Queensland, who had gone to work as a jackeroo after two years of secondary school at Gatton Agricultural College. The 'Tony' came from his second given name, Livingstone; his mother preferred 'Tony' as a name, and adapted the 'tone' from Livingstone. He was gentle, honest and steady by nature, a fair-to-good student. In 1936, he had graduated from the then Gatton Agricultural College, now Queensland Agricultural College, with three As, three Bs and a C. He went back to the family property, 'Wetheron', working there in the midst of the worst drought recorded in the district. It was an outdoor life, spent with his brothers, mainly devoted to keeping their cattle alive.

Boyd's first flight was Brisbane to Sydney in 1938, to attend the wedding of his sister, Dorothy, and it made such an impression that he decided to join the RAAF. He was told that he needed two more years' education, so he joined the Australian Army signals unit nearby, while he studied for the necessary examinations, which he passed.

He began flying training at Narromine, New South Wales, and wrote home about the course, his confidence in passing, and excitement at the prospect of going to Canada. 'The flying is just marvellous. I have 41 hours now, half solo, and can do anything with a Tiger Moth.' His good results in the blind flying segment worried him a little, as it could have meant a posting to bombers, 'a more responsible job but not as exciting as fighters'.

'I practise forced landings in people's back yards for relaxation. It's rather a ticklish job and strictly against Regulations. Gosh, it's fun being able to do what you like with the old crate, turn it inside out, almost. They stand up to an awful lot. I always wear a parachute as moral support. I shudder to think of the high-speed jobs ahead. They will be just as good to handle with a bit of practice. Wirraways and Ansons next, or their equivalent in Canada.'[2]

Tony had only been in England for four months, before volunteering for the move to Malta. He liked the UK, despite its small size compared to Australia, and wrote home of the beauty of the autumn countryside. There had been a fall of snow during his move to embark, and he added that he was not sorry to be leaving the cold weather behind.

On the matter of parcels from home, he suggested cigarettes, 'as they are always acceptable' and canteen orders had not been able to be met. (This was well before the days of the anti-smoking activists.)

He had progressed through the various training phases in Australia, Canada and England, and at the end of October 1941 was a member of 242 Squadron with a total of 203 hours flying in his logbook. On 12 November thirty-seven Hurricanes of 242 and 605 Squadrons took off from the aircraft carriers *Ark Royal* and *Argus*, for the 3 hour 40 minute flight across the Mediterranean to the island. Three Hurricanes, flown by Sergeants Grey, Jones and Massey did not make it, landing in enemy territory. All three pilots were taken prisoner. Tony Boyd noted their names in his log-book as 'missing'.

As well as British, there were Canadian and New Zealand pilots in the batch, reflecting the growing international nature of the RAF. Pilot Officer Howard 'Chuck' Lester, 605 Squadron, was the only other Australian among them.

Since the beginning of hostilities, the Royal Navy had made fourteen aircraft carrier voyages into the Mediterranean to launch Hurricanes and torpedo-bombers destined for Malta or the Middle East, losing some 29 aircraft to various causes, while 352 arrived safely. One hundred and fifty Hurricanes had flown on to Africa, and the rest remained on Malta.[3]

To the end of December, Boyd only flew three times, with no enemy contact. January was to be quite different.

On 22 December 1941, the German Luftwaffe returned to Malta, and the most painful and bitter period of the war began for the island defenders and population.

By the end of the year, the island fighter defences claimed 199 enemy destroyed, 78 probably destroyed, and 79 damaged (199:78:79). Axis records admit 196 destroyed and 70 (Italian) damaged. RAF losses had been 94 fighters lost in action, plus many more destroyed on the ground and in accidents. The Luftwaffe claimed at least 84 victories. Many bombers had been lost in attacks from Malta, on land targets and convoys, as well as on flights across the Mediterranean via the island. The Blenheim light bomber squadrons had suffered badly while executing low-level attacks on shipping.[4]

On 1 January 1942, the RAF on Malta consisted of Hurricane fighters of 126, 185 and 249 Squadrons, Wellington bombers of 40 and 104 Squadrons, and Maryland reconnaissance aircraft of 69 Squadron. The Hurricanes were based at Hal Far and Takali, the Wellingtons at Luqa and the Marylands also at Takali. The recently arrived pilots of 242 and 605 Squadrons had been unaccompanied by ground crews, and their aircraft were serviced by men from the other squadrons, while the pilots began and continued to fly as members of those squadron formations. Eventually the two squadrons were dissolved on Malta, and re-formed with other pilots and aircraft in India and Burma.

The headquarters was located in Valletta and the radio station at Kalafrana, with five radars located at Dingli, Maddalena and Ta Silch, with two more at Fanuma and on Gozo becoming operational in February.

The Hurricane II was still the fighter the pilots would have to fly against attacks on the island, though it had been with-drawn from operations in daylight over France since the previous

August. The latest Messerschmitt Bf 109, the 109F, was markedly superior. The Spitfire V now equipped over eighty squadrons of Fighter Command, but none were deployed outside the United Kingdom.

However, it was the Bf 109F tropical version which had flown into the Sicilian bases of Comiso and Gela, along with the other German units of Generalmajor Bruno Loerzer's II Fliegerkorps. One hundred and sixty Messerschmitts of Jagdgeschwader (JG) 53 and II Gruppe Jagdgeschwader 3 (II/JG 3), at San Pietro, as well as being newer and better aircraft, outnumbered the RAF Hurricanes by about three to one.

Loerzer commanded about 200 Ju88A-4 bombers from Stab (Staff) and I Gruppe Kampfgeschwader 54 (I/KG 54), Stab, II and III/KG 77, Kampfgruppen 606 and 806, plus 40 or so Ju87 Stuka divebombers of III Gruppe Stukageschwader 3 (III/SG 3).

Loerzer's mission was to destroy the RAF fighter force and achieve air supremacy, then to attack barracks, depots, ports and communication facilities in preparation for a combined airborne-seaborne invasion called *Operation Hercules*, which was planned for May 1942.

The initial level of Luftwaffe operations was relatively small, with about fifty to sixty sorties a day, flown by all three types of aircraft available to Loerzer. The winter weather and, presumably, settling-in problems, kept the rate of operations down. However, the 109s began standing patrols over the island and soon made flying a hazardous matter for the reconnaissance aircraft and the Blenheims of 21 and 107 Squadrons which had flown in.

The Hurricanes also suffered, and on 25 January 126 Squadron was attacked by 109s during a scramble, losing seven of their fighters. Tony Boyd wrote that his formation was 'jumped by three 109s at 14 000 feet. Five Hurricanes shot down, four pilots baled out, one missing. P/O Russell (126) missing.'

Earlier, on the 22nd, in Hurricane 'P', Boyd had seen six enemy aircraft, and left formation to attack. 'Shot all ammo into a Ju88, starboard engine caught fire; claim one Ju88 probable.' He added that Sergeant Neale had crashed.

During January, there were about 1500 bomber sorties against the island, many at night and many daylight attacks by small formations of bombers with large fighter escorts. Much of the effort was directed at Luqa.

10

On 1 February, London informed Malta that Spitfires would be sent to even the balance against the Messerschmitts, but it had to be borne in mind that their undercarriages were not as sturdy as that on Hurricanes, so proper runways were needed. At the time, in winter, rain often made the grass airfields unserviceable; Luqa was overcrowded, and the Luftwaffe was making craters faster than the airfield personnel could fill them in.

Keen to get Spitfires, Air Vice-Marshal Lloyd did not remind London of the technical problems which the new fighters would cause. No one in the ground crews on the island had been trained for or worked on Spitfires; everything about them would be unfamiliar, and learning would have to be 'on the job'. Even such a relatively simple matter as towing a wingless fuselage to and from workshops off the airfield presented additional transportation demands: the Spitfire wings contained the wheels, whereas on the Hurricane the wheels were part of the fuselage construction, and it could be moved easily with the wings detached.

Every part of a Spitfire would be new and different, and servicing would require new procedures. These would have to be learned under pressure from the enemy, with few spares, no modern maintenance and support system, and with only one-third the number of men available for such tasks in the UK.

A group of Spitfire pilots was assembled, placed under command of Squadron Leader Stan Grant, and sent with their crated Spitfires to Gibraltar. There the aircraft were to be assembled, loaded on the aircraft carrier HMS *Eagle*, and flown off the carrier deck when it had brought them to about 700 miles from Malta. The pilots were a mixed lot, reflecting the wartime composition of the RAF: English, Scots, Rhodesians, New Zealanders and Australians. One of the Australians was J. W. 'Slim' Yarra, and the other was Paul Brennan. Yarra had arrived back at 64 Squadron from leave, to find that Brennan and Peter Hannan had been posted, possibly to the Far East, but Hannan was still on leave. Yarra volunteered without knowing where he was bound, as he had 'seen enough of England to suit me'. (Hannan ended up flying in Burma; such are the quirks of fate.)

Yarra then found the posting was to Malta, 'which sounded pretty grim'. But after hurriedly packing, he was on the train in two hours. Another passenger bound for the Spitfire unit was Pilot Officer Peter Nash RAF, and after discussing the situation in the Mediterranean, the two 'came to the conclusion that we might have a lot of fun in Malta'. Yarra continued, 'I'll be glad to get back to a decent sun and to some sea water that is not below freezing level, like the English Channel.'

Like Tony Boyd, Jack Yarra could perhaps be regarded as a typical young Australian of his generation. He grew up in Grafton, northern New South Wales, son of a World War I winner of the Military Medal at Mont St Quentin. He was a healthy young Aussie, active in sailing, boxing and cycling, once riding 65 kilometres with his friend Norman Rankin to the beach at Yamba, and riding back. (However, Yarra had a puncture, and they had to take turns doubling as passenger, wheeling the other bike alongside.) Norm Rankin also became a Spitfire pilot, and recalled Jack (Slim in the Air Force) Yarra as a very steady character, who would do what had to be done with the minimum of fuss; girls were attracted to this aspect of his personality. His constant girl-friend was Doreen, nicknamed 'Ned', and it was for her that Yarra named his Spitfires.

Rankin and Yarra continued their childhood friendship through school, into the RAAF, training in Australia, Canada and to Operational Training Unit (OTU) in the UK, when they were parted. During a conversation at OTU, Rankin referred to 'after the war, in Australia' and Slim Yarra quietly replied to the remark with, 'I'm not going back.' Rankin was sobered to understand that his friend did not believe he would return home.

Like many young pilots, Slim Yarra had indulged in some unauthorised low flying, on one occasion buzzing a country train, and on another a particular farm house, whose occupant reported the exploit. Yarra's denials were neutered by the length of farmhouse clothesline trailing from the rear wheel of his aircraft.

En route to Malta, Slim Yarra was a Sergeant pilot, who had been graded 'average' in the earlier stages of training, and 'below average' at 55 OTU. He had a total of 184.5 hours as a pilot, of which 37.25 were on Hurricanes at OTU, and 22.5 were on Spitfires with 64 Squadron. The only operational flying he had done, if it could be called that, was on several convoy patrols during which nothing happened.

The batch of Spitfire pilots commanded by Squadron Leader Grant arrived at Portreath, did some flying in Spitfire IIs fitted with one auxiliary fuel tank mounted under the port wing, and spent a few more days in London, enjoying nights in the various clubs. Australian Associated Press correspondent Eric Baume made Australian aircrews welcome, and several good parties were enjoyed, including one organised by an American pilot in the Eagle Squadron, which was attended by several girls from the famous Windmill theatre. Slim Yarra described the girls as 'typical hard-drinking types. Very amusing.'

On 8 February, the group arrived at the RAF base at Kirkham, and none were impressed by the accommodation or facilities, and even less by the discovery that 'the damned place is a Physical Training School, and they expect us to get out of bed at the ungodly hour of 6.30 a.m.' The pilots refused to take part in the Kirkham rites, to the fury of some of the senior staff, but submitted to inoculations, and sailed for Gibraltar on what Yarra described as a 'dirty little 5,000-tonner' called the *Cape Hawk*.

They were then told officially that their destination was Malta, and that they were to be the first to fly Spitfires from a carrier deck. Before that event, they had to endure the very poor living conditions aboard ship.

The voyage took eleven days, recalled by Yarra as 'the worst sea trip I've ever done.' He believed that after the war the British government would be embarrassed by the tales which would come out about the conditions in which men were sent to war. 'It was absolutely shocking. How in hell do they ever expect to win a war when they treat their fighting men like cattle. I am getting sick of seeing Churchill stick his bowler hat up on his cane so the populace can cheer him as their saviour and think we are winning the war. The sooner the people in England realise that we are losing this war so far, the better it will be for everyone.'

Like a generation of Aussies before him, Yarra was becoming disillusioned with British command at high levels, and treatment of junior ranks. The ship plodded on to Gibraltar, but Yarra may not have considered that in early 1942 anything that could float was valuable, as the U-boats were sinking ships faster than they could be built.

Over Malta, the Hurricanes were flying intensively. The lack of ground crews and maintenance facilities resulted in aircraft being provided to the pilots as the machine was available, with little regard for squadron 'ownership'. Tony Boyd's log-book shows that on days in February he flew Hurricanes with the squadron

13

letters GN (249), HA (126), LE (242), GL (185) and UP (605).
On the 11th, they had attacked three Ju88s escorted by nine
Messerschmitts, and he fired point blank at a 109, 'while a second
shot at me', with no results seen because of cloud. His claim for
a damaged was not allowed.

An Australian already on Malta, Howard Lester, had arrived
by flying a Hurricane off an aircraft carrier, and was with 605
Squadron. On 12 February he shared in the destruction of a Ju88
which was chased and sent into the sea some 20 miles south-
west of Cape Passero. It was grey and overcast, and the 605
pilots could not understand why the Ju88 did not escape into
cloud, surmising that the rear gunner did not warn the pilot. But
Messerschmitt Bf109s at once attacked the Hurricanes, shooting
down Flight Lieutenant George Allen. A convoy set out from
Alexandria on 12 February, but failed to push through to Malta
due to operations of the Italian fleet and bomber attacks from
X Fliegerkorps, based on Crete.

On Malta itself, Luftwaffe attention turned to Takali, and the
modern buildings there were converted to ruins after two attacks.
Also bombed was Chateau Bertrand, or 'the Mad House', built
with examples of various styles of architecture and furnishing,
which was used by the RAF as a Sergeants' Mess as it was close
to Takali.

By mid-February, the island had been attacked by 2000 bomber
sorties in the previous thirty days. With the Air Force unable
to cope with construction tasks and repair work to the airfields,
the Army was called in. This force would grow to about 3000
men, and units were allotted to a specific airfield. The Royal West
Kents and the Buffs worked at Luqa, the Manchesters at Takali
and Devons at Hal Far. Men worked on a roster of twelve hours
on duty and twelve hours off.

The sheer physical effort involved in using unskilled labour to
construct aircraft pens with materials at hand, with little or no
heavy transport or machinery, is another of the unsung,
unglamorous tasks which were part of the struggle for Malta.
The pen for a Wellington bomber required the shifting of 3500
tons of earth or stone; an area 30 metres by 30 metres had to
be cleared and levelled; the walls were made of petrol tins filled
with earth or stone, or blocks of stone; the base was twelve tins

14

deep, the top two tins deep; 60 000 tins needed for each pen. Two hundred men could build one with tins in 21 days, or 28 days if stone were used; a fighter pen required one-quarter of the effort and material, and one for a Beaufort torpedo bomber, or Beaufighter required one-half.

At the end of ninety days, the units had constructed forty-five kilometres of dispersal track, fourteen large pens for bombers, 175 for fighters and 101 for other aircraft, and more for protection of the valuable petrol trucks and steamrollers. In addition, craters had to be filled and other repair work done. Without this manpower, the airfields would have been rendered unusable. Without the airfields, Malta would have been unable to defend itself, or to send out aircraft to attack the ships steaming to resupply the Axis forces in North Africa.

15 February had been a clear day, and the Luftwaffe had used it to the utmost, keeping the island under air raid alert from dawn until after dark. The Junkers 88s attacked in small groups with up to fifty Messerschmitt 109s as escort, feinting with a series of small dives and changes of direction before finally bombing Luqa. The defending Hurricanes found it difficult to cope, and by the end of the day there were only eleven fighters left serviceable of the 26 available at dawn.

It was clear to Air Vice-Marshal Lloyd that the Luftwaffe was about to achieve undisputed air superiority. As well as aircraft destroyed or damaged in the air and on the ground, the attacks were eliminating the invaluable ground support machinery and vehicles such as petrol tankers and steamrollers. For a time, bad weather continued to close Hal Far and Takali, adding to the problems of defence.

The continued destruction of aircraft, the pressure of Luftwaffe bomber and fighter attacks, and the lack of protection and maintenance facilities forced the evacuation of the Wellington and Beaufort strike force to North Africa.

On 14 February 1942, Sergeant A. P. 'Tim' Goldsmith, RAAF, found himself at very short notice aboard a Sunderland flying boat bound for Malta. He had taken part in a variety of operational flights over the English Channel and France, but had no enemy aircraft to his credit. He had been married only since 10 December 1941 to Rosemary, an English girl. He was twenty years old,

15

with a total of 307 hours in his log book. On 30 September 1941 he had graduated from 57 OTU with an 'Average' grading and 183 hours total flying time.

One of Goldsmith's friends was a New Zealander, Ray Hesslyn, who had left earlier for a secret destination. Goldsmith's posting to Malta had been quite open, but speedy, with only a few hours' notice. After a brief stopover in Gibraltar, Goldsmith arrived at Kalafrana, on the eastern end of Malta, on the morning of 17 February. While the darkened flying boat had been plodding across the Mediterranean night sky, young Goldsmith had noticed a distant twinkling and flashing on the northern horizon. He asked the pilot what it was, to be told it was Malta under attack. His next question, why didn't they head in that direction, brought an abrupt reply.

The new arrivals settled in, and one of the first people Goldsmith met was his former Flight commander, E. B. Mortimer Rose DFC, who had taught him squadron and operational flying, and to whose instruction Goldsmith was later to say he owed his life. However, at this meeting, Mortie was acting as fighter controller in the operations room, with one foot in plaster after being wounded and shot down. He had insisted on the line ahead formation used in Europe, and also maintained that the reason the 'weavers' tasked with keeping a look out behind were shot down so regularly was that they were not alert. To prove this, he flew as weaver. An enemy formation was identified ahead, and he stopped weaving to look for it, making a nice target for the Messerschmitts diving on his tail.

On 20 February, Goldsmith had a severe disappointment, noted in his diary: 'Posted to 126 Squadron, Takali, Hurricanes. Hell!' But serviceable aircraft were so scarce that many days were to pass before he could even be allotted one for a familiarisation flight. He spent the time seeing some of the sights of the island and learning what he could of the air war situation.

Coming from England, where 'the operational egg' was a luxury reserved for aircrew, he found the Maltese often kept chickens on their flat roof tops, and eggs were in greater supply. The Queen's Hotel was closer than the Sergeants' Mess, and served better food. Like most young Australians of the time, he was a healthy eater, and the rationing of wartime England had not impressed him. The Queen's was to have many good customers in the pilots, as the owner, Carrie Busuttil, made particularly good chips. Food presumably featured high in Tim's interest, and the diary records entries such as '25 Feb. 7 eggs today.' and '28 Feb. Dinner at Queen's. Two pork chops, two eggs, chips.'

Far removed from Tim Goldsmith's delight in the food and relative warmth of Malta, the Axis planners were organising to bring the war over Malta to a crescendo, battering it with the air power which had spread such destruction across Poland, France, the English Channel, the Balkans, the Soviet Union, and which, ten months before, had cleared the Mediterranean of Royal Navy ships. The offensive was to begin in earnest on 21 March.

Meanwhile, the first batch of Spitfires and their pilots had arrived at Gibraltar. While the fighters were being assembled, the pilots enjoyed the available food, drink and relaxation of the wartime austerity prevailing in the UK. Then they went aboard the ship, and began thinking seriously about flying from it. *Eagle* was capable of 20 knots, and if a 20 knot wind could be found at sea, the Spitfires would need to accelerate to 40 knots to fly off. But the flightdeck was only 600 feet long, and the pilots had been accustomed to runways of at least 2000 feet or more; no one knew if they could do it successfully. Once airborne, they were faced with a flight of over 1000 kilometres, over water, in a single-engined plane, to a small cluster of islands.

'This seemed a pretty tall order to all of us,' wrote Slim Yarra, 'and although nobody gave away what he thought, I know we all had our doubts. However, we were in Gibraltar and there was plenty to drink, so why worry.'

During night hours, *Eagle* set off east into the Mediterranean, and was about to launch the Spitfires when it was discovered that the auxiliary tanks were not functioning properly. The ship turned back to Gibraltar, an expert was flown from the UK, and the necessary work completed.

The pilots so recently unimpressed with shipboard accommodation en route to Gibraltar were more pleased with the Royal Navy facilities on the carrier, and Yarra commented on the good relationship quickly achieved with their counterparts, Chief Petty Officers 'who had none of the snobbery that goes under the name of Navy tradition.'

One of the Navy CPOs had a reputation as a teller of tall tales, and after a group arrived back on board in a convivial mood, he offered to establish a seance, to make contact with loved ones at home. The group settled around a table, the CPO began to go into a trance, but revived himself to eject an unbeliever from the circle: Slim Yarra. He went back into his trance, and those around the table became very serious and avoided making undue noise . . . the table began to move, gently but firmly . . . teetering on its legs, it lifted, lifted . . . the believers cried out—the words and oaths are unrecorded for posterity—and bolted, joined by the CPO, who had made an amazing recovery from his trance.

The mystery was unexplained before they went to sleep, but more sober minds next morning deduced what had happened. The unbeliever Yarra had managed to crawl under the table, braced his back against the top, and raised himself . . . The pilots never did tell the CPO, who believed he had psychic powers but dared not try again.

Meanwhile, Tony Boyd had destroyed his first enemy. On 23 February, in LE-P, he had searched for a dinghy, then joined the rest of the squadron which scrambled to engage an estimated '6 plus' formation. Boyd saw the enemy, but the others did not, so he dived to attack. He came in behind the 109s and fired a short burst at 300 metres, with no result, then from below fired a four-second burst and 'obviously got him; two others in the line of fire; cannon fire whizzing by so returned. Sgt Gardiner shot at one on my tail. 3 down in all, 1 to Gardiner, no losses to us.'

Records indicate that the 109 was destroyed; 'White 5' of 10 Staffel, Jagdgeschwader 53 (10/JG53), flown by Gefreiter Otto Butschok. Tony Boyd had no other combats in February, and by the end of the month had 240 hours flying time. It had been a long way from practising landings in paddocks near Narromine, revelling in having forty hours in a Tiger Moth.

The dangerous Messerschmitts were leaving their mark, and he had noted RAF losses: 4 Feb, P/Os Hulbert and Maine and Sgt McDowall missing; 12th, F/Lt Allen missing; 13th, P/O Stuart crashed; 15th, P/O Lowe shot down, crashed; 22nd, S/Ldr Chaffe shot down, missing; 24th, P/O MacNamara killed by a bomb; 24th, P/O Tedford shot down, missing.

Nightfighters were among the aircraft making the long over-water trip from England to Gibraltar, Malta and Egypt. Among them was one crewed by Pilot Officer Mervyn Shipard RAAF

18

and Sergeant Doug Oxby RAF. They had crewed together at 54 OTU Church Fenton, on Blenheims, then spent from September to December 1941 with 68 Squadron, destroying one He111. The AI Mk4 then in use was not accurate and difficult to operate, and Douggie Oxby wonders if he was ever really proficient at assisting his pilot to intercept enemy aircraft. As inexperienced as they were, and with the equipment they had, the memory of that first successful interception and victory remains as 'the outstanding thrill of my operational career' for Oxby.

With other crews, they had gone to the Bristol factory and taken a brand-new Beaufighter, done fuel consumption tests and navigation exercises, and on 17 February set off for the Middle East. Not having any navigational training, Oxby 'hadn't a clue about how to get to Gibraltar, but Ship was perfectly capable of getting us there so we landed without incident.'

After rain delayed them for five days, they departed for Malta, but were intercepted near Lampedusa by Italian CR42 fighters. The Beaufighter was completely unarmed, so Oxby flashed red Aldis light bursts at the fighters, but to no avail. Shipard took the Beaufighter down to sea-level and out-paced the Italians, but for the first time in his flights with Shipard, Oxby was frightened.

When they arrived at Malta, they were worried when the local authorities began to talk about keeping their new Beaufighter there, but Oxby pointed out that it was totally unequipped for operational flying, without radar or guns, and convinced the would-be pirates that they should take the fighter on to Egypt. The Fates must have decided to amuse themselves with Shipard and Oxby.

Leading two other Beaufighters, Shipard took them on to Africa, but a swirling dust storm made land-fall difficult, and after following the dimly seen coast for a time, he saw an airfield below, so went in to land. The strip was only 700 metres long, and the Beaufighter ran off the end, damaging the undercarriage and propeller tips. The other two landed safely.

It was a Royal Navy Fleet Air Arm strip, and the RAF visitors were looked after as well as possible. Next morning, Shipard told the pilot of the leading Beaufighter to hold it with the brakes while running up the engines to full power, then to release the brakes for the shortest possible take-off run along the available

700 metres. This was done, the Bristol Hercules roaring, then the brakes were released, the fighter surged forward, and almost at once the powerful torque effect of the propellers swung the heavy Beaufighter to the right, off the strip and into a revetment occupied by a Naval aircraft. Both machines were written off, and unfortunately two Egyptian labourers were killed.

Having witnessed one unsuccessful landing, one unsuccessful take-off and with three wrecked planes on their airfield, the Navy had enough, with the result that the six Beaufighter crew members went the rest of the way to Cairo by train. On reporting to the relevant headquarters, but having delivered none of the expected three new aircraft, Shipard and Co. found themselves persona non grata. Ship was sent to tow targets for a time. However, they were to return to Malta.

Elsewhere in the war, the German ships *Scharnhorst, Gneisenau* and *Prinz Eugen* had steamed up the English Channel, in a daring move back to German ports, embarrassing the Royal Navy. The Japanese seemed to be unstoppable in the Far East, rolling forward with almost daily conquests. In Russia, the Germans had held the line against massive Soviet winter offensives, despite severe losses in men and materiel. Apart from pinprick counter attacks, the Allies seemed to be losing everywhere.

In January, enemy sorties over the island totalled 2450. The monthly figure would not fall below this for ten months. In February it rose to 3090.

Malta was isolated in the Mediterranean.

2

Approaching Thunder

Malta—March 1942

On Malta, Air Vice-Marshal Lloyd had 21 serviceable Hurricanes. Nine hundred and ninety tons of bombs had been dropped on the island during the fine days in February which allowed such operations. But the weather was clearing as winter receded, and everything was in the Luftwaffe's favour.

On 1 March, Howard Lester destroyed a 109. This was described by Philip Wigley—'Wiggles'—as 'the near impossible by shooting down a 109F. To do this in a Hurricane armed only with .303 inch machineguns was a notable feat, as the 109F was so very much faster. Also, the .303's hitting power was very low, compared with that of the 20mm cannon with which some of our Hurricanes were armed.' Lester's victory was probably the aircraft of Feldwebel Alexander Kelbuth, 5 Staffel JG53, who made it back to Syracuse in the damaged Messerschmitt, had to force-land and was injured, while the fighter was severely damaged.

Another young Australian arrived on the island: Gordon Tweedale, who was to make his mark, and be remembered by some as the bravest man they knew on Malta. He was born in Brisbane in 1918, and after a few years as clerk with an insurance company, left to work on a cattle station. With interests including music—he was a good violinist—building model ships, poetry and tennis, he was not the generally accepted idea of a stockman. When war was declared he returned to Brisbane and studied mathematics, navigation, fitting and turning, as well as obtaining his A-class pilot's licence with the Royal Queensland Aero Club. After joining the RAAF in July 1940, he completed his training, went to England and flew Hurricanes in 43 Squadron. He applied

21

to go to Malta in mid-February 1942, departing on the 21st, and arrived to go to 242 Squadron, joining Tony Boyd, a fellow Queenslander.

Tony Boyd began to get into his stride. On 5 March he flew his Hurricane—LE-P—against a formation of Ju88s, claiming one as a probable, and two more as damaged, setting the starboard engines on fire. 'Six of us attacked five Ju88s and 10 Me109s, intercepted north of Grand Harbour. I attacked the rear three in turn, causing black smoke pouring from engines of two and strikes seen on the third. First one attacked slowed up and lost height. Attacked by 109s throughout; lost P/O Kidson.' Incomplete German records show that one of the Junkers damaged was from 4/KG77, and the rear gunner was wounded.

However, that day Air Vice-Marshal Lloyd signalled Cairo to state that the daylight attacks on the aerodromes were 'very serious', as little work was possible due to the continuous alerts, and accumulated minor damage to aircraft made them unflyable. He had seventeen damaged Wellingtons on the island, and added a request for more fighters 'as soon as possible. Delay in Spitfires is annoying.'[1]

On 6 March, Tim Goldsmith was watching a gaggle of Messerschmitts overhead, when suddenly one had its tail shot off by the island's ack-ack, and as the engine pulled the wings and cockpit earthwards, the pilot managed to bail out. Tim thought, 'Lucky man!' and noted in his diary that Ragbags Rabagliati had promised to get him a flight in a Hurricane as soon as possible. [Wing Commander A. C. Rabagliati DFC.]

Off to the west, south of Majorca, HMS *Eagle* was preparing to launch its cargo of Spitfires. Slim Yarra's had gone unserviceable, and could not be repaired on the ship, so he had to stay behind while the others flew off.

The pilots were in the cockpits half an hour before the navigational guide, a Blenheim, arrived. The carrier turned into wind, the Rolls Royce Merlin engines started, Squadron Leader Grant was in position, and was signalled to go. Yarra and the rest watched, with varying degrees of interest, as the Spitfire was given full throttle, went roaring down the deck, lifted off the deck, sank slightly, 'and sailed away, gaining altitude, proving that a Spitfire can take-off from an aircraft carrier'. The others quickly followed Grant, formed up, and set course for Malta.

Eagle swung away, back to Gibraltar and another load of Spitfires.

The weather was clear, and the Spitfire pilots could see Malta from some distance. The colours struck many of them, attracting notice by their brilliance and clarity. Below was the deep blue of the Mediterranean, extending in all directions. Close to the islands, the blue suddenly became a pale clear green, with a necklace of foam where the waves splintered against the rocky cliffs. The islands presented a mosaic of brown cliffs, white stone buildings, and bright green tiny fields, with white stone walls dividing them. Overhead was the bright African sun in the pale sky stretching south to the deserts.

The pilots also could see Sicily, 100 kilometres to the north, visible as a flat dark strip with a patch of cumulus over it, and away in the distance the snow-capped peak of Mount Etna. It

AERODROMES AND SEAPLANE BASES—AXIS FORCES

ITALY

REGGIO

TRAPANI

BOCCO DE FALCO

MARSALA

CASTEL VETRANO

S I C I L Y

BO RIZZO

GERBINI

CATANIA

GELA

AUGUSTA

BISCARI

SIRACUSA

COMISO

PACHINO

5 AIRFIELDS & GLIDER FIELDS

GOZO

MALTA

20 0 20 40 60 80 100
miles
km
20 0 80 160

was from Sicily that the Junkers and merciless 109s flew against Malta. That hundred kilometres looked very narrow.

There had been rumours floating around the island that Spitfires were to arrive soon, and the pilots who had been operating the tired and under-armed Hurricanes were hoping the tales were true.

Tim Goldsmith was in the Mess when 'a familiar whistling brought us tumbling out, and it was true, they were here!' The pilots, and the rest of the population, felt a great surge of elation as the new sleek fighters slipped in to land. The last one seemed to be having trouble with his undercarriage, and the watchers in the Mess observed professionally as the pilot finally put the Spitfire down.

A little later, Tim Goldsmith saw 'half a dozen sergeants, looking pretty tired and with bloodshot eyes, trundled into the Mess and threw down their kit. I was very pleased to welcome another Australian whom I had known in England, Paul Brennan from Brisbane. The man who had undercarriage trouble turned out to be Ray Hesslyn. So this was his mysterious assignment!'

Brennan, yet another Queenslander, was to become one of the well-known fighter pilots before his departure. One of the flight commanders was Laddie Lucas, who described Paul Brennan in the following words: 'He did not compromise in the air or on the ground. He was splendidly aggressive, but he tempered his aggression with an engaging brand of humour which saw the funny side of things when our fortunes were at their lowest ebb. He was a marvellous squadron member.

'It took him some little while to determine what his judgement was of a colleague. He sniffed around a character rather as a dog gives a doubtful dinner the once over, but when once he had made his mind up about a guy and that person measured up to his requirements, then he would offer 250 per cent support. Paul was solid and loyal to a point in his friendships.

'I fancy he looked at me to begin with and said to himself: "Wait a moment! This looks like a stuck up Pom. Better watch him." But after a week or so in the flight we had sorted one another out and there never was a pilot who gave me, on the ground or in the air, finer or more devoted service.'

That evening, a conference for fighter pilots was called at the Officers' Mess in the Point-de-Vue Hotel. Woodhall informed the gathering that more Spitfires would be sent, but he did not know when. In the meantime, the new arrivals were to be used sparingly, four at a time, to give top cover to the Hurricanes, which were to attack the bombers. It was found that in practice, there were so many Germans that everyone was to try for the bombers and avoid the Messerschmitts, which Goldsmith commented was 'easier said than done!'

The new arrivals began to make their mark. On the 9th, Gordon Tweedale, who had arrived by Sunderland on 1 March, and gone to 242 Squadron, claimed a Ju88 damaged. Next day, he destroyed one.

For all his aggressiveness, even Tony Boyd missed on what could have been a definite victory. On the 9th, in GL-K, he was escorting a Blenheim east of the island when a Messerschmitt flew up behind and tried to join the little formation. Thinking it was a Hurricane, Boyd turned gently towards it, but the 109 pilot must have woken up, and 'by the time I realised, he was 400 yards ahead. Gave him a futile burst.' On a second sortie for the day, Tony had a 'mishap with helmet in the dive and lost formation' as the squadron was attacking three 88s and the six 109s escorting them. Two 109s were claimed as probables, and two of the 88s as damaged.

In the faraway Welsh skies, at 53 OTU, Sergeant Noel Pashen was writing 'Whoopee!' in his diary, after his first 'bash at the old Spit today', adding, 'she's a beautiful kite and responds as if she were part of you'. Pashen was one of a draft of Australians who had sailed from Australia on 15 October after completing Service Flying Training, and gone to the UK via the Panama Canal. The English winter played havoc with training schedules, and also with the innocent preconceptions held by the young Aussies about the British Isles. When the bad news of Japan's advances in the Pacific continued to come in, many of them wished to return to defend their homes, and to do so in a warmer climate. Apart from the weather and lack of flying, some of the Australians were annoyed by the class structure of British society, and its reflection in the armed forces, while some of them were shocked to a lesser or greater degree by the wartime morals displayed by some of the local womenfolk.

Distant sunny Australia, with its beaches, sports, fragrant gumtrees and wholesome Aussie girls, became something of a paradise to them. When the survivors of wartime operational flying over Europe or North Africa at last returned to Australia, some of them were shocked again by the wartime morals displayed by some of the local womenfolk.

But as the March days passed, some of the pilots who would be flying to Malta in a few weeks were learning to master the Spitfire over the Welsh hills.

On 10 March, Tim Goldsmith had 'a touch of the dog', meaning Malta dog, the common stomach and bowel complaint which afflicted everyone sooner or later. He was watching a combat overhead. Jack Mayall, another Australian, was dog-fighting with two Messerschmitts at 10 000 feet over Takali, when a third 109 slid down out of the sun, fired a long burst of cannon, 'and Jack and his Hurricane came screaming down like a bomb and crashed near the outskirts of Hamrun. I saw him go in a terrific flash and flame.' Tim Goldsmith had lost the first of his friends on Malta.

German records indicate that Hauptman Karl-Heinz Krahl, Kommandeur of II/JG3, almost certainly shot down Jack Mayall. Krahl himself had little more than a month to live.

In his pocket diary, Goldsmith tallied the losses for the day: three 109s, two 88s, two Spitfires and two Hurricanes.

One of the 88s had been shared between Tony Boyd and Flight Lieutenant Kee and Pilot Officer Morrison-Jones. Boyd, in HA-F, was one of a formation of fifteen aircraft. Four Spitfires flew as top cover, while the Hurricanes attacked two 88s and six 109s at 14 000 feet. He had attacked the 88 'after F/Lt Kee caused an explosion with cannon. I followed it ten miles, using all ammo, causing smoke to come from both engines; claim one-third of it.'

On the 11th, Goldsmith at last had his first flight in a Hurricane, but only for fifteen minutes, after which he noted 'Not in the same class as a Spit, but easy to land.' Later in the day, he was able to go to the cinema, and saw 'The Wizard of Oz'.

Tony Boyd had flown, this time in GL-K, in an interception of six 109s, but did not claim, and noted that the bombers turned back before releasing their bombs, while the Spitfires claimed one Messerschmitt.

On the 12th, seven Hurricanes were made unserviceable by a raid of Ju88s. However, Ragbags Rabagliati flew out to Egypt, taking mail for posting there.

That day, Generalfeldmarschall Albert Kesselring had senior officers of the Luftwaffe and Regia Aeronautica attend a conference at Catania, when it was stated that the air offensive against Malta would be comprised of three parts:

first, neutralisation of the anti-aircraft defences,

second, mass attacks against airfields and aircraft,

third, attack naval forces, dockyards and installations.

This was not a rigid order of priorities, but could be changed as the situation demanded. Unspoken, but in Kesselring's mind, was the knowledge that he would have to redeploy his force to Russia for the 1942 summer offensive.

The Germans employed their numerical superiority in the obvious way, by saturating the sky over Malta with fighters. About thirty minutes before a raid, the first wave of 109s would arrive over Malta. The defenders had unenviable choices: either take off and engage the advance wave of 109s, and be short of petrol and ammunition when the bombers arrived, or wait until the bombers were en route, then take off under the circling 109s and try to climb to engage the bombers. In addition, when the raid was over, a further wave of Messerschmitts would arrive to harass the tired Spitfires and Hurricanes as they were trying to land. As Tim Goldsmith noted, 'It is no fun being attacked when your wheels and flaps are down and your petrol gauge is flicking near zero.'

The intensity of the waves increased, as did the numbers of German aircraft in them. Always the Spitfires and Hurricanes were outnumbered, by six, ten, or fifteen to one.

Tweedale chased a Ju88 a little too far one day, and was shot up by a 109. He managed to get back for a crash landing, and was sent to Imtarfa Military Hospital to recover from shrapnel wounds to his foot. He was visited by several people, including Tim Goldsmith, who was 'surprised at the number of limbless patients in the wards. The daily bombing was certainly inflicting some casualties.' There being little else to take as gifts, Goldsmith and Tom Freeman presented Gordon with bunches of flowers, much to his disgust.

One day in March, Goldsmith went across to Hal Far to ferry a Hurricane back. He was pleased to have the chance to meet a RAF friend, Ernie Broad, again, but was interested to see the

Hal Far Hurricanes scrambling just as he arrived, so he and Ernie went to the operations room to find out what was happening.

A large raid of 80-plus was coming in from the east. A little blase by this time, the two young pilots stood outside peering into the sky while other personnel went into a large shelter about 25 metres away. They noticed puffs of smoke from the ack-ack guns across the bay, soundless as the noise of firing had not reached them, but still could not see the raiders. Goldsmith glanced directly above, and said to Broad, 'Look, there's a Hurricane coming straight down with its undercarriage lowered.'

Broad needed only a quick look. 'Hurricane be buggered! That's a flaming Stuka! Let's get downstairs!'

Suddenly, Goldsmith could see a dozen Ju87s diving on Hal Far from three different directions, and higher up another twenty or so were queueing before diving, with the ever-present Messerschmitt 109s sweeping around, and then the noise came to him— the nearby Bofors 40mm cannon began firing, as did the 3.7 inch Heavy Anti-Aircraft guns, the high-pitched scream of falling bombs, whine of diving aircraft and rattle of machineguns as the Hurricanes engaged.

'We leaped down the operations burrow like a couple of rabbits just as a couple of explosions indicated a very near miss,' said Goldsmith. The raid went on for about twenty minutes, ending with the 109s coming down to strafe.

Goldsmith and Broad came out into the sunlight and looked around. The Officers' Mess was destroyed, and part of the airmen's quarters was demolished; a Swordfish was burning in its revetment; a Stuka smouldered in the middle of the field, along with its pilot, but the gunner had managed to parachute and was taken prisoner by the crew of a Bofors . . . and there were two craters where the nearby shelter had been; 26 airmen died there.

Goldsmith stayed to help excavate the wrecked shelter, and decided to stay overnight at Hal Far, using a spare bed in the Mess. As they entered it, they noticed a five-metre long steel girder near the porch. It had been tossed 'like a stick' from the Officers' Mess 70 metres away.

He commented that 'at Mdina, night raids were defeated by pulling the blankets over one's head, but the Hal Far boys wisely went to earth very briskly.'

One of the raiders had been shot down by Tony Boyd, of whom Tim Goldsmith wrote at this time, 'He had a lot of trouble getting his victories confirmed, but his list of probables and damaged was already in double figures.'

Next morning, Goldsmith flew the Hurricane to Takali, 'keeping low and rubber-necking all the way across. I had no ambition to be shot down on a ferry flight, as happened to one of the 249 pilots about a fortnight previously.'

On the 17th, formations of Luftwaffe bombers and fighters attacked, not always being intercepted, but six Spitfires of 249 Squadron had climbed to 20 000 feet, looked down and saw six Ju88s about 10 000 feet below, with an escort of 109s. The Spitfires dived, Paul Brennan swung in behind one 109 and fired all his cannon ammunition at a range of 150 metres. The 109 rolled over onto its back and went down, while Brennan banked onto another Messerschmitt and fired his machineguns at 300 metres range, but the 109 did not seem to be damaged. It was Paul's first victory.

Next day, seven Hurricanes of 185 Squadron took off to engage Messerschmitt 109s, and in the combat Pilot Officer Howard Lester was shot down into the sea, and wounded, but was picked up by the air-sea rescue launch.

Lester never saw the 109 which hammered his Hurricane from behind, but was saved from the main effect of the exploding shells by his armour plate and the glycol tank. Remembering his COs instruction to bring the aircraft back if possible, Lester tried to do so, but glycol fumes blinded him and he was forced to bale out. In great pain from his wounds, Lester managed to inflate his dinghy but could not climb aboard so he clung to the outside.

Some hours later, the launch arrived, and at first the crew thought he was dead. One suggested a burial at sea, with the rocks and bag they had with them, but another thought he could feel a pulse, and a nip of medicinal spirit revived Lester a little.

He was taken back to hospital, later evacuated to England, and underwent a long period of treatment. (See Appendix 1.)

Frank Mulloy was 'missing' on 19 March, noted Tim Goldsmith in his diary, and on the 20th, Hal Far was attacked by 75 Ju88s, who put the airfield out of action and damaged several aircraft.

On 21 March, another flight from the aircraft carrier USS *Wasp* provided more Spitfires, this time to replace the Hurricanes of 126 Squadron, who, as Tim Goldsmith noted, 'had been there many months and on whom the strain was beginning to tell'.

Off to the west, the weather at the launching area for the carrier-borne Spitfires was not good, with ceiling at about 1000 feet, fog and rain. However, if the escorting Blenheim arrived, they would go. Slim Yarra was third man. 'When my turn came, I taxied into position. I was rather keyed up and my nerves were taut. But as soon as I opened the throttle I lost all the tautness and got that queer kick one always gets when opening up the world's best fighter aircraft. The Merlin engine sounded very sweet that morning as I raced down that little deck and lifted off the end. At that moment, the fact that we had 1100 kilometres to travel over water, and hostile water at that, mattered not the slightest. All that did matter was that I was in the air again after nearly three weeks on the ground.'

The Spitfires slid into formation behind Squadron Leader E. J. 'Jumbo' Gracie DFC, a Battle of Britain pilot who was reputed to shoot down bombers because he could not see the fighters. The formation went on at low level, through rainstorms and patches of mist, tried to climb above the weather, could not do so, and came back down. A formation of Italian CR42 bi-plane fighters was seen near Pantelleria, but as they showed no signs of aggression the Spitfires kept on their way, unable to spare petrol for combats.

'After three hours flying,' recalled Yarra, 'I was very much in need of a cigarette, but as I could not find any matches had to forego the pleasure.' He could see puffs of smoke coming from other cockpits as some pilots indulged themselves.

Closing on Malta, they tightened formation, and Yarra scanned the sky, noticing a twin-engined aircraft approaching from behind and starboard. He immediately identified it as a Messerschmitt 110, and swung into a head-on attack, prepared to fire, and realised it was a Beaufort. 'I very nearly squirted at that guy. He would have been a little brassed if I had.' He rejoined formation and they went in to land at Takali.

The first new pilot Tim Goldsmith saw was fellow-Australian John Bisley, and each was surprised to see the other. Bisley introduced him to the squadron: Squadron Leader 'Jumbo' Gracie, Flight Lieutenants Tony Barton and Johnny (actually, Tim)

Johnston, and Mike Graves from Ireland, Jim Bailey and Shorty Milner from England, Brooker, Ricky Ryckman and Junior Crist from Canada, Jimmy Peck and Mac McLeod from the USA, Dusty Miller from New Zealand, Pat Schade from Malaya, and Jack Yarra.

Then Yarra learned what had happened to the group who had set off from HMS *Eagle*, leaving him aboard to return to Gibraltar. It was obvious that the intensity of operations was much greater than in the UK. However, he also realised that the number of pilots far exceeded that of available fighters, and was a little disgruntled after estimating that he might be on readiness only about once a week.

At dusk, 75 Ju88s attacked Takali with incendiaries, high-explosives and rocket bombs, attempting to destroy the non-existent underground hangars which were presumed to exist.

The pilots crowded out onto the bastion to watch, noting that the Germans were going much lower than normal, some bombs being released at about 500 feet. Streams of tracer from the Bofors and machineguns crossed those of the Germans as they fired back. Bombs crumped into the dispersal bays, ripped a wing off the Mad House, destroyed houses in Mosta village and pierced the dome of the church. This one failed to explode, but another did explode in a wing of Imtarfa hospital, killing thirty patients and two nurses.

But the ack-ack shot down two bombers, one falling into the centre of the airfield, and burning, and another had a wing shot off almost directly over the watching pilots, then spun down onto the perimeter. Two of the crew jumped, but without parachutes. A rain of shrapnel pattered and clunked down, bringing home the dangers of standing about watching an air raid, and one big piece of steel crashed onto Paul Brennan's steel helmet, giving him something of a surprise.

Slim Yarra thought that 'the Jerries really did some spectacular bombing. The dust covered an area of at least five square miles and smoke from burning petrol and oil made black smudges against the yellow dust cloud. I was surprised and shaken to learn that this happened at least three times daily.'

When the raid was over, Goldsmith and Brennan walked down to inspect the damage in the moonlight. For two weeks, the ground-crews had laboured to repair a damaged Glenn Martin Maryland

31

reconnaissance bomber, having parts flown in and using their natural ingenuity. That afternoon, the plane was declared serviceable and was to be test flown next morning. They found it 'upside down, half in a bomb crater, with the port wing and engine about 20 metres away.'

Goldsmith and Brennan picked their way past fresh craters, delayed action bombs, riddled petrol tankers standing in areas of earth soaked in the precious 100-octane fuel, and saw a Spitfire and a Hurricane burning near the eastern dispersal. There was nothing they could do, and they were sent back to go to bed and prepare for the next day.

Later, they found that the Point-de-Vue Hotel had been hit, and six pilots killed, including one Australian, Pilot Officer Guerin.

Next day, Goldsmith was on readiness, and was told to taxi a Hurricane out of a dispersal bay which was located next to Station Headquarters and the commander's office. Just then the air raid warning went, but Goldsmith took two mechanics with him and went across to the Hurricane, climbed into the cockpit and tried to start it. The battery was flat; he called to the mechanics to fetch a starter trolley, 'and was gratified to see them sprinting to the dispersal hut. A burst of cannon fire brought home to me the reason for their haste. Fighter-bombers were attacking the aerodrome, and I threw myself out of the machine, face downwards on the grass, wishing I was a worm.'

The 109s hurtled past, bombs exploded and the Hurricane received several holes in the fuselage fabric. Goldsmith began to check the plane, heard the 4.5 inch ack-ack open fire and saw a formation of Ju88s approaching. Some 25 metres away was the headquarters trench, so he 'shamelessly deserted my Hurricane and disappeared into the trench' as the first 88 was pulling out of his dive.

Also in the trench were the station commander, his adjutant and assistant adjutant and a Maltese gunner. All crouched as the fifteen Junkers bombed, then looked out into the rolling clouds of dust and smoke. The station commander was about to climb out, when the hawk-eyed Maltese pointed to another fifteen bombers approaching. Again they ducked as the air shuddered to the sound of ack-ack guns, diving planes and falling bombs, exploding shells and bombs, but now was added what Goldsmith called 'the beautiful sound of Hispano cannons. Five heads came up simultaneously to see what the Spitfires were doing.

'There were only two, and each was glued to the tail of an 88. One was above our side of the 'drome and was burning fiercely, rolled gracefully onto its back and crashed with a terrific explosion on the far side of the Mad House.' The other disappeared to the west, both engines smoking, losing height, and eventually crashed south of Gozo; the crew were picked up. One of the Spitfires was attacked by a 109, flicked onto its back and crashed in Sijuwi Valley, next to Luqa.

Three more waves pounded the airfield, and when it was over, the commander's office was a heap of rocks and the Hurricane was a wreck. Back at dispersal, Goldsmith found the only casualty was Hall, a Canadian, who had his nose sliced by falling shrapnel as he watched the Spitfires.

Slim Yarra flew his first operational flight that day, when they were scrambled to intercept a plot of '40 plus', and had his first lesson when he was jumped by a bunch of 109s 'and chased home'.

In the afternoon, another 75 bombers attacked Takali, losing four to ack-ack. Two collided while preparing to dive, and five parachutes were seen to open high up, drifting off towards Sicily. It was presumed the men would be collected by the Dornier flying boat which did this between Sicily and Malta.

In 24 hours, Takali had been battered by about 220 bombers, each dropping 4000 pounds of bombs. To Tim Goldsmith, 'it appeared as though it would be weeks before an aircraft could land or take off from it safely'.

Meanwhile, on 20 March, a small convoy, code-named MW10, had left Alexandria with strong naval escort. The freighters *Pampas, Talabot* and *Clan Campbell*, with the supply ship HMS *Breconshire* had been brought through the dangerous seas despite sorties by the Italian Navy and air attacks.

Admiral Vian had positioned the anti-aircraft cruiser *Carlisle* with destroyers *Hasty, Havoc, Hero, Lively, Sikh* and *Zulu* as close convoy escort, and followed behind with cruisers *Dido, Eurylas* and *Penelope* plus more destroyers. The Italian Navy reacted by concentrating a force of one battleship, three cruisers and ten destroyers, intending to meet the British in battle at the Gulf of Sirte. By use of a smokescreen, superior and aggressive tactics and seamanship, Vian repulsed the Italians, with their losses being one cruiser and two destroyers, plus damage to the battleship.

Now the German Luftwaffe took over the assault on the ships, and Malta itself was given a respite. Fifty miles out of the island harbours, the convoy was subjected to determined attacks, despite the cover of relays of Spitfires and Hurricanes. Despite restricting their use in previous days, the island could muster only fourteen Spitfires and eleven Hurricanes.

Then, only twenty miles from Malta, *Clan Campbell* was sunk by air attack. Two Ju88s were shot down, and another eight were damaged or classed as 'probably destroyed'.

Ernie Broad saw a Heinkel 111 flying in to attack the leading ship, opened his engine up to maximum and went after it. The Heinkel dodged into some low scattered cloud with the Hurricane in hot pursuit. Broad saw it silhouetted against a patch of cloud and opened fire, closing in despite accurate return fire from the rear-facing gunner. Both engines caught fire, and the bomber slipped down to a landing on the sea, settling amid a huge cloud of spray. Broad saw the crew climb into a rubber raft before the nose went down, tail swung up and the Heinkel went to the bottom. It was his first victory.

On the morning of the 24th, *Breconshire* was damaged by a fighter-bomber which sped in and dropped a bomb down the funnel, but the other two freighters reached Grand Harbour in Valletta. *Breconshire* was towed into Marsa Sirocco and work began unloading it there. But the Luftwaffe was about to give another demonstration of its power.

At lunch time, Tim Goldsmith was sent to Hal Far, with three other pilots, as 185 Squadron there was short of pilots. He went out to his allotted Hurricane, placed gloves, helmet and parachute ready to wear quickly, and began to walk back to the readiness hut. The air raid warning sounded, but no fighters took off, so he assumed it was for a high-flying reconnaissance plane and kept on walking. Suddenly there was the rattle of Mauser cannon, and he was in the gutter as the bombs screamed down, to burst with four explosions nearby. The waiting pilots got a shock at the nearness, but settled down to play cards. Goldsmith noted that it was 'Grab', as there were not enough for poker and 'we somehow couldn't see any point in improving our minds by playing bridge on Malta'.

Keith Lawrence, who was leading the section, answered the

34

phone. He grunted a few times, put the handset down and told the waiting faces that the controller estimated a raid of over one hundred enemy planes approaching, and wanted to know if the four Hurricanes would combine with four Spitfires to take off and intercept. Goldsmith recalled that, 'I think we all felt the same about it, ready to get into our trenches, and nobody had the courage to admit it.'

Lawrence told the controller to call them when it was time to scramble. They all sat down again, but no one picked up the cards. The four pilots waited. The phone rang, Lawrence answered, shouted 'Scramble!' and they were running for their aircraft.

Goldsmith's fitter saw him coming, climbed into the cockpit and started the engine, then was out and ready to help him with the parachute straps. Thirty seconds after the order, they were taxying out of the dispersal bays and along the track to the runway, fitters standing on the wing, guiding by hand signals.

Goldsmith was last off, lost contact with the others but climbed hard. He saw the Spitfires passing below, then regained contact with the other three Hurricanes, and took up station as the extreme starboard aircraft in the formation.

Woodhall called a warning from ground control about 'little jobs' in the proximity, and Goldsmith saw six 109s flash across above and swing around to the rear, wait, then attack. Goldsmith pulled up his nose to engage one head-on, when Lawrence called out that more were coming in from behind, and 'Get under the mattress.'

Goldsmith 'half-rolled then pulled the stick across and back, and with full starboard rudder, aileron-turned down until I reached the cloud, under which our section re-formed and flew east for a few miles before starting to climb.'

Woodhall called again, informing them of 'big jobs approaching the harbour from the north at 15 000 feet. Try to catch them before they bomb.'

At 10 000 feet over Kalafrana, the Hurricanes saw about 30 Ju88s north of Grand Harbour, gently weaving through the ack-ack. Most dived on Grand Harbour, aiming for *Talabot* and *Pampas*, but one formation flew on to Hal Far, slid into line astern and began diving on *Breconshire*. Lawrence brought the Hurricanes in at an angle to the line of dive, swinging to join the 88s, but they were too fast and drew away.

35

Goldsmith fired at one. He saw the 88 'crossing my nose from port at 250 yards. I gave him a 3-4 second burst and saw ammunition entering the starboard side of Ju88's fuselage without any visible effects. The extra speed from his dive left me behind.'[2]

He fired at the next 88 behind, with no result, and 'at that moment the close escort arrived, interrupting our little party and sending us into tight steep turns. Looking down, I saw stick after stick of bombs straddling *Breconshire*, and what looked like a hit or very near miss amidships. Suddenly the Huns had gone and we were alone again.'

He rejoined the others and the four Hurricanes climbed to about 5000 feet and circled Hal Far, but then Woodhall called again, telling them another wave of bombers, Stukas this time, were on the way. They began climbing, untroubled by Messerschmitts, but on the radio they could hear the Spitfires heavily engaged elsewhere.

Then they saw the Stukas diving onto the ships in Grand Harbour, and again Lawrence swung the Hurricanes on a converging course, timed to catch the Germans at the vulnerable point at the bottom of the dive.

Goldsmith saw a gaggle of six Stukas diving from the south, turned onto them, and picked one. He closed, and saw it as a Stuka silhouette against the sky some 70 metres ahead and slightly above, and 'fired six seconds of machinegun ammunition at him, watched the tracers ripping into his fuselage, but he kept on flying. Then another one appeared above at 50 metres range and I gave him three seconds fire and had the satisfaction of seeing glycol pouring from his radiator as he lost height towards St Paul's Bay.

'Tracer from above reminded me where I was, and I broke sharply down just as a Messerschmitt flashed over—the swastika on his tail was very obvious.'

He swung back after the Ju87, but saw it was too far away to chase and close in to accurate shooting range; there were many other 109s around. The Stuka was smoking and losing height, but disappeared into a cloud near St Paul's Bay. Flight Sergeant Fletcher also saw the Junkers and confirmed Tim's report.

Out of ammunition and with little petrol, he flew back to Hal Far and made 'a very ropey landing, but feeling pleased with myself nevertheless'.

Control rang to say the Spitfires had destroyed five enemy,

the Hurricanes two, for no friendly losses. Goldsmith was credited with a Ju87 probably destroyed, though he felt personally that the German could not have made it back to Sicily with the glycol gone from his engine.

From Hal Far, the distressed *Breconshire* was plainly visible, and the airmen watched the small boats going to and from her side as frantic efforts were made to unload the burning ship.

After being stood down from operations for the day, Tim Goldsmith stayed at Hal Far, and had a few beers with Ernie Broad. Tim was 'very envious of Ernie having collected a "destroyed", while mine was only a "probable".'

Next morning, Goldsmith was dragged out of bed early, but needlessly, as there was no aircraft for him. But the others made him stay up and join in the poker school. A series of explosions brought them all outside, looking around for a raid, until it was realised that the cargo of the *Breconshire* was detonating. Over there in Marsa Sirocco, her shape was noticeably lower in the water.

Goldsmith stood on a blast wall to watch the others take off to engage 25 Stukas arriving to bomb the burning ship. She was hit twice, rolled over and sank, leaving part of her keel above water. Six Germans were shot down, for the loss of a Spitfire and a Hurricane, in which Pilot Officer Fox and Sergeant Frank Mulloy were killed.

At one o'clock the Takali pilots were released and told they could return. But there was no transport, and a group of very disgruntled young men laden with parachutes, helmets, Mae Wests and flying boots arrived back at their quarters after taking four hours to hitchhike the twelve miles (19 km), in four different vehicles which included a horse-drawn cart.

Goldsmith had been trying to get back to a Spitfire squadron, and a few days later was pleased to be informed he would be going to 126 Squadron, with John Bisley.

Slim Yarra flew on two scrambles on the 28th, against radar plots of 20-plus and 60-plus, engaging Ju88s on the first and 109s on the second, but made no claims. He was learning fast. Next day, he flew again, against formations of 20-plus and 40-plus, engaged the bombers but did not claim. Since his arrival, three pilots he knew had been killed: Pilot Officer Guerin, RAAF; Flight Sergeant Cormack, RAF; Pilot Officer MacCarthy, RCAF. He was soon to leave 249 Squadron for 185. His Hurricane flying time was judged adequate, and 185 was short of pilots.

On 30 March, Tim Goldsmith took part in his first Spitfire scramble from Malta, but was so excited that he was well down the strip before he realised the propeller was in coarse pitch, changed it, and cleared the perimeter 'with inches to spare'. Woodhall was directing them to intercept an escorted single Ju88 reconnaissance plane, and 'it seemed to me that my sensitive altimeter needle was spinning like a chocolate wheel, after the Hurricane's slow rate of climb'.

The reconnaissance plane turned back, but they kept climbing as a raid seemed to be assembling over Comiso, patrolled for an hour and were recalled. Goldsmith was rejoicing, as his Spitfire was 'a revelation to handle after the heavier Hurricane and I was quite pleased to be able to get the feel of it again before combat'.

But because of the shortage of aircraft, 126 and 249 Squadrons were using them on alternate days, with the pilots rostered for a half-day on readiness. The result was, as Tim Goldsmith noted, 'a man would be lucky to get half a day on the job every four days'.

On 31 March, a heavy raid developed, bringing with it a mass of Messerschmitts. With some others, Goldsmith stood out on the bastion watching the four Hurricanes and two Spitfires which were all the island could launch.

From the north, fifteen Stukas appeared and seemed to be going for Luqa, when 'the leader rolled upside down', recalled Tim Goldsmith, 'and dived like a stone, releasing its bombs to strike into the hill above the aerodrome. The others followed in quick succession, all dropping their bombs very close to where the leader's had fallen.' This was a puzzle to the watchers, as all that was in the target area was the clothing store, yet the Germans seemed to think something there was worthwhile attacking.

Enthralled by the spectacle of Stukas, bombs, explosions, ack-ack, and the noise, few of the audience noticed two Spitfires, with a gaggle of 109s after them, going for the Stukas. One Spitfire was forced to turn and fight the Messerschmitts, but the other slipped in behind a Ju87, fired and blew it to pieces, then went on behind another, hammered a long burst into it, and sent it flicking over and spiralling down, both crew bailing out.

Then, thirty Ju88s appeared from over Mosta and began dives

on the airfield. The four Hurricanes flew in, joining the line of 88s in their dives. The fourth one seemed unable to keep up with its target, and the watchers were appalled to see a 109 slide in underneath the Hurricane. They waited for the Hurricane to whip around onto the Messerschmitt, but the Mauser cannon rattled and the Hurricane began a graceful left turn, the nose dropped and down it went for 15 000 feet into the hill behind Naxxar.

'Poor bugger,' said someone. Then a Maltese called out and pointed, and there in the sky was a tiny parachute. The pilot came down near Mosta, and Goldsmith was surprised to learn it was Ernie Broad, who had been wounded in the left calf.[3]

The Hurricane was not only unable to cope with the improved Messerschmitts and Junkers, but time did not allow them to be scrambled early enough to gain a height advantage over the raiders. Once it was decided the raid was committed to Malta, there was time for the Hurricanes to climb to only 15 000 feet, but the enemy often arrived at 20 000 or 25 000 feet. In addition, the radar available was affected by the locations at which it was installed, and it was very difficult to get accurate height readings for the oncoming raids. These plots faded from the screen some 25 miles (45 km) from the island, and the enemy could make marked alterations in height before actually arriving over Malta.

A great deal depended on the Controller, on his knowledge and experience, and on his ability to keep the fighters informed with brief, accurate and timely reports on the enemy. Without this assistance from the ground, the relatively few fighters airborne were operating inefficiently. By reacting to inaccurate or out-of-date reports, they were also at a disadvantage.

The Controller, situated underground, had several factors to consider. These included the weather; the size of the approaching enemy formation; the probable target, such as ships in harbour or aircraft on the airfields; the number of fighters available to him and the severe problems with replacement of losses; and the time available to get what was available to height.

He had to decide whether to engage the raid or not, and if so, to do so over the sea or the island. If not, the fighters were to be ordered to land or go to a position out of the danger area. Conservation of the fighter force had to be taken into consideration against the possibility of destruction of some enemy in a particular formation going to a probable target.

In February, 990 tons of bombs had been dropped, but in March, in 5680 sorties, the enemy had delivered an estimated 2170 tons. The torpedo bombers operating from Malta had been forced to cease operations, and in a few days the Royal Navy would be compelled to withdraw the last few ships from Valletta's Grand Harbour. As March 1942 came to an end, the Germans had almost achieved total superiority over the central Mediterranean. All that was required to complete the process was invasion and occupation of Malta.

3

The Fury

Malta—April 1942

Honours and awards were being received on both sides of the
waters between Sicily and Malta, and on 1st April Leutnant
Herbert Stry, St.G. 3, received promotion to Oberleutnant. He
had flown Stukas in Poland, France and over England, and had
been operating in the Mediterranean theatre since December 1940.
He had been credited with damaging HMS *Illustrious* in the 1941
attacks against it. A new Kommandeur took command of III
Gruppe St.G. 3 on the same day. Kurt Walter was thirty years
old, had eight years' service in the Luftwaffe, and had flown
bomber operations since the French Campaign of 1940. He had
been awarded the Iron Cross 1st and 2nd Class.[1]

But Stuka Geschwader 3 had a bad time in the afternoon raid,
when five Spitfires of 126 Squadron engaged them, shooting down
five Stukas. Earlier in the day, Ray Hesslyn had shot down his
first enemy aircraft, a 109, and in the afternoon destroyed his
second, a Stuka. Sergeant Jack Pauley RAAF, who had arrived
on 21 March in a formation of ten Hurricanes from North Africa,
claimed a Ju87 probable and another damaged.

Paul Brennan had flown earlier, without contact, but Tony Boyd,
now flying Hurricanes on 185 Squadron, made the first of fourteen
claims for April. On the first sortie of the day, in GL-M, he engaged
a Ju88 and two 109s, noting 'results uncertain'. On his second
sortie, seven Hurricanes and four Spitfires attacked an estimated
twenty Ju87s and thirty Messerschmitts. He fastened onto a Stuka
and 'had a dogfight with it, several bursts, left it pouring white
smoke from port side. Also attacked two 109s'.

229 Squadron had also scrambled, and Sergeant Jack Pauley

had attacked a Ju88, but his guns jammed after two short bursts; other hits on the Junkers were scored by Pilot Officer Beckett of 185 Squadron. In a second scramble, of only two aircraft at 17.00 hours, Jack Pauley was shot down. His attacker or attackers may have been Oberleutnant Belser, 8/JG53, or Leutnant Neuhoff; possibly both attacked the Hurricane. Belser claimed his 23rd and Neuhoff his 40th victory.

Three Army officers saw Pauley coming down in his parachute, and launched a small boat to go out to collect him. However, HSL128 had also been sent, arrived, took on board all four men, and towed the small boat back to harbour. Pauley was admitted to hospital with shrapnel wounds and a hernia suffered when the parachute jerked open.

On 2 April, Tim Goldsmith and Dusty Miller ferried four Spitfires from Takali to Luqa. The first two were hopped across without any trouble, but when Goldsmith rang the controller to check before the second flight, he was told tersely to 'make it snappy and keep low', which was all the information offered. Miller landed first, Goldsmith second, and was 'just turning off the main runway when I saw those nasty gray streamers sizzling across my starboard wing and immediately afterwards a series of flashing explosions on the ground ten metres away. I twisted my neck around just as a 109 flew over not more than seven metres above me.

'I opened the throttle, and, ignoring the taxiway, went across the rough stuff with my tail up, until I reached the dispersal bay. Dusty raced across from the next bay, laughing his silly head off, but I was unable to see any humour in the situation for quite a time.'

However, in the combats above, Gordon Tweedale exacted a little retribution, claiming a Ju88 as a probable.

On the 3rd, Slim Yarra flew his last sortie with 249 Squadron, engaging a Ju88, firing all his ammunition at it, for no result. This was his sixth scramble, and he was still learning in the hardest pilots' school of all. Next day he was to go to 185 Squadron, Halfar.

On the same day, John Bisley, with 126 Squadron, shot down a Stuka and a Ju88 into the sea, but was set upon by a dozen 109s.

He had waited off Grand Harbour, and when a Ju88 appeared, slid in behind it. 'I got within 300 yards when three miles out to sea and was not gaining, so gave a one-second burst with cannon and observed no results.' He banked port, back to the harbour. At 6000 feet, Bisley saw about ten Ju88s diving in line astern through the anti-aircraft barrage. He positioned the Spitfire and went for one as it came out of the barrage, swinging in behind, firing to within 150 metres and broke to port as black smoke came from the port engine of the bomber. There had been no return fire. Six 109s were above, and discretion demanded he let the Junkers go.

Continually turning, he went back to the harbour, and called Control to ask if any more bombers were coming. The reply was that Ju87s were approaching.

Then at his height he saw two which had pulled out of their dives. He turned onto the closest and attacked, again swinging in astern. The rear gunner ceased fire after the first burst from the Spitfire. Bisley closed to 50 metres, fired, saw the Junkers' engine burst into flames, and then the 87 went down to starboard. Bisley broke port, as there were what he described as 'a large number' of 109s above. Two attacked, and he dived for the sea.

He began a running fight back to Malta, turning tightly as each attack came in, then straightening out for a quick dart to the distant island. But Mauser shells exploded in the bottom of the cockpit, his legs were hit with shrapnel, the instrument panel shattered, the engine was hit and labouring, so he flew in over Grand Harbour, hoping ack-ack would brush off the 109s, but they kept right on after him to Takali, eager for the kill. There was no time to lower the undercart so he put the Spitfire down in the middle of the airfield at 140 mph. Fitters ran out and helped him into a trench as another wave began bombing, and hit the Spitfire. Bisley was taken to Imtarfa 'feeling very indignant about the Luftwaffe'. The Spitfire was Category 2 damage; the Ju88 and Ju87 were later confirmed as destroyed.

In the opposite bed to Bisley was a 109 pilot, Leutnant Kurt Lauinger, who had been shot down by Norman MacQueen, an RAF member of 249 Squadron. Lauinger had broken his leg when landing by parachute. After an initial period of bad temper, he became more friendly and his English improved rapidly. On one occasion, Bisley told him that Germany would be defeated by the end of 1942, at which Kurt laughed and called out, 'Nurse! Bedpan!'

Kurt retained his sense of humour when Bisley asked for the address of his girlfriend in Hamburg, saying he would visit her as a member of the Army of Occupation, but would shut up 'like a trap', according to Tim Goldsmith, whenever Hitler was mentioned.

In tactics discussions, Kurt said that he had been shot down because he was too busy making sure his leader's tail was cleared and not worrying about his own. He sang the praises of his Staffel leader, Herman Neuhoff, who, Kurt said, had flown in Spain, Poland, France, over England and Russia, and was far too good to be shot down. Neuhoff had 38 victories and needed two more for his Knight's Cross. Disappointingly for Kurt, when he recovered from his leg injury and went to the POW camp, Neuhoff was already there, shot down on 10 April by Buck Buchanan, a Rhodesian, of 249 Squadron.

But, around and above the hospital ward and the chatting of the young pilots, the air offensive raged, and by the first week in April, over 15 500 buildings had been destroyed in the bombings, 1100 people had been killed and 2600 wounded.

Tony Boyd again flew on 5 April, against odds of twelve to one, when the fighter force was four Hurricanes and three Spitfires. One Hurricane was shot up before they engaged, but Boyd attacked two 88s and saw strikes, then had a dogfight out over the sea with four 109s, believing that he definitely damaged one. Returning to land, he was 'attacked by two 109s in the circuit, but evaded OK. Machinegun bullet through the starboard wing and one clipped the bottom of the seat and parachute cover. Phew!!'

On 7 April, Malta recorded its 2000th raid since 11 June 1940. What was more important to the morale of the Maltese people was that on this day, King George VI became Colonel-in-Chief of the Royal Malta Artillery.

As there were so few fighters, little flying was done, and all ranks were employed on building revetments for the fighters. Goldsmith noticed that while the pilots built one double bay, the Army built all the others at Takali.

The double bay built by the pilots was, in Goldsmith's words, 'near the Mad House and eastern dispersal, which was bad, but

44

near two slit trenches, which was good'.

Another pastime, which gradually became more organised and had the blessing of authority, was shooting at low-flying enemy with rifles and machineguns. All ranks and callings took part, and it could be dangerous, with some of the teams being killed or wounded. Among the pilots, Tony Boyd and Gordon Tweedale were quite active in this way of hitting back when unable to fly.

On the 8th, Tony Boyd flew three interceptions, in HA-S. On the first, seven Hurricanes and three Spitfires scrambled, and he engaged the Ju88s, claiming one probable and one damaged, from the formation of thirty bombers escorted by another thirty Messerschmitts. The section of three Hurricanes attacked the bombers head-on, and he saw some strikes on one Junkers, then switched to a second, firing a two-second burst, watching his 'tracers enter him from nose to tail, and small pieces like fabric flew off. I made a second attack on the same aircraft from astern as he dived, pouring two seconds in, definitely striking—claim Damaged.'

Pulling away, he saw another Ju88 below, and dived vertically, firing, swinging around on to its tail, still sending bursts at the bomber, and 'his starboard engine immediately poured black smoke and must have stopped as he slowed up. After another burst he began to lose height suddenly, but 109s made me break off. As I looked back there was a large splash. Claim—very probable.' This splash was estimated by Tony to be about six miles (8 km) off Zonkor Point, and later Flight Lieutenant Lloyd reported seeing foam which looked like the results of a large aircraft going into the sea about 4 miles (6 km) off Zonkor Point.

In the second scramble, the same number of enemy returned, and he waited for the 88s on the far side of the anti-aircraft barrage, attacked one, saw strikes on both engines and fuselage, then both engines seemed to be on fire, streaming black smoke, and Boyd last saw the Junkers in a dive just north of Grand Harbour. But the 109s arrived and he had to break away, initially claiming it as a probable.

Then the Hurricanes climbed again, to attack the next wave of German bombers coming in. He shot at one from below, and saw strikes on it, but no other results, then returned to land.

The third sortie consisted of a total of eight Spitfires and Hurricanes. Tony 'went out to help the Spits with the Dornier

45

rescue plane. They had already finished the job.'

Later, Tim Goldsmith recorded, the ground staff managed to supply two Spitfires and two Hurricanes for operations. This was only achieved through great ingenuity and hard work. The four fighters were sent up to intercept a raid of 120 enemy aiming at the harbour and Valletta.

The dockyard area had become a wasteland of craters, destroyed buildings and jumbled lumps of stone. Many pieces had been blown on to the deck of HMS *Penelope*, which still fought on. She was the sole remaining ship of the Royal Navy. Everything else had been sunk or gone beyond reach of the bombers. The destroyers HMS *Kingston* and *Gallant* lay under the harbour waters.

Those on the ground watched the formations of 88s and Stukas dive on to their targets, then pull out and head for home, weaving violently to avoid the anti-aircraft fire. A lone Spitfire appeared, pounced onto a Stuka, closed in, and the watchers waited for the sound of cannon fire, but were dismayed to see the Spitfire disintegrate.

The pilot was Flight Lieutenant Nip Hepple of 249 Squadron, who had been hit by a Bofors shell from the ground. At first, he did not realise what had happened, and wondered what became of his Spitfire, then pulled the ripcord, and after the parachute opened, had an excellent view of the attack as planes and bombs hurtled past him, and he actually landed in a crater which had been blown into existence less than a minute before his arrival.

A few minutes later the other Spitfire came in low, did a tight circuit and landed, finishing its rolling near the pilots' personally built bay. Tim Goldsmith saw the pilot, Ron West of 249 Squadron, climb out, 'soaked in sweat, his face drawn and white'. West had been held at 15 000 feet, alone, for 45 minutes, in a circle of 109s which made diving attacks on him as he turned and turned and turned as tightly as possible, unable to attack the bombers or to get away from the Messerschmitts.

The attack made it mandatory for *Penelope* to leave, or accept destruction in the near future. Seven of the ship's company had been killed and thirty wounded, including the Captain. So, as darkness fell, preparations were made, and that night she limped away to Gibraltar. The hundreds of holes in her hull were plugged with wooden pegs, and for a time she was called HMS 'Pepperpot' or HMS 'Porcupine'.

Captain Nicholl had been so impressed with the performance of the nearby Maltese ack-ack crews that he ordered an issue of rum for them as well as the ship's company. However, another officer countermanded the order, as it applied to Army gunners. It could only have been by the fortunes of war that this officer's apartment on shore was plastered during the next raid—by 40mm Bofors shells.

But with *Penelope* gone, only harbour tugs and similar ships remained in the once-powerful Naval base in the middle of the Mediterranean. Shore-based aircraft had proven again that ships within range are at risk.

Next day, Goldsmith and Tim 'Johnny' Johnston were on readiness, but before they could reach their Spitfires the air raid warning sounded and they were forced to take shelter in a Bofors gun pit, where the crew made them welcome. 'We slunk into the dug-out while the crew pumped up their daily ration at the raiders as they passed overhead. The din was terrific but died away as quickly as it had commenced.'

They went on, found there were no serviceable fighters and strolled off for a look at the newly made craters. The 2000 kg bombs some of the 88s had dropped made a crater in the rocky soil 20 metres across and six metres deep.

Airborne again, Tony Boyd closed on the bombers, claiming a Ju88 as damaged. The raid was reported as '50-plus Ju88s and 40-plus Me109s', which the Hurricanes disrupted with head-on attacks into the formations.

185 Squadron hit the bombers as the Germans were beginning their dives on Takali. Tony, flying a cannon-armed Hurricane MkIIc, fired a three-second burst at an approaching 88, then turned on to the next. Tony's No. 2, Gordon Tweedale, saw 'a stream of pieces fly off the 88' and it went into a dive with bits and pieces swirling back from it. A gun-post observer saw a Ju88 attacked by a Hurricane at about the same time and location, and reported that the Ju88 did not pull out of its dive. Tony claimed it as damaged or probably destroyed.

Next day, he flew another interception, and described it as 'Jerry's biggest effort yet. At least 100 Ju88s and 87s and 50 or so Me109s. Terrific odds. We couldn't do much about the bombers. Five Hurris lost, remainder shot up, but all pilots safe. Sergeant Horricks got a 109, the best flamer I've seen yet.' Fourteen Hurricanes and four Spitfires had scrambled.

This was the third raid of the day, at about 17.00, and the off-duty pilots, as usual, went out onto the bastion to watch. Tim Goldsmith counted the Hurricanes and Spitfires as they climbed to engage, and saw the combats begin at 12 000 to 15 000 feet. The watchers saw one of the distant machines begin to fall, trailing black smoke, going down, down, to explode in a great flash of flame north-east of Mosta. It was a Hurricane, and a parachute appeared high in the blue. Then another aircraft was hit, and began to burn, again a parachute appeared. This time, as the machine fell, it was identified as a Messerschmitt.

The 88s attacked Takali, one was hit, and what seemed to be three men bailed out but only one parachute opened. Later inspection showed the other two to be the rear gunner and a large part of his gun-position; he had not been wearing a parachute, or even a harness.

When the bombers had gone, 109s remained to harass the Hurricanes, and the pilots watched one Hurricane turning and turning as tightly as possible around the chimney of Cisk's Brewery, while 109s made diving attacks on him.

All the Spitfires returned safely, claiming a 109, an 88 and a probable 88. The Messerschmitt had been flown by Kurt Lauinger's Staffel leader in III/JG53, Hermann Neuhoff. Buck Buchanan, a Rhodesian in 249 Squadron, had shot him down. In a reconstruction of events, Neuhoff had attacked a Hurricane and was pulling up, Buchanan did not realise anyone was near him, a 109 appeared in his sights, range and deflection were right, he fired, hitting the 109 so hard that Neuhoff bailed out, though Buchanan did not see him and continued to attack the empty Messerschmitt.

Tim Johnston related that he 'heard later that Neuhoff was vain enough to be disappointed in Buck, who at that time had only one ring and no gong; seemed to think he wasn't distinguished enough to have shot him down.'[2]

Interestingly, in Ernst Obermaier's book on holders of the Knight's Cross, Neuhoff is said to have been shot down by another German. His Knight's Cross was awarded on 16 June, after 40 victories, including 21 in Russia.[3]

In Tim Goldsmith's diary, he records a Hurricane as being shot down on 10 April, when twelve of them and four Spitfires engaged about 50 Ju88s and the same number of 109s.

The days passed, raids continued, but there were too few fighters to have much effect. The pressure seemed to be on Valletta, and it was assumed that the Luftwaffe believed the airfields were neutralised. Building of revetments and pens continued.

On 11 April, a 500-kilogram bomb hit Mosta Cathedral, but failed to explode. It was defused and retained there as proof of divine intervention. A congregation of about three hundred was worshipping when they were showered by debris from the roof, as the monster arrived. Today the bomb is still to be seen, though the entry hole in the ceiling has been repaired.

At a far higher level of command than the pens around Takali, the effects of the raids were being discussed. On 11 April, Albert Kesselring told Mussolini and the Italian Chief of Staff, Cavallero, that 'Malta as a naval base no longer demands consideration'. The Italians were doubtful, but the Luftwaffe had driven the Royal Navy to the distant ends of the Mediterranean.

On 12 April, Goldsmith was again on readiness, and again was caught on the track to the aircraft, taking cover in the same Bofors pit. This time there was a rifle close to hand, and as a strafing 109 flew past, Tim had a shot at it, but when he began aiming for a second, his legs were pulled out from under him, and an angry Johnston reminded him that it cost 5000 pounds to train a pilot, and two-pence to make a bullet. Again, strafing had damaged their prospective Spitfires, so they had to walk back once more.

Far away in the UK, the USS *Wasp* had loaded 47 Spitfires and was leaving Glasgow, en route for Gibraltar and the Mediterranean. Churchill had requested use of a large US carrier to ferry a greater number of Spitfires to Malta, as the Royal Navy at that time had no big carrier available. On 14 April, *Wasp* began steaming south.

The day before, on Malta, 22 and 39 Squadrons prepared ten Beauforts to attack a convoy of four merchantmen, five destroyers and two flakships. On the 14th, a reconnaissance aircraft from 22 Squadron located the ships, but was chased and attacked by 109s, who riddled it while it was landing, killing the pilot and navigator. When the strike of eight Beauforts attacked, the 109s savaged them, shooting them down over the convoy, on the way back and even while they were landing back on Malta. Only

49

one Beaufort was undamaged. Five others were destroyed, and seventeen of the thirty-six men in the crews were killed. Three explosions had been seen on the two ships attacked.

On 14 April, over the island itself, Gordon Tweedale claimed a 109 damaged. Tweedale, Pilot Officer Oliver Ormrod and 'Wiggles' Wigley had been sent to assist the air-sea rescue launch, which was near Filfla and about to be attacked by ten Messerschmitts. Philip Wigley recalled it as 'an exciting but rather one-sided dogfight, but (we) managed to hold our own until the launch reached the shelter of the cliffs and light A.A. guns on Malta's south coast. I do not recall we shot any of the 109F's down, but certainly damaged one or two, and, what was more important, prevented them attacking the launch. Our little fight was observed some of the time by our own squadron groundcrew—that rarely happened during WW2, except at Malta and possibly Singapore!'

During the day, Tim 'Johnny' Johnston witnessed the death of one of the Messerschmitt leaders, Hauptmann Karl-Heinz Krahl, Knight's Cross and Kommandeur II Gruppe. 'Later watched two 109s shooting up Luqa; they climbed to 3000 feet, turned and went back again; this time only one of them pulled up, a column of black smoke showed what happened to the other. Bad tactics.' Krahl had shot down Sergeant Jack Mayall on 10 March.[4]

Krahl had flown in Spain, France and the Battle of Britain, had been awarded the Knight's Cross in November 1940, and when killed was credited with 24 victories, all against the Western Allies.[5]

Slim Yarra was flying on the 14th, in Hurricane HA-D. A gaggle of 109s set on him, hammering the fighter with machinegun and cannon, but he struggled back and crash-landed at Halfar.

Next day, 15 April, King George VI made the announcement of the award of the George Cross to the island of Malta.

'To honour her brave people I award the George Cross to
the Island Fortress of Malta to bear witness to a heroism
and devotion that will long be famous in history.'

Pilot Officer Ormrod RAF, 185 Squadron, was shot down and killed.

On the 17th, Tony Boyd was awarded the Distinguished Flying Medal, and Tim Goldsmith made the following comment: 'It was a very popular award, and nobody had ever done more to earn it than Tony. He had been with 242 and 185 Squadrons since

November and had done a lot of flying and fighting. All his successes had been gained with machineguns, and if he'd been lucky enough to have cannon, his score would have been considerably higher. Up to then, he had destroyed two aircraft, probably destroyed seven, and damaged more than twenty.' The DFM citation mentions three enemy destroyed and four as probables.

On 19 April, USS *Wasp* passed Gibraltar. As always, rumours abounded in Malta, and stories of American aircraft carriers and Spitfires were rife. But rumours had no effect on reality, and the anti-aircraft defences were to fire only half the guns in a battery, due to lack of ammunition and barrels. During the day, 229 Squadron flew to the island from Gambut, North Africa, with a dozen Hurricanes, but the Malta pilots wanted Spitfires.

Tim Goldsmith was on readiness when the phone rang. Squadron Leader Gracie answered, then told the pilots to go to their aircraft, and scramble when a red flare was fired; over one hundred enemy aircraft were forming up over Sicily.

Goldsmith checked his cockpit; petrol on, reflector sight OK, air pressure up, oxygen bottle on, radio cord plugged in, then sat and waited. After a while, he walked over to the next pen and chatted with Jimmy Peck, an American. They decided it must have been a false alarm. They watched the squadron staff car, an impressed civilian vehicle, begin driving around the perimeter, but there was no sign of enemy.

Suddenly the staff car turned and raced back to 'G' shelter, where the operations room had been constructed under ten metres of rock. No red flare. 'Then I heard them', said Goldsmith. 'From the direction of Safi Strip came a swarm of 88s, larger than I had ever seen in one lot before. As I watched, the leader started his dive on Luqa. Where was I to hide? Fifty metres away was a small stone hut, originally a goatherd's shelter. I hit this like a rat going down a hole and crouched inside.'

Through the narrow door, he could see each stick of bombs explode across the airfield, then feel the blast shaking the hut, and several rocks fell on him. Again the world was composed of gun fire, bursting shells, exploding bombs and the high-pitched roar of the bombers as they pulled out of their dives and weaved away out to sea.

After what seemed a long time, the raid ended. The pall of

smoke and dust began to drift away. Directly opposite was a newly arrived Wellington bomber, burning, the usual column of thick black smoke rising above. Off in the distance, another pillar of smoke marked another burning plane. The airfield was covered with craters. But coming through the haze were trucks full of soldiers, who were carrying picks and shovels, and behind them groaned an old steamroller. At once, work began on repairing the runways.

Gracie came around and collected them, explaining that the controller had decided to keep the Spitfires on the ground as a smaller raid was expected in the afternoon, and he had thought the pilots would prefer to engage when they were outnumbered only by six to one. No one was hurt, but the distant machine on fire was Tim Johnston's, and he took Goldsmith's instead, which released Tim from operations.

Shortly after, Slim Yarra came to collect a Hurricane, and the two Aussies had a chat. Then the expected smaller, second raid was detected and Gracie drove around again, dropping the pilots. The Spitfires went off, climbing hard, and soon the Germans appeared—Stukas escorted by thirty or more Messerschmitts. The attack began, and the Spitfires dived into the melee, sliding down to mesh with the Stukas.

The watchers could hear the rattle of cannon and machine-guns, then saw two Stukas on fire, one going down into Valletta and the other falling into the sea outside Grand Harbour. Tex Putnam, ex-Eagle Squadron member, slipped in to make a dead-stick landing, rolling to a halt in the middle of the airfield. He ran to the group of watching pilots and said he had run out of petrol, so it was decided to take the bowser truck and fix this.

When they reached the middle of the open ground, two Messerschmitts leaped up from the Safi end of the strip, and the impromptu crew of the bowser took cover underneath it. Later, they realised it was not the best place to shelter from a raid. By the time the Spitfire had been refuelled and was in a pen, the others had returned and landed.

The raid dislocated the electricity supply, and the rations had not arrived, so 'candles illuminated our supper of eggs and chips at The Queen's', wrote Goldsmith.

On 20 April, forty-six Spitfires flew in from the US carrier, and the island managed to put fifteen fighters up to keep the

Luftwaffe away. Tim Johnston had never seen so many RAF fighters over Malta. There were eleven Spitfires and four Hurricanes, two of which were flown by Tony Boyd and Gordon Tweedale. Paul Brennan shot down a 109, ten kilometres west of Gozo, then over Takali attacked a Ju88, setting both engines on fire. 249 Squadron claimed 8-1-1.

Working on the walls around the aircraft pens, the pilots heard what Tim Goldsmith described as 'that familiar engine note, and watched with joy as wave after wave of Spitfires flew in over Mdina and circled to land at Takali and Luqa. We counted forty-six, and were pleased to learn that they were four-cannon jobs, the first to go on operations.'

At lunch-time, the pilots met the new arrivals, found many old friends from England, and caught up on the doings of others. The old Malta pilots were pleased to find that half the new fighters were to be allocated to 126 and 249 Squadrons, while the others belonged to 601 and 603 Squadrons, led respectively by Squadron Leaders Bisdee and Lord David Douglas Hamilton.

What was not immediately obvious to the 'old Malta hands' was the relative inexperience of the majority of the new arrivals. With fifty Spitfire squadrons available from which to select reinforcements for the flight to Malta, it was inexcusable to send pilots with no operational experience at all, and some with only 25 hours on Spitfires. Many of the RAF squadrons' casualties were these unfortunate men on their first, or an early, sortie, against experienced Luftwaffe pilots.

The sirens sounded, and all the pilots clustered out onto the bastion to watch. Despite the thick anti-aircraft fire, 'the bombers came down as though it didn't exist'. To add insult to injury, one bomb had landed right in the centre of the pen which had absorbed so much of the labour and time of the pilots. The pen was destroyed, together with the Spitfire in it.

In combats with the Ju88s attacking Takali, Tony Boyd claimed an 88, which authority decided he had to share with the ack-ack guns, and three more damaged, while Tweedale claimed two destroyed.

Tony, in GL-L, had been one of the small formation of two Hurricanes and eight Spitfires which had scrambled to engage what he believed to be four waves each of 15 to 20 Ju88s or 87s, with Bf109 escort, totalling over a hundred. He had seen strikes on four 88s, one of them 'a smoker'. As he attacked another it was struck by anti-aircraft fire, there was an explosion, and the crew baled out.

The first 88 was diving on Takali, and Boyd closed to 100 metres, firing a three-second burst, watching strikes on the fuselage centre-section, then broke off. Just south of Takali he attacked another, from port, his four-second burst hitting the fuselage and port wing.

The third was just south of Luqa, but just after his machinegun burst hit the Junkers so did what seemed to be a 40mm Bofors round, pieces flew off, and two crew members baled out over the sea off Filfla. He saw yet another Ju88 south of Hal Far, Boyd went for it from starboard, firing as it turned and went away with black smoke pouring from it. He claimed it as damaged.

Pilot Officer Tex Putnam and Flight Sergeant Ryckman were killed during the afternoon's combats. Putnam's parachute caught on the Spitfire's radio mast, and Ryckman was shot down into the sea.

Slim Yarra, flying 185 Squadron Hurricane HA-C, noted that they had scrambled six Spitfires and four Hurricanes to fight plots of 60-plus and 20-plus, glumly adding, 'Everyone shot down. I crash-landed.' Goldsmith and the others were 'naturally pretty depressed about the performance as we returned to our Mess.' He was on dawn readiness next day, so went to bed early.

The severity of the bombing, by an estimated 89 bombers which concentrated on Takali, had left the area a chaos of smoke, dust, craters and fires. It seemed that the airfield would be out of action for several days, but the British Army units concerned moved in, and systematically began work. By dawn, a runway was ready and flyable aircraft were ferried to the other airfields. Twenty-seven Spitfires remained available, while others needed repair. Two had been destroyed in the attack.

As well as the lack of experienced pilots in the batch of reinforcements, another serious matter was the condition of the new Spitfires. Rather than being sent in ready for action with the minimum of work by the crews on Malta, the fighters had been despatched with unclean cannon, unserviceable radios, and many other minor matters which required attention, and resulted in the aircraft not being ready for operations.

Before dawn on 21 April, Goldsmith and Mick Graves collected two Spitfires at Takali and flew to Luqa, 'as the sun popped over the horizon to see if Malta was still there.' There were six Spitfires and four Hurricanes available. Gracie took four Spitfires, and allocated Jimmy Peck, with Goldsmith as his No. 2, to protect the Hurricanes. They were Wombat White Section.

At 08.00 they scrambled, and the two Spitfires took station above and behind the Hurricanes from Hal Far. However, as they climbed, Goldsmith and Peck drew further and further ahead of the Hurricanes. As they passed through 18 000 feet, Goldsmith looked down and saw the Hurricanes mixing it with some 109s, and called Peck to suggest they go down. But Peck had seen another gaggle of 109s above them, swinging round to attack, and Tim 'forgot all about the party below'.

The Messerschmitts darted in, making a series of scissors attacks from front and rear, and the two Spitfires circled tightly to avoid each lunge. 'Tracers flicked past on all sides,' recalled Goldsmith, 'but I had no opportunity to do any shooting myself, as I was staggering around at less than 100 mph, while they must have been doing 250 as they attacked.'

Goldsmith lost contact with Peck, then 'decided there was no future in this business', and went into an aileron turn, watching his speed build up as he went down to 5000 feet, levelled out and looked around to see if the coast was clear. 'It wasn't. Six of the apes had followed me down and I broke violently into a steep turn as I was attacked from the rear.'

Again Goldsmith was forced to turn, and turn as steeply as possible, while 109s circled above, waiting for an opportunity. He was some twelve kilometres offshore, and each time he eased off the turn and dodged toward the coast, 'down came the wolves. One came down, holding his fire until he closed in, so I delayed my evasive action until he was reasonably close. As soon as I started it, he eased back on the stick and sailed over my head, I immediately reversed the controls and pulled up after him.'

The 109 was turning port above, outlined against the sky, and 'At 200 yards range I gave him a four-second burst with my four cannon and was very pleased to see flashes as the high-explosive shells smacked home into his wing and fuselage. His zoom fell off into a dive and he went down towards the sea. I thought he was going to get away, then suddenly the machine hit the drink and disappeared immediately.'

The port cannon had stopped after two seconds' firing, but Tim continued with his two starboard cannon.

'I was suddenly reminded of his cobbers when I felt and heard explosions in my port wing as Mauser cannon shells struck. Again a 109 pulled up over me and again I pulled up my nose after him and fired. This time only my two starboard cannon fired, making accurate shooting rather difficult. I had the satisfaction of seeing flashes along his fuselage.'

But the next 109 was behind, firing and hitting. The aileron jammed and Goldsmith, 'in a terrific funk', pushed the stick forward, then the throttle and emergency boost lever, heading for Grand Harbour and the protection of the guns there. Tracer flicked by as the 109s followed, hitting the Spitfire again, then they swung away. He crossed the coast at 1500 feet near Sliema.

As he flew towards Luqa, Goldsmith was hit by the reaction to the flight and combat, and had to hold back a strong desire to vomit. Very reluctant to have to clean out the cockpit, he mastered the feeling of sickness, then noticed a Spitfire pull up alongside.

It was Ray Hesslyn, the New Zealander, who told him there was a fight over St Paul's Bay. Goldsmith agreed to go with Hesslyn, then found he was low on petrol, as well as having jammed ailerons. He rebuked himself, and turned back to Luqa.

Jimmy Peck was back OK, but Pilot Officer Brooker was gone, shot down by the 109s. A gun crew on the island had seen Goldsmith's 109 crash into the sea, so he was credited with one Messerschmitt 109F confirmed destroyed, and another damaged.

The Luftwaffe maintained the pressure, and formations of 150 bombers and fighters attacked the island. Paul Brennan, in U-2, was on readiness in the afternoon, and scrambled. Woodhall kept them high while the first wave attacked the harbour, but brought them in to attack the second wave who were going for Luqa. They began to dive on the bombers below them, at 10 000 feet.

Brennan had picked an 88 as a target, looked behind to check, and saw two 109s coming in at him. He estimated the Messerschmitts to be too far away to really interfere with his attack before he finished the bomber, so continued his dive on it. At 300 metres he opened fire for three seconds, then the port cannon stopped. A quick look behind—the 109s were closing fast—in front the 88 was close, so Paul fired again, two seconds, then tracer from the 109s was streaking past his starboard wing, he broke port, saw six more diving, so pulled up and fired at one, but he was going too slowly and the recoil from cannon in one wing only slewed the Spitfire so the shells missed. He decided it was unhealthy in that piece of sky, so dived away.

Woodhall had reported 88s attacking Takali, so he went in that direction, picked an 88 and began to stall turn after it, having looked around and not seen any 109s. But one was attacking, firing, and a shell burst in the cockpit. 'Suddenly there was a flash between my legs and a loud bang in the cockpit. I was paralysed with fear. For a few seconds I just sat there, doing nothing.'

Then, noting a hole in the cockpit near his right boot, he instantly realised the 109 was attacking from that side, and broke starboard. 'I did not see the 109 at any stage—either which way he came or which way he went.' Testing the controls, he found they were intact and decided to land, but after diving to the area could not find the airfield at first because of the smoke and dust.

Then began an exhausting time, flying round and round the airfield, over the hills and into the valleys, dodging the circling, diving, firing 109s, holding back the sickness and tiredness, waiting for an opportunity to get down onto the ground, but always the 109s were there above.

'With all the violent turning and twisting I was compelled to undertake, I began to feel very sick. I wanted to vomit, but somehow managed to choke it back. My neck ached from constantly twisting it from side to side, looking back, and from holding it up, while doing tight turns, against the extra gravity force. I was flying automatically, watching the skies above.'

Paul decided to try somewhere else, so flew out to the cliffs, diving down alongside them, using the rock-faces to protect his port side, keeping low over the water, and began to recover from the efforts of the previous minutes. Relaxation was almost fatal. 'A great streak of tracer flashed past me. I realised that 109s had seen me trying to creep off, and, coming down sun, had got on my tail.'

He broke starboard, away from the cliffs, and the 109s went past. Tiredly, he flew back to Takali, resolved to land somehow. ' . . . I put my wheels and flaps down, did a violent steep turn over the fence, side-slipped my height away, fish-tailed my speed off, and popped my aircraft down right between two bomb-holes. I felt exhausted and dead tired, both physically and mentally. The strain, particularly in the circuit, had played me right out.' One of the groundcrew had to come out and guide him through the maze of craters into a pen. Brennan had to be helped out of the cockpit, and he stumbled along the wing, dizzy and holding on to it.[6] Gordon Tweedale claimed an 88 destroyed during the raid.

Paul Brennan flew another sortie in the afternoon. He had already experienced an uncomfortable time when caught in the open by a strafing 109, and felt very conspicuous wearing his yellow Mae West life jacket. At 15.00, they scrambled, climbing to 26 000 feet. Brennan, in Spitfire U-2, was with Buck Buchanan.

They were engaged by several formations of 109s, who made passes at the tightly turning Spitfires, until 'Three of the four 109s overshot me. The fourth made his turn too wide, and I got inside him. I was slightly below him when I attacked from 200 metres. I allowed some deflection, firing 6 metres ahead of him in the hope that my bullets and his aircraft would arrive at that spot simultaneously. They did. He spurted glycol. I kept on firing, as I was determined to make certain of him. He caught fire. He rolled on his back, and went into a vertical dive.'[7]

The Messerschmitt went into the sea, with Brennan following him down for a distance to make sure, then he broke in case any of the other 109s had come down also. He climbed to 10 000 feet looking for the bombers, and suddenly they were diving right past him, with the Spitfires after them.

Brennan swung on to the tail of an 88, and picked up speed in the dive, closed to 200 metres and fired. After a one-second burst, the port cannon stopped, which normally would have slewed the Spitfire, but its speed this time kept it relatively straight, and he kept on firing until all the ammunition was gone, aiming at the starboard engine and wing-root, which burst into flames. The Junkers, followed by Buchanan's target, crashed into the sea.

The island claimed ten enemy aircraft destroyed and seven damaged for the day's actions. Rations were cut again, though it was already acknowledged that providing adequate food was difficult. If food could not be supplied in large amounts, weapons and ammunition were, and it was announced that groundcrews were to be encouraged to fire at passing enemy aircraft.

Next day, 22 April, another newly arrived Australian, G. M. 'Max' Briggs, 601 Squadron, shared an 88 with three other pilots from 249, 601 and 603 Squadrons.

Tired as they were, facing large numbers of enemy aircraft each day, operating in the knowledge that the Messerschmitts were waiting for them to take off, waiting to fight at all heights, and waiting for them to land, the fighter pilots screwed up their personal reserves and went out to the dispersal pens each time they were on duty. The Spitfire pilots were able to feel compassion for the Hurricane pilots, flying an inferior aircraft against the same odds.

Paul went to Hal Far to talk to Tony Boyd and 'Slim' Yarra, Gordon Tweedale and the other Hurricane pilots. He found that, while they were aware of the shortcomings of the Hurricane, they were personally confident of its ability to dog-fight with any single Messerschmitt, and even thought it superior in that regard to the Spitfire. Their greatest concern was the relatively ineffective armament of .303 inch machineguns, which simply was not heavy enough to destroy the German aircraft. Armour and fuel-tank protection had been added since the hey-day of the Hurricane in 1940. Boyd and Tweedale had each shot down an 88 with machineguns, and were quite pleased about it.

On 22 April, Frank Jemmet had been attacked by 109s, but flew on, and crash-landed in one of the small stone-walled fields near Rabat. The plane burst into flames, Jemmet had been pulled out but died in an Army ambulance en route to Imtarfa.

Next day, Tim Goldsmith and Dusty Miller went into Valletta, looking for excitement and adventure, saw what 'The Gut' had to offer and returned to the squadron to go on readiness. As it happened, Tim did not fly, but sat out the raid while the squadron attacked Stukas with no friendly casualties, and all climbed into the car to return to the Mess 'in high spirits', which were soon dampened when a piece of shrapnel punctured a tyre. There was no spare and they had to wait for the next passing truck to hitch-hike back.

Gordon Tweedale claimed a Ju87 on the 23rd. Tony Boyd flew again on 24 April, in GL-L, when six Hurricanes and four Spitfires engaged 40-plus bombers and the Messerschmitt 109 escort. He attacked five separate Messerschmitts, and claimed two as damaged.

It was 08.00, and at 10 000 feet the Hurricanes were bounced by four 109s. Tony turned into them, swung back as they passed and gave the last one a burst, with no results, as the Messerschmitt was 230 metres away and going fast. But Tony had lost the Hurricane formation. Alone, at 7000 feet, he was attacked by two 109s. He broke into them, swung back and again fired at the last one, 100 metres away, seeing some hits.

Another pair of 109s were after a Spitfire, and he dived on to them. Catching the last one as the German pulled up, Tony fired a two-second burst, but as the strikes flashed on the rear of the fuselage, thin streams of black smoke poured from the 109's exhausts as the pilot went to full throttle and his Daimler-Benz engine hauled him away out of range.

More of the ever-present Messerschmitts were there, and he found himself in 'a private dogfight with six Me's over Hal Far, 5000 feet, for ten minutes.'

He took a fleeting opportunity to fire at a pair, with no result, but then he caught another, from only 50 metres' range on the Messerschmitt's starboard, and fired the last of his ammunition, the hits sparked along the 109's fuselage and starboard wing, and it pulled up very steeply, rocking from side to side. Tony thought the controls may have been hit; the pilot also may have been wounded.

The Germans had been shooting too, and his rudder controls were shot away, but he landed relatively safely. There were three other bullet holes in the wing. It was indeed a long way from practising landings in paddocks at Narromine.

Tim Goldsmith's birthday was on 25 April, and he hoped for a quiet day, perhaps some 'spine-bashing followed by a quiet pub-crawl, not picking fights with bull-headed Germans'. But he was on afternoon readiness, No. 2 to Jimmy Peck once again.

They were scrambled, but his propeller began throwing oil back onto the windscreen, then the cockpit canopy came loose when he tried to close it, and flew off, so taking all this as a sign from the Patron Saint of Fighter Pilots, Tim told Peck he was turning back, and went down to land.

Tony Boyd was airborne, one of a total of seven Hurricanes

60

and Spitfires, in a cannon-armed IIc version with no letters, number 2481, leading a section. They flew 50 km out to sea, orbiting at 25 000 feet, then attacked the last wave of enemy. Twenty Ju88s and escorting 109s were crossing the coast, and the RAF fighters 'jumped them beautifully. I got right in to 50 metres on one and my blasted cannon would not fire!!! Also got a stray shot of machinegun through two oil-pipes; everything covered in oil.'

When Paul Brennan scrambled, he was to fly with Buck McNair leading. Brennan was No. 3, leading the second two in the formation for his first time as leader. McNair gave him some advice while waiting to go. He told Paul there were three rules: first, get the section into a good tactical position to begin; second, attack with decision and unhesitatingly; third, use judgment about when to break contact.

They had scrambled, with McNair's No. 2 being Squadron Leader Lord David Hamilton, commander of 603 Squadron, which had flown in off the latest aircraft carrier reinforcement. Hamilton was getting some experience of local conditions before leading his squadron. Brennan had Linton, a Canadian, on his wing. As they climbed, Paul noticed his airspeed indicator was not working. Bees, undetected by the groundcrew, had built a nest in the pitot-tube. He decided to carry on with the flight.

On orders from Woodhall, the first wave of 88s were allowed to bomb Takali, then the Spitfires were brought in on the second wave, which was attacking Naxxar. The air seemed full of 88s, 109s and bursts from the ack-ack guns. Below, Paul could see the 88s which had attacked Takali speeding out over the cliffs, and the second wave bombing Naxxar. He selected one and dived on it.

Six 109s, guarding the port side of the bomber formation, attacked. Brennan was forced to leave the bomber and turn into them. 'All but the last overshot me. I pulled up ten or twelve metres underneath him. It was point-blank range, and every detail of his machine stood out vividly. I could see his markings, his twin radiators, his retracted wheels, even the rivet heads on his fuselage. I gave him a second and a half with all four cannon. The result gave me a terrible fright. His starboard wing snapped off near the fuselage. It folded back and banged against his fuselage. For a moment I thought it was going to tear away from his machine and come hurtling into my aircraft. I broke down very violently so as to avoid it. Five hundred metres away, dead in front of me, was an 88.'

He went after it, quickly looking around for the ubiquitous 109s. Some were diving, but so far away that he decided to attack the bomber. Speeding in, he ignored the streams of tracer from the rear gunner, and at 250 metres' range opened fire with the four 20mm cannon. The rear gunner stopped firing, and Brennan could see the flashes of exploding shells on the 88. He shifted his aim to the cockpit, but even as smoke began to flick back, he knew the 109s were closing from behind, so kept on firing. More hits flashed on the 88, then it caught fire and began to disintegrate. It crashed near Takali.

Paul broke, and skidded into the bomber's slipstream, momentarily thinking the buffeting there was from hits by the 109s. He righted the Spitfire and looked around. Two 109s sped past, overshooting, and others had taken up position over the bombers. All around were 109s and 88s, and when Buck McNair called, asking if he was OK, Brennan replied that he was, but in the middle of the enemy. McNair was going to attack some Stukas. Brennan told him to beware of the 109s, then dived to Takali; his ammunition had gone on the bomber.

After a few minutes, McNair joined him, and they flew across to Hal Far. Although both were out of ammunition, they intended assisting the Hurricanes trying to land there. The 109s were having sport with the Hurricanes, preventing them from landing. When the Messerschmitts saw the Spitfires approaching, they dodged away, and assembled at 5000 feet, watching.

McNair became annoyed with the Hurricanes, as some confusion arose when they were attempting to land. When one was approaching with wheels and flaps down, another would come flying in from behind, in an attempt to check the runway for his own landing. But the first pilot would see an aircraft coming in fast from behind, assume it was a 109, and break, whipping up wheels and flaps. Not far away was a gaggle of real 109s, probably laughing, working out what next to do to make life miserable for their enemies. Meanwhile McNair and Brennan had no ammunition and were running out of petrol.

Brennan had to land without an airspeed indicator, but managed it with help from McNair, who flew alongside reporting his own speeds. Hamilton and Linton returned soon after, with no victories. McNair and Brennan had got two each, and gave an impromptu amateur wardance in the dispersal area.[8]

Gordon Tweedale claimed a 109 destroyed. He had scrambled with Philip Wigley RAF, Sergeant Dodd RCAF and Sergeant Finlay RAF to engage a raiding force of 100 Ju87s and 88s with Bf109 escort. The RAF launched six Hurricanes and seven Spitfires. 'We succeeded in damaging several bombers,' said Wigley, 'but, being badly outnumbered by the 109 escort, had to try very hard to stay alive. We really needed an additional pair of eyes in the back of our head!'

At about this time, Brennan started to realise that he was considered to be an 'old hand', with other pilots asking him questions about flying over Malta. Pilots who had flown in the Battle of Britain, or who were quite experienced in fighter operations over the Continent, openly admitted that the flying over Malta was tougher.

All 126 Squadron returned 'after sweating it out with the 109s', but 601 lost Pawson, and the Hurricanes lost Fletcher and Corfe.

In the evening, Tim Goldsmith and a few others went to The Queen's Hotel, hoping for some beer to celebrate, but there was none and they were 'forced to work up a mild glow with Spanish port.'

The unrelenting Luftwaffe attacks had again brought the island to a crisis point. Air Vice-Marshal Lloyd knew that fighter reinforcements would not arrive until at least 9 May, but Spitfires and Hurricanes were being lost each day. His losses for April would be 41 destroyed and 87 damaged, and on the 27th he signalled Cairo, describing how close to disaster the island was, particularly if the radar and radio installations were destroyed. He concluded with a request for 'help from outside to counter the bombing nuisance.'[9]

Tony Boyd again led a section on 28 April, in another cannon-armed Hurricane IIc, GL-A. Nine fighters engaged 60-plus, and he fired at two Ju87s and a Ju88, but made no claim, remarking in his log-book, 'I am a bad shot with cannon.'

In the evening, Miller and Goldsmith went to the Naval Chief Petty Officer's Club at Sliema, where they met Tony Boyd and Ernie Broad. There they drank and discussed the war, until 'having decided Malta was in a weak strategic position, we went to bed.'

Even in the relatively restricted world of the fighter squadrons, it was obvious that Malta was in a serious situation. The number of fighters was very small, and in no way adequate to defend the island. While the Germans were sustaining losses, they were able to get through to their intended targets. The RAF bomber force lay in ruins in the pens around Luqa; the naval surface units had been driven out, and from 26 April the submarines were withdrawn. The ceaseless battering by II Fliegerkorps was telling.

Since the beginning of the blitz on 20 March, 5800 bomber sorties, 5600 fighter sorties and over 300 reconnaissance sorties had been flown over Malta by the enemy. The tonnage of bombs dropped on the island was equal to that dropped on the entire United Kingdom in September 1940. And Malta is only seventeen miles by nine miles (27 kilometres by 14.5 kilometres).

Squadron Leader 'Jumbo' Gracie had been promoted from command of 126 Squadron to command Takali airfield itself, as a Wing Commander. He made some positive changes to the organisation of the airfield, aimed at raising morale and improving efficiency. Daily Routine Orders were headed 'It is the duty of every airman to kill the Hun.' Rifles and ammunition were provided to all the dispersal pens so the patient, enduring groundcrews could shoot back at the passing Germans. This may not have had much effect on the Luftwaffe, but did boost the elan of the fitters, mechanics and others who had previously been subjected to attack without being able to retaliate. Some light machineguns were also set up and manned by the groundcrews. Gracie's actions and words created a spirit of determination in everyone.

But a more immediate matter was confronting the anti-aircraft gun crews. By 29 April they had shot down, or claimed and been awarded, 99 German aircraft for the month. They had been told that if the one hundredth was destroyed before 30 April, every man would be given a bottle of beer. Some were worried that the Luftwaffe might not come. But the Germans attacked as usual, and at the end of the day the gunners had been credited with a 109 and a Ju88.

29 April was Goldsmith's first time as section leader. When the afternoon raid was announced, he led his four Spitfires as high and as fast as possible, levelled off at 20 000 feet, then swung

back towards the island from the south-west with the sun behind them.

A staffel of 109s skated past above without seeing them, then Goldsmith saw the ack-ack bursts and the bombers, thirty Ju88s at 15 000 feet, with 109 escorts, and then more 109s some 3000 feet above. The 88s began their dives, and Goldsmith took the Spitfires down after them, but the Germans were so far away and so fast that they had bombed and were scooting out to sea before the Spitfires reached them.

'I closed on one and at about 150 metres range opened up, my port cannon fired a couple of rounds, my starboard fired one and they both packed it in,' recalled Goldsmith. 'Cursing violently, I broke away as the rear gunner's tracers came snaking at me.'

To starboard, he saw Paddy Schade firing and hitting another Junkers, then noticed a 109 swinging onto Schade's tail, and kicked the Spitfire around to menace the German, who dodged away. Another 88 went down burning from Junior Crist's guns, and the 109s swarmed onto the Spitfires, preventing more damage to the bombers.

Not in the mood for 'such frivolity', Goldsmith avoided a head-on attack by diving to wave-top level, and went back to base. As he neared Luqa, he saw a Spitfire coming in to land with its wheels up, and called on the radio, 'Wheels, wheels.'

Back came Crist's Canadian accent, 'Wheels be buggered,' and the Spitfire slithered along the runway, stopping in a cloud of dust. The plane had been badly damaged, and Crist wounded in the hands and arms when shells burst in the cockpit. He and Schade had shot down Ju88s, and Jimmy Peck was credited with a 109 probably destroyed.

After four of 126 returned from a patrol over an air sea rescue launch, and landed at Takali, the pilots saw a Hurricane coming in to land, when 'suddenly a 109 popped up from nowhere', recalled Tim Goldsmith, 'and gave it a brisk strafing'. The Hurricane staggered in and landed wheels up, the watchers ran across to see who the pilot was, and found Tony Boyd, covered in glycol. He climbed out, shrugged and said, 'Oh well, it wasn't a very good kite anyway.'

A total of twelve fighters had been scrambled to intercept thirty Ju88s and Bf109s. The Hurricane leader's radio had failed, and

Tony Boyd took over as flight leader. They made a successful interception eight kilometres east of Kalafrana, and engaged the bombers, upsetting their attack. He claimed one 88 damaged, and was 'strafed by 109s as I touched down; machine riddled with machinegun fire. Armour plate saved my back.' The aircraft had been the cannon-armed IIc, GL-A.

Tony had made claims on six days of April, totalling ten Luftwaffe aircraft as probables or damaged. Only two had been fighters, the others bombers. That simple statement should be read in conjunction with the more detailed descriptions of combats to understand what it meant to persist in closing with the Junkers in a sky filled with swift deadly Messerschmitts, who so often drove the attacking fighters away, and who gave no second chances and no mercy. By the end of April, Tony Boyd had a total of 263 hours 40 minutes.

On 28 April, the Luftwaffe flew 190 sorties over Malta, and 220 on the 29th. But maintenance was needed on Sicily as much as on Malta, and some units were to be returned to the Russian Front. The next few days would see a distinct drop in the number of attacking German aircraft.

But, unaware of this, on the night of the 29th Goldsmith and Ernie Broad went to The Queen's 'for a few ports', and spent the time teaching Carrie Busuttil's children the fine points of Snakes and Ladders.

While the handful of Spitfires was twisting and turning through the shoals of Messerschmitts and Junkers, a crucial conference was held at Obersalzberg. Hitler, Mussolini, Cavallero and Kesselring had decided to go ahead with the invasion of Malta. Kesselring had claimed optimistically that the island was broken, and asked for the operation to be launched on 31 May. But Mussolini and Cavallero pointed out that if this was so, then invasion was no longer necessary, so the original date of 1 August should be observed.

Always alert for a cheaper way to victories, especially since the heavy losses in Russia, added to memories of the severe casualties suffered by the airborne formations in the invasion of Crete, and faced with the vacillating Italians, Hitler refused to permit the earlier invasion, but compromised by deciding on 18 July, after the projected fall of Tobruk.

Hitler's fear was that the parachute troops might land, and

be left in the lurch by the Italian Navy if the Royal Navy came out from Gibraltar or Alexandria. Never comfortable with naval matters, and not believing in the resolution of his southern ally, Hitler hoped that he would not be forced to launch an airborne and seaborne invasion on the tiny island in the Mediterranean. Perhaps Kesselring and Rommel would make it unnecessary.

The Luftwaffe and Regia Aeronautica had flown 10 300 sorties over the island, beaten down the defences, and could attack at will. The Royal Navy approached Malta at its own risk, with the certainty of heavy losses. The only regular contact with the outside world, apart from radio, was the nightly arrival and departure of aircraft from Gibraltar and Egypt.

In February, 993 tons of bombs had been dropped, in March, 2174 tons, and in April, 6728 tons. In April, the dockyard area received an estimated 3156 tons, and the three airfields 2400 tons between them, with the balance on other targets. In the three days 20-22 April, 104 tons fell on Luqa and 337 tons on Takali. On the 25th, three separate attacks were made on 39 General Hospital, and other places hit in raids included 45 General Hospital, the University, the Museum, the Opera House and many private homes.

In late April, an estimated 210 enemy aircraft were available for the attacks on Malta. The daily average was 130 sorties, but on 20 April 325 had been mounted, and on seven other days over 200 sorties were flown. Some crews were flying three attack sorties a day. The air offensive had been doubling every month since January, and the Spitfire reinforcements had been barely enough to retain a defensive presence. Because of unrelenting enemy pressure and lack of adequate maintenance and repair, each batch of Spitfires had lasted one or two weeks. Few, if any, hoped that May would bring relief from the siege. That was too much to wish for.

4

The Tempest

Malta—May 1942

To open the month, 'Slim' Yarra, 185 Squadron, was sent off at night to attempt to destroy the raiding bombers. In Hurricane H-3, he was vectored onto the raider, a Ju88, came close enough to see its exhausts, closed in and fired. The 88 dived, and disappeared from the radar screen, but he could only be credited with a probable. It was his eighth combat, and first claim after five weeks on the island.

This combat of Yarra's seems to have been a turning point. Since arriving on Malta he had been on the receiving end of the Luftwaffe effort, and several times had been forced to return in damaged aircraft. But from this sortie, things were to be different.

On 2 May, the electricity supply was restored. Communications by telephone could be resumed, and no longer need the people scattered around the airfields rely on flags and flares to warn of incoming raids, scrambles, the all-clear and other activity.

On the same day, 249 Squadron encountered its first Italian fighters. Early in the day, while doing an air test on his engine, Paul Brennan had Norman MacQueen and Watts leave him to do a cannon test on the rocky islet of Filfla, where they met four 109s and shot one down; a successful test. Buck Buchanan and Ray Hesslyn went off to engage a reported large formation of enemy, which turned out to be six Ju88s with an escort of 109s and Macchi 202s.

They tried to get at the bombers but the 109 escort was alert and aggressive, continually forcing them away, and both landed without being able to claim more than a 'damaged' by Buchanan. Both were chased and attacked in the landing circuit until the

Messerschmitts went home. The Macchis were seen during the combat to fly on, maintaining a tight echelon starboard formation, throughout the period of engagement.

For the next few days the Macchis were seen coming over, always in the same formation, never engaging, and it was assumed they were along to gain experience of the situation over Malta.

On 4 May, Paul Brennan was flying again, in Spitfire A-2, led by Norman MacQueen. In the pre-flight discussion, MacQueen decided to go well to the south of Malta, gaining height, then turn and come back down, using the speed of a dive to break through the fighter escort and get close to the bombers, which were the target of fighter interception. Pilot Officer Almos, of the American Eagle Squadron, was MacQueen's No. 2. Linton was No. 4 to Brennan.

However, when they scrambled, Almos and Linton were slow getting off the ground and the Spitfires were only at 8000 feet when the 109s arrived. The Spitfires were flying up-sun, just south of Gozo. The Spitfire formation was shattered, and Messerschmitts were all around them. Brennan saw Linton in a vertical dive with four 109s after him, and he had no idea where the others were. He was throwing his fighter all over the sky, avoiding darting 109s, for what seemed an hour, but was probably only a few minutes.

Far below, at only 5000 feet, five Italian Cants droned across the harbour, ignoring the ack-ack fire, keeping formation, one hit, falling a little then closing up again, plodding through and away. The Messerschmitts were keeping the Spitfires away. Watchers on the ground stared up into the blue, hearing the whine of engines and mutter of cannon, unable to see the combats in the glare.

A 109 attacked Paul Brennan from below, missed, and 'pulled up straight ahead of me. He was a sitting target. I gave him four seconds. He went into a spin, pouring glycol.'

By some violent manoeuvring, Brennan broke contact with the other Messerschmitts, called Linton, and headed for Takali, where Linton was waiting. Then Almos called that MacQueen was in trouble, and wanted to land. Brennan saw his aircraft, seemingly under control, and flew towards him. MacQueen's Spitfire gave a couple of lurches, slipping off height, then went into a vertical dive, crashing outside Naxxar. Brennan covered the landings of the other two, but had to endure another session of harassment by the waiting 109s before he could get down.

Apparently, MacQueen's radio had failed, and he did not hear Almos warning him of a 109 darting up from below. It seemed to be making for Sicily, lifted to fire at MacQueen, hit him, then continued on its way. Presumably, MacQueen was badly or mortally wounded, and the aircraft went down vertically.

Denis Barnham, a Flight commander in 601 Squadron, has described the incident as seen by himself and a group of other squadron pilots from the slope outside the Mess at Luqa. They had watched the Italian bombers, and peered into the sky for the fighter combats, seen the two Spitfires dive towards them and circle the cloud of bomb dust, noting that they were two close for correct tactical positioning. A 109 flashed past, banking a little, but going too fast to shoot properly, and kept going northward.

Barnham and the others immediately began looking for the second German; the 109s never flew alone. They watched the Spitfires, the second still too close, circle overhead, then saw the second German diving, speeding low towards the Spitfires, pass over their heads, bank towards the leading Spitfire, and shoot. The watching pilots saw a flash near the Spitfire cockpit as a shell struck, saw the second Spitfire break violently right, the 109 climb steeply into the sun-lit sky, then the leading Spitfire wavered, straightened, and went into a dive. It was visible for a second between the spires of Naxxar church, and was gone. As the cloud of black smoke billowed, Barnham turned to the others, angrily pointed out the fault of the number two Spitfire, in flying too close, and threatened to shoot down any of his pilots who did that.

They ran to the crash, but there was nothing to be done, and Barnham began sketching the scene in his diary. Though the identity of the pilot who had just been killed was yet unknown to them, Barnham seemed to sense the presence of MacQueen. He bid farewell.[1]

Of MacQueen's death, Paul Brennan wrote: 'Everybody was down in the dumps about Mac. We felt his loss very keenly. He was one of our finest pilots and had shot down at least eight Huns. He had been one of the first Spitfire pilots awarded the DFC for operations over Malta, and he had richly earned his gong.

'Mac's death had a sobering effect on me. I had begun to think

I knew all there was to know about air fighting. I had shot down my sixth Hun that very day. The death of such an experienced and capable pilot as Mac brought me to a realisation that I did not know as much as I thought I did. I saw that I could not continue to take the risks that I had been taking, and continue to stay alive. I had held a poor opinion of the shooting prowess of the Hun fighter-pilots. On every occasion but one they had missed me. I had thought that it must always follow that they would always miss me. Now I knew I was wrong, and that I had, rather foolishly, under-rated the Hun.'[2]

It was an opportune time for him to reappraise his flying and the situation. The Germans were sending over fewer bombers and more fighters, and the fighters were more proficient at their given tasks of hunting the Spitfires and Hurricanes, keeping them away from the bombers.

The defending pilots were always outnumbered many times. Their diet was basic and repetitive, below the standard necessary to sustain men subjected to daily stress, exertions and strain in combats. Illnesses and stomach complaints afflicted everyone, and were added to the strain of daily bombing and poor living conditions on a besieged island 1600 kilometres from the nearest friendly land.

The wider war situation had no good news for the island defenders. On 5 May, the Japanese landed on the island of Corregidor, in Manila Bay, and on the 6th General Wainwright surrendered all the Philippines to the Japanese. On the next two days the Battle of the Coral Sea was fought, the US and Japanese navies each losing an aircraft carrier.

In the full moon period, the Germans and Italians increased their night attacks, which meant less sleep for the already tired fighter pilots. The longer days meant more hours on readiness, but little sleep was possible. Paul Brennan noticed the cumulative effect showing on the Maltese, who he thought seemed to have aged, and looked more haggard and nervous.

Destruction in Valletta was widespread, blocks of stone and debris choking the narrow streets. It seemed as if the population was living in the large shelters hewn from the rock. Food supplies were very small, and Victory Kitchens had been established to feed the people in communal fashion. The only private cooking done was with black-market goods, or the chickens and eggs which many Maltese kept. The local goat herds had been gradually butchered, providing a temporary answer to the demand for meat but destroying the milk supply necessary for babies and the aged.

The Maltese consumed great amounts of bread and wheat was the item most in demand for resupply convoys, after petrol and munitions. Even water-damaged wheat was used, and the taste of that bread was said to be unforgettable.

It was obvious to all that the Axis controlled the seas around Malta, and convoys could only be fought through with great loss and sacrifice. If an invasion was not made, the island could still be starved into surrender.

To the islanders, the fighter pilots were living symbols of their own resistance, the extra dimension added to the gunnery of the anti-aircraft crews of the royal Malta Artillery. Wherever they were recognised, the pilots were greeted with displays of affection and made welcome. This made a great impression on them, and is a lasting memory.

Then rumours began of another reinforcement of Spitfires to be flown in from aircraft carriers.

After the previous disasters, when precious fighter reinforcements had been destroyed on the ground within minutes or hours of arrival, detailed planning was done. Each new fighter in the formation would be numbered, and the pilot would look about on landing for the corresponding number waved by a member of the reception committee, who would lead the plane to a protected pen. At the pen would be an experienced Malta pilot, an engine fitter, a rigger, an armourer, 100 gallons of petrol, 20 gallons of oil, and plenty of ammunition. An instrument fitter and radio mechanic would service two bays.

Each new plane would be in a pen, refuelled, re-armed, with a fresh pilot in the cockpit within ten minutes of landing. Each bay had a long pole, on which a yellow disc or a cross could be hung, depending on whether or not the plane was ready. When these were raised, officers at headquarters and positions around the airfield could scan the area with binoculars and swiftly count the number of operational machines.

Pilots and groundcrews were to live at the pens, with eating utensils and cups, and food would be supplied by a converted bus bringing meals around.

One afternoon it was decided to test the reception arrangements, and 126 Squadron set off in a bus for the airfield. But when it was discovered that some had been left behind, the bus was turned around. Tim Goldsmith and Paddy Schade got out and asked to be collected on the next passage of the bus, in about fifteen minutes. The bus departed and the two went across the road to the building which had aroused their interest: Cisk's Brewery.

After a brisk tour of the plant, the two colonials were enjoying samples of the brewer's art, and had almost forgotten the bus. 'A terrific tooting dragged us away, and we found that the bus had been waiting for twenty minutes. Bart gave us the most filthy scowl and wouldn't talk to us for a couple of days. We were a bit full, and it went right over our heads at the time.'[3]

On 7 May, Lord Gort VC replaced General Dobbie as Governor of Malta. Gort flew from the UK, and the hand-over ceremony was done quickly, with a two-hour briefing by Dobbie on the situation, then Gort was in charge. Dobbie had exhausted himself with his responsibilities and was in need of rest.

Gordon Tweedale destroyed a 109 during the day, and Tony Boyd led the 185 Squadron flight when eleven fighters went up to escort a batch of Hurricanes coming from North Africa. He was back in an eight-gun IIa, GL-Y. Some inquisitive Messerschmitts probed, and he fired at one without result, mainly 'as a deterrent.'

The pilots who were to fly off the carriers with the latest batch of Spitfires were a little conservative about the idea, though it had been done before. For Eric Mahar, despite his flying hours, 'it was quite an experience getting on an aircraft carrier, never having been on one before, and being told you were going to fly off it, looking down the flight deck and thinking, "My God, there's not far to go." I remember all of us discussing this; are we going to get off?'[4]

On 8 May, a rehearsal of the fighter reception arrangements was held. Everyone who had a part to play was inspected and roles acted out. The airfield repair teams, stretcher-bearers, despatch riders, meal vehicles, and even the Bren-gun carriers—all that the island had in the way of armoured vehicles—were on hand to tow away any crashed Spitfires on the morrow.

As Wing Commander Gracie was going around checking arrangements, he told Paul Brennan that he and Ray Hesslyn had each been awarded the DFM.

Then, after the rehearsal was over and the squadron pilots were walking back, they were caught in the open by a raid, and had to run for it. Bud Connell, who had flown in from Gambut with 229 Squadron, was wounded.

Defending fighters engaged, and Gordon Tweedale claimed an 88 and a 109 destroyed, with another 109 as a probable. Tony Boyd, leading a flight in GL-Y, destroyed a Ju88. Sixteen fighters had intercepted a plot of eighty-plus. At 09.40, 'we jumped six Ju88s out of the sun at 18 000 feet; I got one, both engines on fire'. He attacked the port-side Junkers, coming in a diving attack from astern, closing to 100 yards (100 m), firing a long nine-second burst. Both the 88's engines began smoking heavily and many pieces were shot away, and suddenly the port engine gave out a great stream of white smoke. The pilot jettisoned his bombs and went down in a steep spiral, going north-east but losing height rapidly, and was last seen by Tony at 12 000 feet, when Macchis forced him to break away. He turned with ten Macchi 202s but dived away, entering a fight with 109s at ground level, and was 'hit in engine by cannon, glycol tank blew up, drenching me; belly landed Takali.' It had been his last flight in a Hurricane.

That evening there was a conference, at which Gracie declared everything was ready for the arrival of the new Spitfires, and passed out to each pilot a duplicate set of instructions, one to be retained and one to be handed to the incoming pilot.

At dawn on 9 May, off to the west, 62 Spitfires launched from USS *Wasp* and HMS *Eagle*, and set course for Malta. There were several Australians in the formations, including Fred Johnson, Ken Mitchell, Eric Mahar, Ray Sly and Alan Yates. Ray Sly had been a prominent member of 452 and 457 Squadrons RAAF in operations from the UK over Occupied France. A Flight Lieutenant, he was only 20½ years old.

Eric Mahar had no trouble getting airborne, and believes that Spitfire crashes off the carriers were due to pilot error. 'One chap forgot to put his airscrew into fine pitch and he just went to the bow and trickled over into the sea.'

They formed up and set course along the northern coast of

Right
Hal Far Airfield (*Len Reid*)

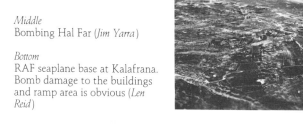

Middle
Bombing Hal Far (*Jim Yarra*)

Bottom
RAF seaplane base at Kalafrana.
Bomb damage to the buildings
and ramp area is obvious (*Len
Reid*)

Above
View from the deck of
HSL 128. The pilot in his
dinghy is close, and in the
distance is the smoke used to
mark his position (*L. G. Head*)

A happy pilot after rescue,
aboard HSL 128 (*L. G. Head*)

HSL 128 moving out to sea
from Kalafrana (*L. G. Head*)

Left
HMS *Eagle* (*Ruth Pashen*)

Middle
Bags of precious wheat being unloaded in Grand Harbour, 1942

Bottom
Sergeant L. G. Head with the 'scoreboard' on HSL 128 (at that time, 59 aircrew rescued) (*L. G. Head*)

Marsa Scirocco Bay from Hal
Far. The keel of the SS *Breconshire*
is visible in the centre (*Len Reid*)

Right
Paul Brennan in a Miles
'Master', Aston Down, United
Kingdom, 1942 (*Philip Wigley*)

Below
'The Mad House' against a
background of bombing

Below right
Chateau Bertrand, with bomb
damage (*Jim Yarra*)

Above
Spitfire V being lifted to flight deck of HMS *Furious*, August 1942 (*Paddy O'Brien*)

Right
Tony Boyd in readiness, Hal Far (*Philip Wigley*)

Bottom
The Cant Z506B captured in flight by Flight Lieutenant E. T. Strever and his Beaufort bomber crew, and flown to Malta, 1942 (*Colin Parkinson*)

Left
Accommodation and dining facilities in aircraft pen (*Jim Yarra*)

Middle
185 Squadron Spitfire in pen (*Jim Yarra*)

Bottom
MC 202s of 360 SQ 155 GR ready for take-off at Chinisia, 14 June 1942. Earlier they escorted JU87s of 102 GR attacking the *Harpoon* convoy (*Chris Dunning*)

Above
Gibraltar. Spitfire being ferried
to an aircraft carrier (*Guthrie
Hore*)

Right
Gordon Tweedale, RAAF (*Hugh
Tweedale*)

Below left
Tony Boyd, RAAF 185
Squadron (*Boyd family*)

Below right
Colin Parkinson, landed after
destroying a Messerschmitt
(*Colin Parkinson*)

Hurricane of 229 Squadron RAF taking off from Malta

The gallows and noose erected at Takali by Wing Commander Gracie to back his threat of execution for any act of sabotage (*Colin Parkinson*)

605 Squadron Hurricane II B 12 guns, October 1941. Pilot Lester, RAAF. Photo taken from another Hurricane at 5000 ft (*Philip Wigley*)

Africa, flying east into the Mediterranean.

Even though the new Spitfires were not expected over Malta until 10.30, people were at their allotted places around the airfields by 08.00. John Bisley was in the pen next to Tim Goldsmith, and after a while they went off for a cigarette and a check of the nearby slit trenches. At 10.00 the sirens sounded, and a number of 109s appeared overhead. Three Spitfires took off from Takali, and headed west, climbing fast, to give cover to the arrivals.

More Messerschmitts appeared, and Goldsmith counted sixty, at heights between 500 feet and 15 000 feet—waiting.

Further out to sea, some of the arriving pilots could also see the waiting 109s, but at that distance did not recognise them, and in their innocence thought they were friendly fighters providing cover. Eric Mahar's 'anticipation of protection was short-lived. They were 109s, and their intention fell far short of protection. Baptism by fire would be an understatement.'

Though the new arrivals had been told they might have to fight their way in, they assumed some fighter cover would be given. 'But these things had big black crosses on them,' noticed Mahar, 'and I kinked my neck looking around at them.'[5]

Then the Spitfires began to come in over the coastline, heading for their airfields. The 109s dived, the ack-ack opened up with every type of gun, and the three Spitfires had their hands full with the marauding 109s higher up. Goldsmith saw one Spitfire approaching to land, wheels and flaps down, then a Messerschmitt lunged, a long burst of cannon, and the Spitfire fell into a dive, crashing in flames at the airfield boundary.

But that was all he had time to watch, as the other Spitfires were slipping in to land, coming along the runway, pilots peering out for their reception teams, and for the next twenty minutes it was bedlam. Clouds of dust, taxying Spitfires, people running out to meet their allocated fighter and leading it back to a pen, banging ack-ack, flights of 109s passing over, and then the Spitfire he was waiting for appeared, it was brought into the pen, and the pilot climbed out while the ground crew 'leaped onto it, whipped off panels, loaded guns, refuelled, checked radio, oil and glycol, while I stowed my parachute aboard and told Ted the score on what happened in Malta.' The new pilot was Sergeant Ted Graysmark, RAF.[6]

Meanwhile, Paul Brennan had similar experiences, and briefed his newcomer, Pilot Officer Barnefather, RAF. The Spitfire was coded U-3. Then a Spitfire which had not been 'adopted' taxied up to the pen, and the pilot asked what he should do. This was a Canadian, Williams, later to be well-known as Willy the Kid.

Ken Mitchell had come from 131 Squadron in Shropshire, off the carrier into the sky over Malta. 'When we arrived it was chaotic, and there were 109s and other aircraft there. They were actually in the circuit. It was the first time I'd seen head-on attacks. I saw these 109s coming towards us, and there was a sparkle—it was the cannon shooting through the spinner, they were firing at us head-on, quite a new experience, really. Everybody was tired after a long flight, bottom numb after sitting on the CO_2 bottle for the dinghy.

'We'd been told not to drop the belly tank, as they needed them, but we were too unwieldy with them, we'd have been sitting ducks. It was very fortunate everyone got down; we had very small losses. It was chaotic, not like anything I saw at any other time.'[7]

Eric Mahar: 'When we landed, the enemy were flying around the circuit with us, and they'd do quick dives along the runway. It was quite a nerve shattering experience. There was someone in Control with an Aldis lamp, and if there was a 109 close behind you as you were coming in to land, he'd give you a red light, and (you'd) go around; it was as close as that—when you first land, the enemy has complete air superiority. We had to taxi immediately into a revetment. When we got out, there were bombs lying everywhere! We didn't know they'd been defused. The whole thing was rather shattering. Mitch and I had come from nice quiet 131 Squadron in Shropshire . . .'[8]

Ray Sly had been killed during the landing actions. It is not clear whether he crashed on landing, or decided to try to take off again to assist the younger pilots, obviously in trouble, who had not landed. McKay, a Canadian, noted in his diary that 'Sly hit a pen when trying to take off again, and crashed. He was alive when taken from the aircraft, but died in the afternoon.' Opinion of the experienced survivors is that he would not have tried to take off again, as he would have had very little or no fuel. However, eye witnesses apparently saw him begin to take off again.

The 'old Malta hands' were ready to go in their new Spitfires. Ten minutes later, they were scrambled to engage a raid estimated to be over one hundred bombers and fighters approaching from Catania in Sicily. At 18 000 feet over Luqa, 126 Squadron was bounced by about twenty 109s, and Goldsmith spent some time avoiding a bunch of them who 'obviously wished me no good'. He heard Woodhall, the controller, call that Ju88s were bombing Valletta, and aileron-turned down, down, to 4000 feet, where he saw the Germans. Goldsmith attacked one, and when last seen it was smoking from the starboard engine.

Tony Boyd had climbed into Spitfire J-3, as a section leader among the 25 Spitfires scrambling. 'First trip in a Spit. Two minutes after take-off was squirting at 88s. No claims. Got on well, wizard machines. Six of us covered the remainder in, and landed at Takali.'

Apart from cockpit drill on Spitfires, he had not flown one before taking off directly into combat. Such were the necessities of operational life on Malta in May 1942.

Boyd flew back to Hal Far, then scrambled again, as section leader. 'Six of 185 sent off late. Fired at two 88s and one 109, windscreen oiled up. Covered the other 20 while they landed. No claims. Pretty hot time, lost Sergeant Tweedale.'

Gordon Tweedale had been shot down in the hectic fighting, crashing in Spitfire BR248 into a street in Lija, killing Seraphim Gauchi, a Gunner in the Royal Malta Artillery. On 7 May Gordon had claimed a Messerschmitt, on the 8th another and a Ju88, added to three 88s and an 87 destroyed in a four-day period in April. It is possible that he was shot down by Leutnant Beckmann, Stab III/JG53.

Paul Brennan was plagued by mechanical problems, and was unlucky to be in the target area whenever the Luftwaffe returned and he was trying to take off. The second time, he was strapped in, ready to start the engine, when the groundcrew looked up, saw the bombers close and beginning to attack, waved at Brennan and ran. After a false start following them, brought to an abrupt halt because he had forgotten to disconnect himself from the Spitfire, he arrived in the trench 'beating the bombs by the narrowest of short heads.'

He was impressed by the nonchalance of one of the mechanics, who had been swapping his tools for a rifle throughout the day, shooting at passing Messerschmitts. In fact, a 109 which flew over the airfield was shot down, going into St Paul's Bay, and naturally everyone who had fired claimed it. That sort of event gave a tremendous boost to morale.

Tim Goldsmith also was getting into his stride. In a section of four, they had engaged five Cant Z1007s, with Macchi escort, at 20 000 feet. His cannon had set one on fire, falling out of the sky ablaze with pieces falling off it.

Other Australians claiming victories in the swirling actions were Bisley, a Macchi Mc202 destroyed, and Max Briggs of 601 with a 109 destroyed.

For the new arrivals, it was an abrupt change from life aboard ship, and an even greater change from the relative civilisation of the airfields in the United Kingdom. Apart from the climate, the enemy presence was almost overwhelming. What stuck in Eric Mahar's mind was 'the number of unexploded bombs lying around, and the number of 109s that flew just above our runways did not boost the morale.'[9]

However, even after the dramatic fly-in, and, later, the daily succession of combats, witnessing losses and victories, in his first action, Mahar was a little unaware of what was happening. He noticed 'pretty red lights going over my starboard wing. "I wonder what that is?" Suddenly the penny dropped!' By the time he finished his evasive action there were no enemy aircraft in sight, but no friendlies either.[10]

After a restless night, kept awake by the Luftwaffe, the pilots began moving back to the airfield at 05.00, a drive made nerve-wracking as the night bombers had scattered delayed action bombs which were impossible to see in the darkness.

10 May dawned fine and clear, with Sicily visible and distant Mount Etna seen distinctly.

Tony Boyd had flown as one of a formation of four, patrolling at 20 000 feet; his No. 2 turned back, and Tony lost the formation, but found a pair of 109s, so 'chased and caught them, made a fight, many squirts but no results,' and went back to land.

Around the airfields, the pilots waited, and waited, but it was not until just before 10.00 that the red signal flares shot up, and the Spitfires began rolling out of the pens, dragging banners of dust behind them. . . .

Paul Brennan, in the new Spitfire coded U-3, was flying with Johnny Plagis, the Rhodesian. The first four had gone, led by

Stan Grant. Brennan and Plagis climbed steeply, knowing that already 109s were above and that the bombers were not far away.

At 14 000 feet over Filfla they were attacked by 109s, and more could be seen up higher, circling, waiting. With Brennan and Plagis were Buck Buchanan and two others. All began turning tightly to avoid the Messerschmitts; then Woodhall called that Stukas were diving over the Harbour. So Plagis and Brennan went for the Junkers, while Buchanan stayed to fight the 109s with his three Spitfires.

As they dived towards Grand Harbour, Brennan saw the ack-ack barrage over it, so intense that the puffs of smoke from the bursts seemed to form a dark cloud, with the Bofors shells sparking up through it. The two Spitfires went straight into the barrage, and as they flashed out the far side, Brennan saw so many aircraft that he first thought of the risk of collision—Stukas were pulling out of their dives, Spitfires were coming from all directions, and the ever-present Messerschmitts were diving in to the melee. He looked down and saw a couple of parachutes, sharp against the blue sea, and a 109 go into the water, tracer flickered over his port wing . . .

He broke starboard, saw a Stuka ahead and fired, missed and shot past it, going too fast, saw a 109, fired, missed and sped past him as well, then heard Buchanan call a warning to the Spitfires over the harbour to climb, 'They're up here!'

Brennan climbed out of the melee, firing into the belly of a Stuka as he went by, saw shells explode on the engine, then was past, above the Stukas, and hauled around into a steep climbing turn, looking for a target. Spitfires and Stukas were everywhere. Then he saw one alone, and dived onto its tail, noticing another crash into the sea. He fired and the Stuka went into a very steep turn, Brennan followed, still firing, the Stuka kept turning, Brennan began to wonder why it did not blow up, still turning and firing, watching the shells hitting, then the Stuka 'literally blew apart.'

'Rather dumbfounded', he was watching the remains spiralling to the sea when he heard Plagis call a warning, looked around and there was 'the big yellow spinner of a 109 about 50 metres from my tail. Flashes were coming from his guns. I got a hell of a fright, and pulled the stick back to turn. By this time my speed had fallen away, my aircraft gave a hell of a shudder, flicked over onto its back and started to spin.'

It was all so sudden that Brennan did not realise he was spinning, but thought the 109 had got him, then automatically recovered from the spin and almost began to spin the other way. The 109 had gone, presumably to claim a victory. Plagis told Brennan that the German had been firing for about ten seconds.

It all happened so swiftly that when he looked down, the Stuka was still falling, just hitting the water about 100 metres from the one he had watched go into the sea as he began his attack.[11]

Paul flew back and landed, so tired that he slept all afternoon, despite all the activity outside and above. Ju88s attacked in the afternoon, and were engaged. At the end of the day, the defenders claimed 23-20-20, for a loss of two Spitfires. Radio Rome admitted a loss of 37, and it was not given to exaggerating Axis losses.

In 601 Squadron, Max Briggs, in Spitfire BR282, was killed, possibly by friendly anti-aircraft fire. His death shattered his friend Scott.

Tony Boyd thought it was the 'most terrific air battle ever seen here. Astounding, plus an appalling barrage. There were about 25 Spits, eight Hurris, 30 Stukas, fifteen Ju88s, twenty 109s all mixed up in one enormous milling fight. We lost one Spit, I got one 88 probable, one 88 damaged.'

He dived onto the tail of a Ju88, firing a five-second burst from the four 20mm cannon. The 88 was only at 1500 feet, going north to Sicily after bombing. The 20mm shells flashed around the rear of the cabin and wing roots, then there was a large explosion and black smoke poured from the hole, possibly fed by a fire inside. The Junkers went nose-down, in a shallow dive, three miles (5 km) outside Grand Harbour, but Boyd had to pull up and away. 1500 feet was a dangerous place to be with the Messerschmitts about. In his combat report he claimed the 88 as destroyed, but noted it in his log-book as a probable. He also noted damaging another, but made no mention of it in his combat report.

He flew again, still in J-3, but 'our lot had bad luck, missed the bombers. I had one squirt at a 109, no claim. Then I went up after the recco [reconnaissance aircraft] but too late.'

In 126 Squadron, Tim Goldsmith was with a section of four, when they bounced two 109s. Goldsmith fired but had cannon trouble after only twenty rounds fired. These struck home on the wings and fuselage, the Messerschmitt dived away, and Tim claimed a damaged. However, the 109 was seen to crash, and his claim was upgraded to 'destroyed'.

On his next scramble, his cannon would not fire, and the terse annotation in his log book is ample comment: 'SFA'.

Then on the third flight, he again mixed it with the ever-present 109s, firing on one which went down smoking. Then he attacked another head-on from below, cannon hammering into the nose and belly of the Messerschmitt, which went diving into the sea. The Spitfires were circling Luqa at 8000 feet when two 109s came through going north to south. Tim fired at the second, from the side, turning with it as it passed, and saw flashes on the fuselage 150 yards (150 metres) away. The 109 nosed down, diving towards the sea, watched by John Bisley and Ted Graysmark from the ground. It went over the cliff edge, diving, and no one saw it reappear.

Then over St Paul's Bay he saw a 109 coming head-on, slightly higher, and he fired six seconds cannon at it, seeing many flashes along the bottom of the fuselage and the 109 flicked past 20 feet (six metres) overhead, diving straight on into the water. This was his fifth victory.

At his headquarters, Albert Kesselring declared that Malta was neutralised. All ships there had been destroyed or were out of action; the Libyan routes were safe; the blockade was still maintained; the most important military installations had been destroyed; and enemy air activity was severely restricted. This had been achieved with 5807 bomber, 5667 fighter and 345 reconnaissance sorties since the beginning of the attacks. RAF losses were claimed to be 73 aircraft shot down or probably shot down, with a further 78 destroyed or probably so on the ground.

He had said that he intended to remove two Gruppen of Ju88s and two of Bf109s, for service elsewhere. These were to be replaced by Italian fighters and bombers.

However, the Italians disagreed with the German opinion, and regarded Malta as still dangerous. They noted that there had been a total of 65 anti-aircraft batteries identified on the island on 20 March, and on the 10th of May there were 66, in spite of the heavy attacks. Aircraft identified on 20 March were 43, on 28 April there were 58 and on 10 May this number had grown to 87.

The Italians concluded that any neutralisation of Malta was

partial and temporary, that the blockade should continue, that operations as outlined on 12 March, against anti-aircraft defences, shipping and airfields-aircraft, should continue, and that the forces needed for this should remain at the level with which the offensive was begun.[12]

Kesselring was quite experienced in the ways of the Luftwaffe High Command, as well as in directing air operations. There is nothing in writing, but it is possible he hoped to create a good mental impression in the minds at Rastenburg and Berlin, after which convincing them that the invasion should go ahead would be easier.

Next day, on Malta itself, there was a definite feeling of having won a great success with the new arrangements and the Spitfires. The people had stood out in the open, cheering the fighters as Luftwaffe planes went down burning or smoking. Not only the fighter pilots but the average Maltese were aware of the success, and Paul Brennan noted that 'the gloom and depression that had hung over Malta for so long lifted and vanished.'

The new feeling of achievement was immediately converted into aggressive action. On 11 May, Johnny Plagis, Brennan and two of the new pilots took off on a sweep to Sicily. Such a flight would not have been considered seriously a few days earlier, when the swarms of 109s would have made it wasteful and suicidal. Brennan, still in U-3, had to land with engine trouble, one of the new pilots became separated from the others and returned, but Plagis and Willie the Kid found and engaged eight Macchi 202s. Plagis was in a turning contest with one at sea level when the Macchi stalled and went into the water, after which Plagis tried unsuccessfully to shoot down some of the others. Then they returned to Malta.

Plagis told Brennan the Italians had flown well, and it had been difficult to get away from them, but the Spitfire was superior. It was the first time 249 Squadron had engaged them, and the pilots were keen to know what one of their own thought of that part of the opposition.

There was little enemy activity until seven o'clock, when a formation of bombers was followed by radar as they flew to the south-east of the island and began to circle 15 kilometres off Kalafrana Bay. The Spitfires were at 18 000 feet over Filfla, and went in to attack as one of the three bombers in the raid dived on Hal Far.

Plagis and Willy the Kid turned and went down after the Ju88, Brennan looked up and saw eight 109s diving on the two Spitfires, called a warning, and began to fight the Messerschmitts. But, with the advantage of height, they dived at him from behind, shot at his tightly turning Spitfire, then zoomed up and swung back to make another pass.

He was soon in trouble and calling for help. Woodhall alerted the others and gave them Brennan's position over Kalafrana.

Brennan had 'lost all my speed in my turns. My aircraft was shuddering, and on the point of stalling. Once or twice it did flick, and somehow I managed to maintain control. At last, after an agony of waiting, Pete Nash and another Spitfire arrived and chased the 109s away. I was feeling pretty shaky. It was the most determined attack the 109s had made on me.'

As the other two Spitfires took the pressure off him, Brennan climbed and turned towards the harbour, looking for some 109s that Woodhall had reported there. He saw two, low down on the sea, tails towards the sun. He dived after them, but the Messerschmitts were going fast, and it was not until they were north of Gozo, about one-third of the way back to Sicily, that he caught up with them.

He fired at the rear 109, but saw no result, the German began to turn, Brennan turning with him, firing, both only a few metres above the waves, when, 'suddenly his right wing hit the sea. He cartwheeled on his wingtip and tail once or twice and then blew up. The leading 109 escaped. I found Pete Nash behind me.' Nash, higher, covered Brennan back to Malta.

It seems, from German records, that the Messerschmitt pilot was Gunther Freiherr von Maltzahn, one of the leading Luftwaffe fighter pilots. He was rescued by the Dornier Do 24 flying boat which picked up pilots of both sides. Given Brennan's description of the combat, von Maltzahn was lucky to survive the crash.

At Takali, Paul Brennan found that Plagis and Willy had been credited with the Ju88 as a probable. It was the only bomber to cross the coast, as the other two had dropped their bombs in the sea and flown back to Sicily. This was a marked change in Luftwaffe behaviour. Only a few days before, Ju87s and 88s had been attacking any place on the island which was designated a target. However, the Messerschmitts were as dangerous and determined as ever, and quite obviously had been told to destroy the Spitfire force. The few bombers were probably bait to lure up the defending fighters.[13]

During the day, Tim Goldsmith flew only once, and he and Tony Barton, the squadron commander, chased two 109s back to Sicily. Even with the engines 'through the gate' on full boost, the 109s maintained their lead, and Tim tried a shot at extreme range, but saw no results.

In the 72 hours to 22.45 hours 11 May, the island defences claimed 36-31-45. 249 Squadron's tally for the campaign was close to eighty enemy destroyed, higher than any other Spitfire squadron on Malta.

The intense activity, with no proper diet, was draining the physical reserves of the pilots, despite the recuperative powers of youth. Though they were tired, the recent successes had kept morale high, and people like Paul Brennan and Ray Hesslyn 'were as keen as ever to get into the air.'

On 12 May, led by Stan Grant, they scrambled at about 10.30, but Hesslyn discovered his oxygen was not working, restricting him to heights lower than 10 000 feet; Brennan told him they would stay together. They went to 8000 feet and flew up and down the island, seeing no enemy, then turned to go to Hal Far, and saw 'a beehive a mile south-east of Filfla and about our height.'

It was a massive formation of 109s, and they watched a single Spitfire pull up towards it, fire, and turn in a dive for the island. A 109 darted after it, closed to 100 metres, fired, and the Spitfire went on in a straight line into the sea at about 300 mph. The pilot was a New Zealander, Mitchell, who had called Woodhall on the radio to say he 'had it.'

Hesslyn and Brennan were after the 109. Hesslyn chased it, hit it with several bursts and it flicked onto its back and dived into the sea. Brennan was fighting with a bunch of 109s who had come down for them.

Again, the turns to avoid the series of diving passes were wiping away his speed. The Spitfire was becoming harder to control at the low speeds; he began to think he would not get out of the situation, and had been a fool to bite off more than he could chew. The leading 109 turned back in a head-on attack. 'I could see the flashes of his guns firing from the centre of his slow-revving spinner and the leading edges of his wings. His shells and bullets tore past the top of the cockpit. I believed they would all miss me, but to make sure, I trod on bottom rudder. 'There was a sharp crack as though somebody had hit my cockpit with a sledgehammer. Something hit my left arm and knocked it off the throttle quadrant. A tingling pain shot through it, but I found I could still use it. For a few seconds, expecting a row of bullets across my body, I did nothing. But the bullets did not come.'

The 109 had ceased fire and pulled up, away from a collision; Brennan had stalled the Spitfire. It spun, and he recovered a few hundred feet over the sea. The 109s had turned away, possibly believing that the explosion on the canopy, and the spin, meant the end of the Spitfire.

Brennan flew over the cliffs and landed at Takali, arm aching, blood staining his sleeve. One 20 mm cannon shell had exploded on the port side of the windscreen, the spalling effect flinging splinters of windscreen into Paul's arm. He was given a 'good stiff whisky' and taken to hospital.[14]

'Slim' Yarra, on his fifth scramble in two days, in Spitfire GL-K, was climbing as one of a section of four to engage a plot of 25-plus enemy. He fired on a Ju88 but saw no results, then the watchful 109s attacked, forcing him away. Four Messerschmitts sped past; he aimed and fired, shooting down the leader, and damaging a couple of others. His first confirmed victory, in an outstanding series to be scored over the next two months, had been claimed.

Tim Goldsmith had a day off. Ted Graysmark was flying, but was shot down, ending up in his rubber dinghy in the sea. When his body was found, it was obvious he had been machinegunned in the water. This event hardened the already tough determination to resist. Goldsmith noted in his diary, 'the rotten bastards. Pilot Officer Graves baled out OK.'

While the island was under continuing heavy attack, large flights of troop carrying aircraft had been flying past taking reinforcements from Italy to North Africa. On this day there was a disaster for the Axis when RAF fighters engaged the formation, shooting down thirteen transports off the North African coast. Few on Malta realised that these troops had been assembled for the invasion of the island, but were being siphoned off to Rommel.

Next day, 13 May, Goldsmith was flying again. The new spirit of aggression had him chasing two Macchis back to Sicily, closing to 70 metres, carefully lining up one in his sights and firing, first shells hitting . . . the cannon stopped again.

Tony Boyd, leading a section in C-3, scrambled with four others to catch a formation of Italians, noting that 'the dingos heard we were up and turned back. No interception.'

Later they scrambled again, trying to get height to catch the expected reconnaissance aircraft, and were 'up at 30 000 feet for some time waiting, but missed him in the end. The Spit gives wizard performance at height.'

Nick Ferraby, an Englishman in 185 Squadron, flew with Tony Boyd on this sortie after the German reconnaissance aircraft, but though the Spitfires saw the German, they could not catch him. Ferraby noted in his diary that it was good to be flying Spitfires again 'after the ropey Hurricanes we've been using for the past six weeks or more. Boyd and Finley due to go home tomorrow night.'[15]

On 13 May, Kesselring signalled Hitler that Malta had been eliminated. Some writers have cast aspersions on Kesselring because of these optimistic messages to the Fuhrer about the plight of Malta. His own memoirs notwithstanding, it could be that Kesselring was trying to encourage the leaders and staff at OKW and Commando Supremo to mount the invasion of Malta. Once it was underway, it would have to be seen through. Certainly a man with the experience Kesselring possessed must have had an idea of the real situation.

Paul Brennan watched the next raids from the verandah of the hospital, seeing three Ju88s shot down, one after the other, as they dived on Takali, and two Spitfires collide as they converged on a damaged 109, with all three pilots parachuting.

He was discharged at lunch time, and walked across to the Mess, where a discussion was going on about the new Luftwaffe tactics. The intention seemed to be destruction of the Spitfires, either in the air or on the ground. By sending several small waves of bombers to entice the Spitfires into the air, the Luftwaffe hoped to catch them on the ground, refuelling after those combats, with a larger formation which would be able to repeat the bombing successes of March and April, when the RAF fighters were destroyed in their pens.

However, the tactic failed when the first three waves were attacked so fiercely, and it was obvious to German radar that a large number of Spitfires were still airborne and more were known to be available.

On 14 May, Tim Goldsmith was scrambled in the morning, but was unable to engage the bombers, and was fighting the Messerschmitts. He got into position on one, fired and kept on firing in one long 12-second burst, watching the German fighter hammered into flames and go down. He landed, refuelled and re-armed, and waited.

The signal to scramble went, he started the engine and taxied out of the pen, out to the runway, opened the throttle, lifted off, up with flaps and undercarriage . . . and found he had taken off with 601 Squadron by mistake. They got past the 109s, and he found a Ju88 in front of him, opened up and closed to 150 metres, then 'fired everything' at the bomber, setting both engines and fuselage alight, seeing pieces of the plane fall away, and watched it go down to crash.

Later, he was disgruntled to find that 'a sod from Takali is claiming a half share' in the destruction of the Junkers. Tim was awarded it.

Tony Boyd had gone on readiness at dawn, with Nick Ferraby as his No. 2. Ferraby did not know Boyd well, but thought he was 'a steady experienced chap whom everyone looked up to.' They had scrambled at 09.00, and climbed fast to engage. Ferraby shot at six different Messerschmitts, but did not lodge a claim. Then they were scrambled again at 12.00, and attacked twelve Macchi 202s; odds of six to one. In the combat, Ferraby called to warn Boyd of a Macchi on his tail, but the Italian fired and hit the Spitfire. Boyd's plane spun out of the combat and he crashed close to Takali.

Denis Barnham, a Flight Commander with 601 Squadron, had been talking to a new pilot waiting to make his first operational flight, not realising anything was wrong with the Spitfire they were watching, 'descending slowly in a medium turn. How beautiful it looks, as graceful as a bird, yellow-brown on the top surface of its elliptical wings—now pale duck-egg blue on the underside as it passes us and murmurs away again. Round and round, getting steadily lower. Lower and lower. It's getting very low, dangerously low. I jump to my feet as it disappears behind 'G' shelter—a roar of flame, a bubble of fire fifty feet high, searing its way over the grass in front of us, a monstrous trail of exploding petrol with blackened fragments being spewed out of the bottom of it. It's plunged into the valley—it's gone—no trace of it, not even a wisp of smoke, just the roar, now silence.'[16]

That afternoon, Paul Brennan was told Tony Boyd was dead, killed attacking the Macchis. Boyd's final victory, on that day, had been a Messerschmitt 109 from the first scramble. Incomplete records show his claims to have been four destroyed, five probably destroyed, twelve damaged, shares in the destruction of two others, and claims for two others which could not be ascertained as probable or destroyed.

His own log-book 'line page' lists entries for two and two shared destroyed, which excludes the final Bf109 on 14 May, five probables, and nine damaged. He had taken part in 67 scrambles, of which 42 resulted in combats, almost all in the Hurricane armed with eight .303 inch machineguns. 'He was generally regarded as the greatest Hurricane pilot on Malta,' said Philip Wigley RAF.

Paul Brennan described Tony Boyd as 'not only one of the most capable, determined and courageous pilots on Malta, but he was also an outstanding personality. He was cheery and happy at all times, and throughout the depressing periods of April and early May he had been inspiration to every one of us. We felt Tony's death keenly, and it cast a gloom over his fellow Australians.'[17]

Ferraby had claimed a probable in the combat, and later noted in his diary that both Boyd and Finley had been lost that day. Both had been due to leave that night.

Later in the day, with Bud Connell, Paul went into Valletta. He noticed that the spirit of the recent successes was evident in the attitude of the people, in the new determination to clear away the rubble from bombing attacks. For a time, it had been left, the fatalistic view being that the next raid would only leave more. But now it was being cleared away and the streets made passable. When the shopkeeper he asked about ribbon for the DFM found Brennan was a Spitfire pilot, he found it difficult to refuse the gifts the man wanted to press on him.

On 16 May, 'Slim' Yarra, in GL-K of 185 Squadron, was one of two Spitfires scrambled to engage an enemy formation. He attacked seven 109s, and went for the leader, but only damaged him. Then he was attacked by four Mc202s, turned into them, and in the combat hit one, which suddenly collided with his own wingman. Yarra fought the other two until he was out of ammunition, then dived for home. The combat took 35 minutes.

Paul Brennan flew again on 17 May. Beset by a deep feeling of nervousness, he prepared, took off in Spitfire Vc coded C-25 and climbed. He was 'getting back on the horse after being thrown', and found the nervousness disappeared as soon as combat was joined. He fired at some 109s, with no result, but was his old self again.[18]

Buck Buchanan was forced to bail out, and a 109 dived, firing at the parachute. Buchanan was killed; he had nine victories. Pete Nash, 13.5 victories, was killed in a combat with 109s, both his Spitfire and an enemy aircraft crashing at the same time.

After two days off, Tim Goldsmith also flew. Going head-on at a 109, firing from below it, he saw no results and the Messerschmitt flicked past overhead, gone into the blue. Slim Yarra, in GL-K, was one of a two-Spitfire scramble from 185 Squadron. They engaged 15 Macchis; he hit one but did not claim.

On 18 May, Stan Grant's aircraft went unserviceable as they were preparing to take off at 05.45, and Paul Brennan, again in C-25, was told to take command of the three Spitfires. As they climbed, Ron West, a flight commander, followed, but told Brennan to keep leading and he would take over the sub-section of two of the four planes. It was Paul's first time as leader, and he 'got a hell of a kick out of it.'

Messerschmitts were reported in the area, presumably searching for one of their pilots who had gone into the sea the day before. The Spitfires flew to various places as directed but saw nothing, then noticed two elements of two aircraft each below them. Brennan identified them as Macchis. He dived on the pair on the right, leaving the others to West.

Paul came in astern of one, fired and saw hits on the port wing, the Italian broke across Brennan's No. 2, Gilbert, who fired, and the enemy was last seen trailing glycol, as Brennan went for the other, who rolled into a vertical dive.

Brennan followed, waited till he came out of the dive at 2000 feet, and gave him a long burst, watching as 'he hung there for a second, rolled on his back and hit the sea. As he crashed I saw another aircraft spin into the sea half a mile away.' He called on the radio; West said he had just shot down an Italian, and the other Spitfires answered.[19]

When they landed, it was discovered that the first one engaged by Brennan and Gilbert had landed at Zonkor Point, so three of the four had been destroyed. It was also discovered that they were Reggiani 2001s, the latest Italian fighter. The pilot who had crashed on Malta, Tenente Remo Cazzolini, of 2 Gruppo, was taken prisoner, but claimed he had shot down a Spitfire first. It was certainly not from the 249 Squadron section which bounced his flight of Reggianis . . .

On 18 May 'Slim' Yarra won his DFM. In company with a New Zealander, Shaw, he had a brief clash with some 109s protecting the first wave of Ju88s, then was told by Woodhall to cover the air-sea rescue launch, which was trying to pick up a Luftwaffe pilot. Shaw had to return to base with a damaged aircraft, so Yarra, in K-3, was alone with about 'thirteen Messerschmitt 109s to myself', as he wrote in his log book.

What had happened was that four Hurricanes of 229 Squadron were sent to attack some Italian motor-torpedo boats sighted off Sicily. But some twenty Messerschmitts appeared, and Spitfires were sent to the rescue. Pilot Officer Norman Fowlow RCAF was shot down, and reported to be in the sea a few hundred metres from the coast. HSL 128 was sent to pick up Fowlow, and set off from Kalafrana at 11.03.

Four Hurricanes of 229 Squadron were to give close escort to the launch, while two Spitfires from 185—Yarra and Shaw—were to give high cover. The numerous 109s set on the Hurricanes, shooting down Sergeant Jim Pendlebury as they chased him over the launch, and the crew saw the Hurricane cartwheel into the sea about three km ahead. They found some pieces of wreckage, but the pilot was gone.

Higher overhead, Slim Yarra had engaged more Messerschmitts, shooting down Uffz Johannes Lompa in White 3, 4/JG53. Lompa baled out and the HSL crew saw him come down by parachute near Filfla. They went over and picked him up, but though he was visibly relieved at such prompt rescue, claimed to know nothing of the missing RAF pilot, which was quite probably true.

The launch, commanded by Flight Lieutenant Crockett, continued and found Fowlow. As he was hauled aboard, Lompa shook his hand and congratulated him, then both pilots fell asleep in the relative safety of the launch, while overhead the Spitfires and Hurricanes fought on.

'I arrived over the rescue ship,' Slim Yarra said later, 'to find at least thirteen Messerschmitts there. I stayed, but it wasn't a case of bravery. I couldn't get away; I had to stay.'

He was forced to circle the launch, turning into each attack as the yellow-nosed 109s flashed in. One dived on the launch and sprayed the area with bullets, Yarra whipped onto its tail and fired, but it climbed away.

'I sat above the launch, and the Jerries kept coming to have a crack at me. I kept turning into them, firing for all I was worth, and driving them away.'

He was out of ammunition, but remained over the launch, making dummy attacks into the diving Messerschmitts for some forty-five minutes, until the launch was back in harbour. When he did get back to Takali, four 109s attacked him in the circuit, and he was forced to manoeuvre with them.

'I had to turn in against four 109s which attacked me,' he recalled. 'It nearly cost me dearly, for it caused me to run out of petrol. My motor cut out as I got into the circuit near the aerodrome, and I had to pancake in a hurry.'[20]

He continued with his landing, but his fuel was exhausted and he glided in to touch-down. The flight had lasted one hour fifty minutes. It was his sixteenth combat and the 109s claimed were his fourth and fifth confirmed victories.

The combat over the sea grew as more flights of Spitfires were fed in, with other pilots claiming two destroyed, two probables and one damaged, though the 109s also claimed two destroyed. One of the Messerschmitt pilots, Unteroffizier Gerhard Beitz, in Yellow 2 of III/JG53, was shot down also, and picked up three days later by the same launch, HSL 128. In fact, 7 Staffel lost an aircraft, but the pilot was picked up by Axis ASR aircraft, and an aircraft of 8 Staffel crashed on landing at Vittoria, being completely destroyed.

After this, Yarra was given leader positions in the formations, first leading two, then four, and at the end of the month, eight aircraft. For the rest of May, he would make another nineteen operational flights, with combats on seven of them. But he made no more claims though he fired at several enemy. Leading four on the 20th, he engaged four Ju88s but was 'shot up by Me109Fs'; on the 26th, ammunition in both wings exploded and caught fire so he returned to base; on the 26th, scrambling to intercept 70-plus, while attacking forty Ju88s, he was 'shot up by Re2001 escort'; on the 28th, 'chased Ju88s back to Sicily, Me109s chased me home'; and on the 30th, when landing, eight 109s attacked the airfield. It was a hectic month for Flight Sergeant J. W. Yarra.

That day, John Bisley destroyed a 109, and T. W. Scott, of 601 Squadron, destroyed another.

That evening in the 249 Squadron Mess there was some excitement. Ray Hesslyn RNZAF had received a bar to the DFM, now having eleven victories, the last five between 10 and 14 May.

As well as 'normal' bombs of all sizes, the Italians and Germans had begun dropping a variety of booby-trap devices. One of these was the fountain pen bomb. Paul Brennan related how a bomb-disposal team member was cycling along and saw, in the dust at Hal Far, one of these bombs. He left his bicycle, carefully carried the bomb to the workshop, made all the preparations to work on it, set it into a vice, carefully began to dismantle it, and found that he had discovered a genuine fountain pen.[21]

After 18 May, emphasis in enemy bombing changed to high-level diving attacks by 109s. They approached at about 25 000 feet, swept down to 10 000 and dropped their bombs as they sped away north to Sicily. Italian bombers would appear at great height in formations of three or five, bomb inaccurately and depart, sometimes losing one or two from their formation.

Tim Goldsmith flew once more on 19 May, with no contact, and on the 20th had a day off with the prevalent 'Malta dog'. It was a mixed day, for along with the illness, he was told he had been awarded a DFM, and DFCs had gone to Johnny Johnston, and to two Americans, Jimmy Peck and Reade Tilley. Tim did not fly for the next four days, and on the 23rd was told that his commission had come through, dated from the 15th. His diary comment was 'so I had my first reasonable meal for ages'. The day before he'd written, 'Bloody awful lunch'.

On 25 May, he engaged Italians again. The first flight was fruitless; nothing was seen. On the second, the Spitfires got through to the bombers, and there was a Cant Z1007 in front of him, but other Spitfires were firing, and Tim claimed a quarter share of it, damaged. Similarly, he attacked a Reggiani 2001, but was only able to claim it as damaged.

He flew a night patrol, saw nothing in the way of enemy, but was illuminated by searchlights and fired on by friendly ack-ack, then had to land at Takali as Luqa was bombed. The diary contains the small comment 'While at Takali Mess got a bit full.'

On the world scene, the Allies seemed to be retreating or defeated everywhere. The island defenders were isolated in the Mediterranean, constantly under attack, with little good news from other fronts. On the 15th, British forces in the Far East had retreated from Burma into India. Next day, the Germans captured Kerch, on the peninsula separating the Black Sea from the Sea of Azov; on the 17th the Soviet offensive was halted by the German forces east of Kharkov; on the 20th, the whole Kerch peninsula was captured by the Germans. Next day, though no one on Malta knew it, Hitler decided to postpone indefinitely the invasion of the island. It could probably be starved into submission.

On 26 May, Rommel attacked the Gazala Line in North Africa and next day Reinhard Heydrich was wounded in an assassination attempt in Prague. He would die of poisoning from horsehairs in the seat padding forced into his body by the explosion. In retaliation, the Germans would destroy the village of Lidice, believing the assassins had been assisted by the villagers. On 28 May, the Germans destroyed large Soviet tank forces in the Kharkov area, and Rommel's offensive in North Africa continued.

Paul Brennan had been flying Spitfire C-25 since the 17th, except for two flights. But, despite seven scrambles, he could not achieve any successes, though he damaged an Re2001 on the 25th. His log book contains comments such as: 'could not catch them'; 'no interception made'; '109s becoming very hard to catch'.

Except for uneventful patrols on the 28th, Tim Goldsmith did not fly again until 30 May. On the first scramble, nothing was seen, and they returned to base. Then the Italians came again. They got through and bombed Luqa, but the Spitfires were among them. Goldsmith was one of four Spitfires which attacked a BR20, sending it down to destruction. He then swung onto another Reggiani 2001, shooting off its radiator, and the stubby Italian fighter went down. The Spitfires again landed at Takali, and Tim 'got a bit tipsy', but flew back to Luqa next morning.

Throughout the weeks of bombing, after the heavy daylight raids and the harassing night attacks, the airfield repair crews had been working at the unglamorous labouring tasks necessary to enable the fighters to get into the air to engage the Italians and Germans.

The last days of May were so quiet that the new boys could be sent up with the 'old hands' for some practice flying. How greatly the situation had changed in a few weeks. Up to 9 May, practice flying had been out of the question; every flight was operational. Now, enemy presence was scarce enough to allow training activity.

In his log book, Slim Yarra listed those killed during the month: Fletcher RCAF, Tweedale RAAF, Sly RAAF, Williams, Barclay, Mitchell, Finlay (sic), Boyd RAAF, Ryckman RCAF, Nash, Willis, Hall, Kidd, Dick, Wallis, Henry and Wills. Yarra's total flying hours were 258.

On 30 May, the RAF launched the first 1000 bomber raid of the war, with Cologne as target. This was 'Bomber' Harris' first great effort to demonstrate that Bomber Command of the RAF was a part of the Allied war effort which could contribute to achieving victory. He was beset by enemies who wanted the bombers used for their own purposes, and to have the air forces allocated to the Army and Navy, in effect disbanding the RAF. Maximum publicity was wrung from the raid, but this did not excite appropriate interest on Malta, where their own problems were seen as paramount.

Chase Italians and Germans back to Sicily as they might, and revel in the new spirit of aggression, the fact remained that they were besieged. Great efforts were being made to force convoys through, but the Luftwaffe and Regia Aeronautica, with submarine and surface fleet co-operation, were to show once again the power of aircraft against ships forced to proceed along a known route to a known objective.

On the 31st, Albert Kesselring, Commander-in-Chief of German forces in the theatre, sent to the Italian High Command his plan for the invasion of Malta—Operation *Hercules*. The Italians also had studied the problem, titling their paper 'C3'. Kesselring intended that eight to fourteen days after the present offensive in Africa ended, the Luftwaffe forces of X Fliegerkorps and Fliegerfuhrer Afrika were to combine with II Fliegerkorps in Sicily

94

and commence preparations for the invasion. The invasion date, to be known as X-Day, was to be 18 July.

The German forces for the actual assault would begin moving from France on or about thirty days before X-Day, completing their concentration at X—two days; no training was to be carried out near Sicily, all was to be in France; the transport aircraft massed for the operation were to arrive in Sicily at the last minute; rumours were to be spread that these preparations were for a move to Russia. Kesselring had between seven and nine Gruppen of Ju52 and He111 transport aircraft available, totalling about 450 aircraft. The Italians had a force of 140 of their big Savoia S82s available for their part.

Before the invasion, intense reconnaissance was to be made, searching in particular for new defence works and installations, and also to take horizontal and oblique photos of the selected landing areas. The installations and positions would be heavily attacked by the Luftwaffe and Regia Aeronautica, and the RAF was to be destroyed in the air.

With control of the air, systematic attacks, aided by low-level reconnaissance flights, would be made on all defensive positions, especially anti-aircraft. This pressure and intensity of attack was to be maintained for more than a week, and if necessary, up to fourteen days. These were preliminary operations, deemed successful when Malta could be declared 'out of action as an air base on X—1day', and the air, ground and coastal defences had been reduced to a minimum.

It was realised that strategic surprise would not be possible, but tactical surprise could be achieved. On X-Day, early morning attacks would be made as had been done in the past weeks, but at 08.00 a full scale attack would be made on defensive installations in the landing area, on anti-invasion measures and on the airfields. Pressure would be maintained, in waves, for the next five hours.

Meanwhile, the Luftwaffe transport aircraft would have been assembled on the eastern side of Italy, at Foggia, Bari, Brindisi and Lecce, and would have flown to their forward airfields where troops waited at Gerbini, Comiso and Catania. When the troops had been loaded, the aircraft were to have taken off again, flying east from Sicily, then turning south into the corridor to Malta. At a marked point, they would turn west and later turn south, taking them around Malta, finally turning north for the approach to the targets around the southern side of Marsa Sirocco and Kalafrana. The Italian transports, from Castevetrano and Sciacca, would join them as they flew along the southern side of Malta before turning north for the final run-in. All were to fly at low-level, with fighter escort, and at this time the island radio and radar was to be jammed, to disrupt fighter control on Malta.

As the transports were taking off from Sicily, the seaborne assault force would begin moving out to sea.

On Malta, the waves of fighters and bombers would have been rolling across the island, and as the first transports were crossing the south coast, the attacks would have concentrated on all gun positions in the areas of the landing zones. H-Hour was 13.30.

Nine battalions of German and Italian paratroops, with their heavy weapons, were to drop in selected areas, seize and hold them. If possible, a further wave would be flown in that afternoon. There would be constant air cover, with Luftwaffe bomber formations allocated to particular paratroop units, to react to calls from them to deal with gun positions, troop concentrations among the defenders, and any tanks seen in the battle area. The Italians were to attack the forts at Benghaisa and Delimara.

At H+6 hours, at dusk, gliders and paratroopers would land between Kalafrana and Benghaisa, capture the coastline and establish a defensive line. This would be assisted by bombing the forts, if necessary, by a smoke screen, and by dummy paratroopers dropped to confuse the defenders.

By midnight, the sea-borne force was to be going ashore in the area held by the airborne troops. Priority was given to assault troops, guns, tanks, then infantry and supplies.

Next morning the island of Gozo would be assaulted and various diversions carried out on other parts of the coastline of Malta. The German-occupied landing area would be developed, and Hal Far and Krendi captured for use by the air forces. Gradually, but ever more quickly, the island would be occupied.

For this operation, Kesselring had available the Messerschmitt Bf109s of two Gruppen of JG27, two of JG53, and two reconnaissance units, 1(F)22 and 2(F)123; two Stuka Gruppen of StG3; the Ju88s and Heinkel He111s of Gruppen from LG1, KG77, KG100, KGr606 and 806, plus the nightfighters of I Gruppe NJG2, totalling about 500 aircraft. Some 580 Italian aircraft would be available, coming from all parts of Italy and the combat areas. In round figures, one thousand aircraft would be available to blanket Malta and its immediate area.

To deal with any Royal Navy thrust from either end of the Mediterranean, the Regia Aeronautica had bases in Sardinia, the Aegean, Libya and Sicily, with a total of six torpedo groups, three bomber groups, eight fighter and one dive-bomber groups.

The paratroop units came from the Luftwaffe 7 Parachute Division and 4 Parachute Regiment, plus the Italian 'Folgore' Parachute Division. Five Italian Divisions were to be landed by sea—or air if the situation allowed—led by assault troops of the 'San Marco' Regiment and a Blackshirt detachment.

This was Kesselring's plan. General Kurt Student, commander of German airborne units, prepared another, in which the airfields were captured first by his paratroop and glider units, with 'Folgore' taking the high ground overlooking Takali, and the sea-borne troops coming ashore at small beach-heads seized in the bays on the steep south coast, after which the invasion front was to have moved north across the island.[22] But Hitler had to be convinced of the necessity for an invasion.

A young RAAF pilot posted for inclusion in the next batch to fly Spitfires to Malta was Sergeant Colin Parkinson. He had staged through West Kirby, which he thought was the worst camp he had experienced, with filthy accommodation, few working facilities, and a commander who hated people from the Dominions. After travelling in buses to Liverpool, the 36 pilots in the group embarked on a cargo ship, which had been modified to carry the crated Spitfires, and had had its passenger cabins painted. The smell of new paint, combined with a rough sea and large amounts of alcohol, made many of the passengers, pilots and ground crews feel ill. 'I have never seen so many people sick at one time,' Parkinson wrote in his diary. 'Some of them sat for days in one spot on the deck and stared out to sea with glassy eyes.'[23]

The June convoys were gathering.

5

Whirlwind

Malta—June 1942

The quiet days continued into June. Reconnaissance aircraft arrived and departed, high-flying Messerschmitts sometimes dived to scatter a few bombs, but the Luftwaffe presence was markedly less than it had been a month before. Luftwaffe losses from all causes had been about five hundred aircraft. Italian bombers made the most of the attacking sorties, in close formation, escorted by Macchi 202s and Reggiani 2001s. The Italian fighter pilots were generally agreed to be accomplished and could perform beautiful aerobatics, but had little knowledge of combat tactics.

Among the Luftwaffe units, promotions and awards continued. Gerhard Michalski became Kommandeur of II/JG 53 on 1 June, and on the same day, Herbert Stry, of the Stukas, received the German Cross in Gold.

Far away in Germany, of more import to the course of the war and German victory or defeat, Hitler had called General Kurt Student to report to him, then told Student that the invasion of Malta was cancelled. Rommel had taken Tobruk, but the Italians were not performing well. General Cruwell had reported from Rommel's headquarters that morale and fighting ability of the Italians was low; Hitler did not trust the Italian fleet to remain at sea, despite the considerable Axis air power massed to attack if the Royal Navy mounted an operation toward Malta.

After the war, when asked why the invasion did not take place, Goering replied, 'You try to carry out an invasion with Italian forces!'[1]

But on the besieged island, no one knew of this. The nearest Allied position was still 1600 km to the east or west, and enemies lined the approaches. The fighting went on.

However, on 1 June, 'Slim' Yarra destroyed a 109. In the preceding month, he had destroyed five fighters, damaged two more, and claimed a Ju88 as a probable. On this day, leading a section of four in GL-K, they engaged eight yellow-nosed 109s, chased two and Yarra shot one down. But Andy Macnaughton was killed.

HMS *Eagle* at Gibraltar collected a batch of Spitfires, and was to make a dash into the Mediterranean to launch them, then return for another batch just before the convoys later in the month. One Australian abroad for the first flight was Len Reid, who had been in Gibraltar testing re-assembled Spitfires. Like many others, he had begun flying training in Australia. In December 1940, he went to Canada to No. 1 SFTS at Camp Borden, Ontario, and then to 52 OTU, Debden, Essex in July 1941. He then went to 504 Squadron, and to 130 Squadron, before posting in May 1942 to RAF Station Gibraltar. He had some 258 hours flying time.

He had got to know some of the crew of HMS *Eagle*, and noticed that 'they were always scared aircraft would get them, that the dive bombers would get them.' Eric Mahar said, in support of this attitude, 'If you were in the Royal Navy in the Mediterranean, wouldn't you have been nervous? They'd lost a lot of ships there.'

Reid's batch of pilots had been told not to take off if the speed of the wind over the deck of the carrier was below 26 knots, which was the absolute minimum allowable.

Eagle set off into the Mediterranean with its load of Spitfires, which were launched some 1000 km from Malta. Len Reid, in BR230, was in a flight of nine, led by the experienced Malta pilot from Rhodesia, Johnny Plagis. The formations followed the route along the coast of North Africa. But near Pantelleria, about 330 km from Malta, Reid saw some Messerschmitts 'sitting out there watching us for five minutes.' Then they began positioning themselves to attack. Flying next to him was an American also watching the 109s.

Then Reid noticed other pilots dropping their belly tanks, so released his own. It was clear something was about to happen.

Reid said nothing himself, but heard other pilots shouting that the 109s were coming in. 'I could see them getting in position, saw them closing, I recall Tex shouting the 109s were attacking, I saw them coming . . .'

99

Suddenly, the 109s attacked from behind, and Reid waited for Plagis to give the order, at the right moment, to break, but nothing came from Plagis, who suddenly rolled over and dived for the sea as the 109s were upon the Spitfires.

'He left the rest of us up there like sitting ducks,' recalled Reid. 'Those 109s just flew in behind us and shot Tex out of the sky. I can still see him . . . Tex was alongside me, he was shot, obviously, as the stick came back into his stomach, and I saw him go up, smoke coming out, he was probably dead, and it was a matter of rolling over and diving for the sea. Everybody had to look after himself.

'I had one or two on my tail, tracer bullets flying past but fortunately they didn't hit me, and followed right down to the sea. I remember zig-zagging madly across the water, and in the finish I was on my own, I didn't know where I was, but knew I had to steer a certain course which might bring me to Malta. It did. I was supposed to land at Takali, but landed at Hal Far, as I came in from that direction. Eric came out to meet me.'

He found that four Spitfires had been shot down. He was posted to 185 Squadron, joining Ken Mitchell and Eric Mahar, presumably because he happened to arrive there rather than at another airfield.

Len Reid found that the memory of, and example set by, Tony Boyd was still the subject of conversation. He and Boyd had trained together in Australia on 7 Course, and at Camp Borden in Canada, but had gone to different OTUs in the United Kingdom. They had met again in London, quite by chance, during a leave late in 1941. Len Reid recalled that, 'Unfortunately Tony was killed in combat before I arrived, however his reputation at Hal Far lived on, and he was greatly admired by all Squadron personnel, particularly the airmen who serviced his aircraft. Tony had earned the reputation of being an outstanding Hurricane pilot, and many of the squadron praised his skill and tenacity in air combat.'[1A]

In Gibraltar, the convoys were forming to push through to Malta, and the younger members of the ships' crews were enjoying life. Some Spitfire pilots relished the change in climate and lifestyle after drab, wintry England. Colin Parkinson had plenty of money, as he had had little leave in the UK, so splurged on items in the shops. He also tried 'Spanish rice', but lost his appetite when he found pieces of octopus tentacle in it. He had a weakened stomach, after five days' serious drinking, and octopus was a little too much.

The Spitfires had been assembled and taken aboard HMS *Eagle*, then the pilots also boarded her. The NCO pilots slept in the hangar, under the wings of aircraft, while the officers were in the wardroom. This drew comment from the egalitarian members from the Dominions, including Parkinson. The ships prepared to sail.

On Malta itself, enjoying the relative respite after the hard days of May, but aware of the impending convoy operations, the fighter squadrons tested their Spitfires with long-range tanks fitted, preparing to go out and cover the precious ships when they came within range. Ninety-five Spitfires were available, an almost unbelievable number compared with the situation at the beginning of May when the defences were sometimes able to gather a maximum of ten or twelve.

126 and 601 Squadrons moved into a new Mess at St Julian's Bay, described by Tim Goldsmith as 'nice and clean, right on the edge of the bay. Wizard spot with fine swimming in the bay.' It had been the home of an English lady who had recently been evacuated. Close by were anti-aircraft guns, whose firing must have made life difficult for her.

Jimmy Peck, the American, John Bisley and Goldsmith hired a five-metre yacht and went sailing, having 'a wizard time just falling in the water.' Now and again, they saw the minesweepers trudging back and forth outside the harbour, making 'little tingles go up and down our spine.' They were well aware that the mine-sweepers were preparing for the imminent convoy actions.

There was little flying for them, just some air tests, and scrambles with no result, as the squadrons prepared for the convoys. Slim Yarra's collection of current musical hits was played constantly on the gramophone in 185 Squadron, and the popular Glenn Miller tune 'In The Mood' was repeated over and over. More than forty years later, in some of the surviving pilots who heard it, the tune evoked memories of Yarra, the gramophone, and the squadron on Malta. In addition to the music, contract bridge became popular with the squadron pilots, who were obviously more refined than the 126 Squadron group described by Tim Goldsmith!

Ken Mitchell recalled that Yarra 'liked the American Negro type of singing, and used to astonish us by repeating perfectly all the

101

1939-42 songs. He loved jazz. But he didn't abide perfectly by rules, he wasn't perfect with discipline, which I suppose made him the perfect fighter pilot. Forrester, the Rhodesian, also entertained us with the accordion.'[2]

'Transport between the squadron's [accommodation] and the airfield was terribly difficult, very short,' said Ken. 'You had to rely on gharries, the Maltese horse-drawn cart. Cars and trucks were scarce as hen's teeth. We used to get out to the aircraft with Dave, a dispatch rider of the Royal West Kent Regiment, who had a lovely big Harley-Davidson motor-cycle. We used to hop on the back, parachute pack over shoulder, making sure the straps didn't get caught in the back wheel, and he'd drive us out, one at a time.'[3]

The war outside their horizons went on. On 4 June, at Midway, the US Navy won, more by luck than good management, a decisive victory over the Japanese and changed the course of the war. If the Japanese had won Midway, they would have gone on to bombard the West Coast of the USA. President Roosevelt would never have been able to convince the American people that Germany should be defeated first, and most of the US war effort would have been used to protect the west against Japanese attacks. There would have been no immediate supply of US tanks at Churchill's request for them to go to North Africa, no campaign at Guadalcanal and in the Solomons, no invasion of Morocco in November 1942, and no resulting invasion of Sicily and Italy in 1943, no great build-up in the United Kingdom for the invasion of Europe in 1944; nothing until the West Coast of the USA and the Panama Canal had been made safe. The war would have taken an entirely different course.

But the US Navy did win at Midway, though the effects were not to be felt for some months. In Russia, the Germans besieged Sevastopol; the Japanese invaded the Aleutian Islands; in North Africa the Germans attacked and took Bir Hakeim.

Malta prepared for the convoys.

Far away from the warmth of the Sicilian and Maltese skies, naval forces were being assembled to fight their way through to the island. On 5 June, from England, one component set out for Gibraltar: five cruisers and ten destroyers escorting five merchantmen. At Gibraltar and Alexandria, other ships were preparing for the battles.

On 6 June, Johnny Plagis led four Spitfires against a formation of ten Reggianis, which turned for home. Plagis chased them, caught up and shot down two some sixty kilometres out from Malta. Slim Yarra, 185 Squadron, was leading a section of four in GL-W, engaging about 25 Reggianis, but did not claim.

Next day, Yarra damaged two more Reggianis. He had been leading a four in GL-N, but turned back with engine trouble. Three Reggianis appeared, and in the combat he damaged two before they left for home.

On 8 June, HMS *Eagle* sailed with its component of Spitfires, which were launched at dawn. Colin Parkinson was one of a section of eight, which was 'led by an inexperienced Flight Lieutenant. His speeds varied from 160 kmph to 320 kmph. On the way we saw a sub being refuelled by a depot ship just off the coast of Africa. It took approximately four hours to get to Malta, where we all landed safely without too much damage to the aircraft, but two were pranged.'[4]

The new pilots were all briefed on the situation, and they began to take in the surroundings. Parkinson noted that 'we were told all sorts of tales about how the Huns and ice cream merchants used to come over and fly round the circuit, shooting up aircraft on the ground. Met Jack Yarra, who has the DFM. I'm in 603 Squadron, Squadron Leader Lord Douglas Hamilton is the CO. I'm in B Flight, so won't see much of him, thank goodness. 603 is very much an officers' squadron; the sergeants don't get a fair deal. Both officers and NCOs have very poor food, though it is quite possible to buy meals of eggs, pork chops, tomatoes, fresh beans, lettuce and potatoes at various Maltese shops, so while I have some money I won't starve.'[5]

On the day the new Spitfires arrived, Slim Yarra, in GL-N, scrambled twice, once to engage an estimated 60-plus, and when attacking a formation of twenty Ju87s, used up all his ammunition for no known result. Next day he again scrambled twice, the first time having return fire from the bomber gunners hit his windscreen, flinging glass fragments into the cockpit and his face.

The very core of the decision to persist in holding Malta, as a base for offensive operations, was reinforced when a new torpedo-bomber squadron arrived on 10 June. 217 Squadron flew in, but none of its Beauforts were ready to use, as the bomb-bays had been used for installation of extra fuel tanks, which had to be removed. Only two members of the squadron had actually flown on operations.

On the 11th, the second anniversary of the commencement of hostilities over Malta, *Operation Harpoon*, the convoy thrust from the west to Malta, began at Gibraltar. On the same day, *Operation Vigorous* began from Alexandria, with the same objective. From Gibraltar, a total of one battleship, six cruisers, seventeen destroyers, four minesweepers and a supply ship were to escort five merchantmen and a tanker to Malta. From Alexandria came eight cruisers, twenty-six destroyers, four corvettes and two minesweepers with eleven merchantmen and a tanker.

In total, one battleship, fourteen cruisers, forty-three destroyers, four corvettes, six minesweepers and a supply ship were marshalled to take sixteen merchantmen and two tankers to Malta. Such was the power of land-based aircraft, even though it was supplemented by a fleet of proven poor fighting ability.

By this time, Malta had been subjected to 2537 raids, losing 1215 people killed. Tens of thousands of homes had been destroyed or so damaged that the population lived in the shelters and were fed communally, by authorities who were plagued day and night with the responsibilities of office, all of which revolved around the date to which food and fuel could be stretched. Starvation was always close, despite stringent rationing, and though some vegetables and fruit were grown on Malta, the staples such as flour and potatoes, as well as meat, simply were unobtainable. Everyone, from highest to lowest, lived on much the same diet.

On 11 June, John Bisley destroyed a 109, with a second credited as a probable. Paul Brennan was commissioned, followed two days later by Ray Hesslyn.

Night bombing became more intense, particularly during full moon periods. By this time, radar-equipped Beaufighters were on the island, and, together with the ack-ack and searchlights, took a steady toll. Radio Rome described the tough life of the night bomber crews over Malta, giving some comfort to those on the island. Some of the Beaufighter pilots ran up respectable scores, including Moose Fumerton, a Canadian, who destroyed four enemy in two nights' flying. He was to accumulate twelve victories over Malta, ending the war with fourteen.

On 12 June the RAF's greatest star over Malta opened his account, when George Beurling damaged a Messerschmitt 109.

He had flown in on the recent carrier-borne Spitfire reinforcement, after a less than happy time with 41 Squadron, with which he had destroyed two Focke-Wulf 190s, but by leaving the formation to attack alone.

Len Reid, who had survived the interception of the Spitfire formation en route to Malta on 3 June, had gone to 185 Squadron. Flying BR112, he was in a formation which engaged Ju88s and 109s on 12 June. He fired, but made no claim.

But the main offensive force of the Axis air arms was now applied to the convoys coming from east and west. The convoy battles are themselves worthy of books, and have been well-described in the past. For the purposes of this account of the RAAF pilots on Malta, the battle details are not necessary, but the courage and determination of both sides should be remembered.

Savage attacks were made on the convoy from Alexandria. After losing one cruiser sunk with all hands, plus three destroyers and two merchantmen gone, and two others turned back because of damage, the force returned to Egypt. The ships from the west fought on, and closed on Malta. On the 15th, the sound of battle out at sea could be heard on Malta itself.

The island Spitfires took off, flying west to give cover to the ships. The first four, Tim Goldsmith and three others from 126 Squadron, arrived at 10.40. They began patrolling over the ships, having noted, during their approach, two Italian cruisers, one sinking and one crippled, the result of battle between the opposing navies. Earlier, Beaufighters had reached the ships, but had to return when their fuel was gone. Stukas had attacked with deadly accuracy, sinking one ship and damaging the tanker, *Kentucky.*

Herbert Stry, Stuka pilot and leader of 5th Staffel, St.G. 3, was credited with sinking a 10 000 ton freighter and damaging a destroyer in the convoy battles.[6]

Goldsmith, flying as Jumbo Harry 3, found the western convoy 240 kilometres from Malta. He could see that there had been a naval battle between surface ships, and began to circle the scene. Low on the water, heading for Pantelleria, a small Italian island with an airfield and military garrison, was a Cant Z506 flying boat. He dived on it, lined it up and fired a three-second burst. Again he had cannon trouble, the starboard pair jamming after one second. But the shells struck home on the Italian, sparking along the starboard side of the fuselage and on the wing, it surged up sharply to the left, rolled onto its back and fell into the water. Italian records show that this was actually a Fiat RS14 of 144 Squadriglia, flown by Tenente (Lieutenant) Antonio Carnielli, which had been acting as a convoy shadower.

Other pilots continued hammering at it as it lay in the water, one wing poking up vertically. Later, there was some harsh joking at the supposed consternation of the crew down there as the Spitfires speared in, guns churning the water around the Cant.

The convoy fired on three BR20s, and the Spitfires attacked these bombers. Goldsmith climbed to 6000 feet and picked a BR20. His Number 2, Flight Sergeant Evans, fired at it, but Tim saw no results, so fired another short three-second burst. He opened fire at 150 yards (135 m), closing to almost collision point. Again the persistent cannon problems interfered, and only the port cannon fired, but it was enough. He broke left as the starboard engine of the bomber began smoking, the fuselage began burning, pieces fell away, the BR20 began spinning, then burst into flames and went down. Two parachutes appeared before it hit the water.

These parachutists were part of the crew of one of two S84s (not BR20s) which were lost from a formation of nine from 4 Gruppo, carrying out a high-level bombing attack on the ships. Flight Lieutenant Winfield claimed one shot down, identifying it as a BR20, while Flight Sergeant Farquharson claimed a 'damaged'. Goldsmith made no reference to anyone else sharing his victory, but Flight Sergeant Evans seems to have been allocated a share.

Three members of the crew, piloted by Gruppo commander Maggiore (Major) Gastone Valenti, baled out and were rescued. A stowaway, Sottotenente (2nd Lieutenant) Zezon, was in Valentini's bomber, and was killed while manning a gun. It was thought he shot down two Spitfires, and he was later awarded a posthumous Medaglia d'Oro. But no fighters were lost. None of the crew of the other bomber, flown by Maresciallo (Warrant Officer) Aldo Pinna, survived.[7]

On the way back to Malta, Tim Goldsmith saw an aircraft over to port, broke off to investigate it, and found it to be a Macchi 200. He moved onto its tail, and after a short turning and diving contest, during which he fired three bursts, using all his remaining ammunition, left the Italian streaming oil, with a long distance to cover back to base. He described the Italian's flying as 'mild evasive action, turning one way, then the other.' In view of the amount of oil streaming from it and the 100 km the Macchi would have to cover to get back to Pantelleria, he claimed it as a victory, but no Italian record shows a loss for this day. Goldsmith turned back for Malta, and landed after two hours and forty-five minutes flight 'with bugger-all petrol'.

Every effort was made to keep an umbrella of Spitfires over the battered remnants of *Harpoon*. Over 300 Spitfire sorties were flown, and no ship was lost to air attack while they were overhead. The Beauforts of 217 Squadron set off to attack the Italian fleet which was moving to intercept the convoy. The torpedo bombers made one hit on the cruiser *Trento*, and left the Italian ships manoeuvring in all directions, their mission disrupted. The cruiser was later sunk by submarine torpedo, and Wellington bombers of 38 Squadron later damaged the cruiser *Littorio*.

Through the night, the remaining ships of the Allied convoy dashed for Malta, leaving behind damaged vessels which suffered further losses from the Italian fleet. Both sides were bloodied in the actions.

Next day, the merchantmen *Oran* and *Troilus*, with HMS *Welshman* made their way into harbour. Nothing else of the desperately needed supplies reached the island. Between them, they carried 15 000 tons; starvation and surrender had been postponed for a short time. No one knew when the next great concentration of ships could be readied for another battle across the Mediterranean.

Having learned from the experiences of the past convoys, when precious cargo had been lost because unloading ships had been not given a high priority, everything in the harbour area was subordinated to the swift dispersal of the goods in the ships' holds. The unloading plan included stevedores, vehicles and the local road system, all directed to removing the merchandise from the danger zone as soon as possible.

There were seven air attacks from Sicily, but the Spitfire defence was adequate, and the cargoes stayed safe. Tim Goldsmith intercepted what he described as a half-hearted attack by four Ju88s, with an escort of Messerschmitt 109s and Reggianis. The 88s dropped their bombs into the sea outside Grand Harbour, and turned for home. Goldsmith and the others gave chase, and in a combat with 109s about fifty kilometres north of Malta,

107

shot one down into the sea. He was attacked head-on by another, who put a cannon shell into the port wing of the Spitfire, but did little apparent damage. Goldsmith swung onto another, lined him up and fired . . . one round came out of the cannon, so Tim disengaged quickly 'and came home smartly!'

'Slim' Yarra, leading a section in GL-J, was attacked by twelve 109s. He was hit by a bullet through the exhaust, but destroyed another 109. He noted in his log book that 'Tex and Mac baled out,' and had the Messerschmitt listed as 'damaged'.

It was obvious that raids on the ships would continue, and next day the Spitfires repelled another six attacks. Following radioed orders, Tim Goldsmith's formation made a 'wizard interception of 109s, but a little low'. In the swirling aftermath, he put two bursts into one Messerschmitt, but could only claim him as damaged. Then he and Dusty Miller chased one back to Sicily, but could not close in to get a shot, and reluctantly swung back. They were to be Goldsmith's last claims over Malta.

The Italian fleet returned to port, and was photographed there on 17 June. British attacks on Italian and German ships trying to make the crossing between Europe and Africa resumed, in some cases forcing them back to Italian harbours. One Axis convoy for Africa did finally make it, after a series of advances and retreats lasting sixteen days, instead of the normal two-day crossing.

Again a lull descended over the island. The fighter pilots, and gun crews, could not really relax when on duty, and the waiting stretched many nerves. After the recent bursts of activity during the convoy battles, few realised that the Axis naval and air arms were now repairing the damage, and concentrating on the battles in North Africa.

On 19 June, one of the Spitfires' adversaries died in a take-off accident at Tripoli. Helmut Belser, a Staffel leader in III/JG 53, crashed; he had claimed 36 victories, 24 against the Western Allies. He was awarded the Knight's Cross posthumously.[8]

Tim Goldsmith was having two days off duty and one on. On the 20th, he wrote that 'these few days have been blissfully quiet and dull. Bags of swimming in between time. Very few scrambles. 17 hours a day on a hot dusty aerodrome with no transport to the Mess, and bloody food, is no fun at all.' Paul Brennan was flying, but, like his New Zealand friend, Hesslyn, had no success. They flew against Italians and Germans, but were unable to claim any destroyed. The targets were there, but they seemed unable to score.

However, Slim Yarra, in GL-W, was still having successes. While attacking a formation of bombers, his flight was set upon by the fighter escort. Yarra took his section of four in on four yellow-nosed 109s, slipped behind one and shot its tail off, though Terry, an RAF pilot, was on the receiving end of Messerschmitt fire. Yarra's Spitfires continued after an 88. Yarra was hitting it when three more 109s arrived and attacked him, but he shot one down and 'beat it for home.'

Terry brought his Spitfire in for a crash-landing but was unhurt. In a later scramble, Flight Sergeant Bob Sim RNZAF, claimed a 109 destroyed and another damaged. German records show only one aircraft of 5/JG53 crash-landed at Comiso, with no losses.[9]

That day at Takali, for 249 Squadron, interest centred on the shooting down of the hundredth enemy since the squadron had been equipped with Spitfires. While using Hurricanes, 27 enemy had been destroyed, and the combined total for both types of fighter had reached 100 during the intense May actions. Now all were waiting to see who would get the hundredth with a Spitfire. On 19 June, the score stood at 99 confirmed destroyed. Among others, Brennan and Hesslyn waited for enemy to appear. While on readiness they hoped for a scramble, but it was not to be. Next day they were on leave, there was a combat, and the magic total was reached. They also missed the party in the Mess to celebrate.

But, off to the south, the war in North Africa was reaching a crisis point. On 20 June, Rommel attacked and captured Tobruk, a victory which led to his eventual defeat in North Africa. At the time, the Allies were shaken by this latest triumph of 'The Desert Fox', but, buoyed up with the surrender and the acquisition of the large amounts of supplies, Rommel decided he could go on to Alexandria. Never having overly concerned himself with logistics, he now relied on his legendary luck and battlefield skills to go the rest of the way to Suez. He decided that he could not wait for the invasion of Malta, and asked that the units allocated to that operation be allocated for his use along the North African coastline. And had not Kesselring repeatedly said Malta was neutralised? The recent convoy battles had been Axis victories, and the small amounts of supplies which had reached the island

109

could only stave off eventual surrender, not prevent it. Rather than waste time, men and machines on invading an island which would fall anyway, those men should be used to develop this opportunity to push on to Suez.

On 22 June, Kesselring went to Rommel, to ask for the return of his Luftwaffe units which had been used in the recent desert battles, and which Kesselring needed for *Hercules*. But Rommel, about to be promoted to Field Marshal for the victory at Tobruk, was able to retain them.

Kesselring pointed out that the recent upsurge in supplies had been achieved because Malta's offensive capability had been greatly reduced, but attacks from the island would resume unless pressure was maintained, or the island invaded and its threat negated.

Rommel, reportedly in a raging temper, took matters into his own hands and made personal approaches to other, higher authorities. He sent his personal media aide, Dr Ingemar Berndt, to speak to both Dr Goebbels and Hitler on Rommel's behalf. Next day, after another heated conference with the Italian High command, he signalled the chief German military representative in Rome, von Rintelen, asking him to gain the approval of Mussolini for the advance intended by Rommel in North Africa.

The Italo-German forces in the desert had been in action since 26 May, overcoming the British defence of the Gazala Line. Rommel was now to push his formations eastwards, ever east, but with no respite, as there were no fresh formations released from Europe by OKW. After learning of his promotion to Field Marshal, he wrote to his wife saying he would rather have had another division.

In Russia, the Germans were penetrating the defences of Sevastopol. On the 24th, Rommel advanced to Sidi Barrani, and next day Auckinleck took personal command in the desert, while 8th Army retreated to Mersa Matruh. On the 27th, the Germans advanced to Mersa Matruh. Next day the British began withdrawing to El Alamein. In Russia, the German offensive at Kursk began. Two days later, Rommel reached the El Alamein position and at once began to attack, intending to bounce the British back from this, their last position before the Nile Delta.

But Rommel had at long last reached the end of his advances. Aircraft from Malta had attacked and sunk or damaged ships carrying replacement troops and tanks outside Tripoli on 21 June;

a tanker on the 22nd; two more ships were damaged on the 23rd and had to be towed back to Palermo, and a similar result was achieved on the 30th.

Rommel's old faithful Afrika Korps (15 and 21 Panzer Divisions) and 90th Light Division, with the few reliable Italian units, again and again went into the attack, now often in captured British vehicles and with captured artillery firing in support. Time and again the Germans had been held and seemed unable to break through, and each time the British command had lost its nerve and ordered a withdrawal. But on 25 June, Auchinleck sacked Ritchie, last in a string of British generals defeated by Rommel, and took personal command. Mersa Matruh would be the last battle where Rommel was to push the British off balance and dominate their command staff with his personal legend.

Ever eager for a victory parade, Mussolini arrived at Derna on 29 June, with the necessary white horse for his triumphal entry into Cairo.

So far, it had been dayfighter pilots in the RAAF who had been so heavily involved in the combats, but with the introduction of the Beaufighter for night interceptions and intruder attacks, several Australian night-fighter pilots were to make their mark. 89 Squadron had been formed for service in the Middle East, and, after arrival in Egypt, sent a detachment to Malta. Mervyn Shipard arrived on 22 June. He had already destroyed a He111 in the previous November, over the UK. At this time, his radar operator was Sergeant Doug Oxby RAF, who was to go on to become the top-scoring operator in the Allied forces, assisting his pilots to destroy more enemy aircraft than any other.

In the Spitfire squadrons, other RAAF pilots began to claim victories. On the 23rd, C. L. Baxter, 249 Squadron, damaged an Re2001, and Sergeant Colin Parkinson, 603 Squadron, shared a Mc202 with Pilot Officers Newman and Smith.

Parkinson described the combat in his diary. It was his fourth flight in ten days, and he had taken off with the wrong section, becoming 'White 5', in the formation led by Flying Officer Mitchell. The Spitfires climbed to 24 000 feet, and found three Cant bombers flying west, into the sun, south-west of Gozo Island. The Spitfires came down from the north, across the sun.

Parkinson stayed with Mitchell as they dived to attack from astern, but had to break when a Macchi slid in behind him, and another attempt to attack the bombers from below was foiled by the fighter escort. Parkinson then went in again, under the bombers, hanging on his propeller, firing at the centre bomber, when 'a stream of bullets like tram lines went past my wings, so I broke away down to about 6000 feet.'

Below him he saw a Spitfire and a Macchi, with the Macchi seeming to get the better of the contest. 'I sailed in and the other Spit sailed out. I made one three-quarter head-on attack. The Italian flicked and presented his tail to me. I was about 200 feet behind, dead on and firing, I saw something break off the fuselage and then the pilot bailed out. His kite went into the sea. I circled the pilot, whose chute had opened. He looked dead to me, so I eventually flew straight at him, and then decided he wasn't dead because he started to wave his arms frantically.'

Records indicate that the Italian was Aldo Buvoli, of 360 Squadriglia. Parkinson went back and landed at Takali, where squadron claims were for three destroyed.[10]

During the day, the air-sea rescue launches picked up their hundredth pilot from the sea. In two more weeks, the Malta launches and tenders would establish a world record.

Next day, 24 June, Parkinson wrote that the food was 'very bad', and that only two of the expected six ships had arrived. While sitting in his cockpit, ready to take-off, he heard the sound of a Spitfire in a power dive, looked up, and saw one diving for the airfield, but with glycol streaming behind. The pilot tried to land, but his engine cut, he tried to turn at too slow a speed and at only 20 metres height, stalled and spun to the ground. The fighter burst into flames, and exploding ammunition kept rescuers and the fire engine away. When he was able to get close to the wreckage, and could see the pilot's body in the cockpit, and smell the burning clothes, Parkinson found it was the man who slept next to him.

The orderly room staff asked Parkinson to sort through the belongings of the dead man and make a list of his belongings, but he was unable to do a proper job, as another pilot had 'carefully ratted everything'. Parkinson was ashamed to find the man who did this was another Australian, who had arrived on Malta in the same batch of reinforcement pilots as Parkinson himself.[11]

During combats with Italians and Germans attacking Luqa, Flight Sergeant Irwin RAAF claimed hits on a Bf109.

After an attack by Wellington torpedo bombers of 38 Squadron

RAF on a convoy in the Gulf of Taranto, some thirteen enemy aircraft were detected on radar approaching Malta. Pilot Officer John Ross RAAF, a Beaufighter pilot in 89 Squadron, intercepted a Ju88, and attacked. He and his observer, Sergeant Thompson RAF, reported it going down in 'a shower of red flashes—it apparently fell into the sea.'

At the end of the month, Kesselring moved units back onto the Sicilian airfields, for a renewed offensive in July. Ju88s of II and III/KG 77, and the 109s of I/JG 77 flew in from the Russian front. He had moved as many aircraft as possible to Africa to assist Rommel, but now these were too far to the rear, as Rommel could not wait. When June drew to a close, the Axis land forces were at the forward edge of the radius of action of their supporting aircraft, but the British forces were much closer to the RAF and Commonwealth air bases, and well within their protective range. Consequently, air attacks were placed on the hapless Germans at regular 30-minute intervals by bomber formations, and other attacks could be made at any time.

Now another serious fault in the direction of the Luftwaffe became obvious, as the Messerschmitts preferred to attack the British fighters, against whom there were more kudos to be won in the fraternity of aces, rather than the militarily more important bombers.

June had seen 2890 enemy sorties over the island, well down on the peak of 10 300 of April, but still a significant effort. There had been 106 daylight alerts of air raids and 65 night alerts, but only sixty tons of bombs had been dropped. Most of the enemy effort had been directed against the convoys, with reconnaissance and fighter sweeps across the islands. Attacks on shipping by the RAF had clearly reflected the North African battle-front location, its closeness to Malta and distance from Egypt, with the requirement for Axis ships to steam relatively near to the island. Only 35 sorties had been flown from Egypt, with attacks on twelve ships, but 71 had been flown from Malta, with attacks on at least 42 ships. This pendulum effect became obvious as the front line in Africa surged back and forth.

As June ended, Malta was again watching friendly forces being forced to retreat into Egypt, which meant that any convoys had an even more dangerous journey. There was little to give encouragement to those examining the local situation, or that of the Allies around the world.

6

The Storm Continues

Malta—July 1942

On the first day of the new month, Mahar, Mitchell, Parkinson and Ross registered claims. Mahar and Mitchell damaged a Mc202 and Bf109 respectively, while John Ross, Beaufighter pilot in 89 Squadron, claimed a Ju88 probably destroyed.

Parkinson found an enemy fighter 'with finger trouble. I flew out to one side, recognised it as an Re, flew in behind, gave a long burst, saw strikes, the kite faltered, glycol poured out and [it] went into a vertical dive. A shower of enemy fighters attacked me, so I went into a vertical dive and escaped them. Last I saw of the Re it was still heading for the drink at 5000 or 6000 feet. I went home and reported. Ballantyne was shot down. He bailed out and was picked up OK. Bullet in the neck or something. Claims he shot down a 109.'[1]

At Gibraltar, meanwhile, the next batch of Spitfires and pilots were ready, and Noel Pashen and the others were busy with last-minute purchases. They went aboard HMS *Eagle* at 18.00, and Noel thought the quarters not too good, but decided the situation could be borne as it was for a few days only. He also thought that the flight deck was short, but reasoned that everyone else had managed to fly off successfully, so he could.

On Malta itself, any feeling of nonchalance about the harassing night raids was jolted that night. About 02.00 next morning, Parkinson and the others were awakened by the sound of a low-flying aircraft, followed at once by the sound of falling bombs, 'the whole building shuddered (so did I), showers of rocks hit the walls and roof and a smell of dust filled the air; but no explosion. We all decided to get out of the building in case it was a delayed action bomb.'

They trooped out onto the bastion and watched the raid, seeing two fires at Luqa. After the 'All Clear' was sounded, they went to look for the bomb. A Maltese waiter found it. 'I've never seen anyone move so fast in all my life. He took one look, gave a loud yell, and was off like a streak of greased lightning. I took one look and didn't stay too long either.'

The bomb had hit various buildings nearby and come to rest about twenty metres from the sleeping quarters. The pilots went up to the Mess to await the dawn. It was 03.30, there were no beds, and some had to be on readiness at 05.45. They went to their aircraft still tired from the flying of the day before.[2]

It had been decided to reduce the length of time spent on Malta for fighter pilots to three months, as the intensity of operations was putting great strain on them. On 1 July, Tim Goldsmith flew, but there was no interception. Next day, his diary entry expresses his feelings: 'Whoopee! Told to get ready to leave today, but didn't.' The relief from pressure was helped along with a few drinks, and even those were of doubtful strength. Any feeling of light-headedness was probably due more to exhilaration at the news than to alcohol.

On 3 July, Goldsmith 'Left tonight in a Whitley for Gibraltar in the middle of an air raid. Good bye old Malta.' He had 347 hours in his log book, only forty more than when he arrived in February. Since his first claim for a Stuka damaged on 26 March, he had been credited with twelve enemy destroyed, seven damaged and a quarter share in destruction of another. Goldsmith was the first RAAF pilot in WW2 to be awarded both the DFM and DFC. He was twenty-one years old, had been married for five months, and was to go to 53 OTU in Wales. Further air fighting awaited him against the Japanese over Darwin, in northern Australia.

In his happiness, Tim probably did not know, and may not have cared, that on the same day the Soviet fortress of Sevastopol fell to the Germans, and next day, further to the north, German forces reached the Don River, while in the deadly Arctic waters, convoy PQ 17 was ordered to scatter. Twenty-three ships would be lost to air and submarine attack, only leaving eleven to struggle into Murmansk and an unsympathetic, ungrateful Soviet reception.

None of the pilots, and few on Malta outside the Special Liaison

Unit staff involved with the 'Ultra' signal intercepts of Axis messages, would have been aware that in Africa, Rommel had tried to punch through the El Alamein position, 100 kilometres from Alexandria and the Suez Canal, and failed. After nearly two years of military operations back and forth along the northern edge of Africa, the British command had at last organised its artillery and tank forces into masses rather than small dispersed weak blobs.

The exhausted Germans and some Italian formations had tried to bounce the British off balance, as they had for the past five weeks, but failed. The German troops were so tired that they fell asleep immediately they halted, sometimes sleeping under artillery bombardment from British guns. Petrol, tanks, artillery, fresh troops and air support were all lacking on Rommel's side, but each day saw more of those arriving on Auchinleck's.

The petrol, ammunition, tanks, trucks, aircraft, men and supplies which would have given Rommel just that necessary weight to shove through to the Canal had been lost to aircraft from Malta. These few crucial hours at El Alamein justified the retention of Malta through its months of suffering and sacrifice, and the Axis tide began to ebb. Rommel would try, unavailingly, to break through, attacking throughout July and August, but sheer weight was now accumulating on the British side. Together with the correct use of artillery, Rommel's new opponent, Montgomery, did not intend to make the mistake of engaging the German in the loose, free-flowing melee at which Rommel was superb.

Montgomery was going to call the tune and make Rommel dance to his beat. But, in the early days of July, all most people knew was that the unstoppable Desert Fox was at the gates of Alexandria.

The carrier-borne force of Spitfires at Gibraltar was delayed, and the pilots went back ashore, being told that word of the sortie had leaked out. They were to remain for nine more days, the pilots playing cards, swimming and sunbaking, watching films or enjoying Gibraltar within the limits of their finances.

On Malta, the Ju88s of two Gruppen of KG 77, and the Messerschmitts of I/JG 77, began their attacks, maintaining them throughout the month.

185 Squadron had scrambled three times on 2 July, and on

the third occasion, at 19.00 hours, Sergeant Len Reid was one of four sent to intercept a plot of six-plus. Flight Sergeant Haggas, the leader, and Flying Officer Stoop each claimed a Mc202, while Reid damaged a Bf109F; his first claim.

On that day in 603 Squadron, Colin Parkinson had damaged a Re2001. He noted that the squadron moved into a Maltese school for billets, and commented on the relative comfort and soft beds. But he also noted in his diary the results of the day's flying: 'Pilot Officer King landed with his kite shot up; Pilot Officer Glazebrook did the same; Pilot Officer Johnny Hurst is missing, which means that he's had it.'[3]

The intensity of the night raids made Parkinson change his mind about staying in the billet, and go to the shelter instead. He had 3 July off flying, and used it to catch up on some sleep. That night when the raids began, he went to the shelter, and 'had to listen to the bombs dropping outside while Maltese people in the shelters raved louder than the bombs.' Further irritation was added when the electricity was cut off due to bomb damage, but he noted that two Ju88s had been destroyed by the night-fighters.

Early on the 4th, he took off to search for possible survivors of a Beaufort which had gone into the sea about 85 kilometres to the east. He was not overly awed by rank or hereditary position, and observed that the squadron leader was not fit to lead a practice flight 'let alone an operational flight. Being a Lord has a hell of a lot of influence.' On return, Parkinson's undercarriage would not go down, so he had to force-land, but nothing was said to him about it. He flew three times, with no results, as his windshield became covered with oil.[4]

In combats on 4 July, 'Slim' Yarra destroyed a Ju88, claiming a Bf109 as a probable and another damaged. He was leading the squadron formation, scrambled to intercept an 18-plus raid. They found four 109s, and Slim 'crawled up on them and fired like hell. Broke off and saw nine Ju88s with eight 109s as escort; attacked the rear 88 and shot it down; chased back by 109s, shot up badly. Crash landed.' GL-W was taking a beating.

He had already flown four sorties in July, on the 2nd frightening an Italian pilot in his dinghy by making a series of dummy attacks on him. But next day the fates provided a form of balance by

117

having eight 109s attack while he was one of a pair escorting a minesweeper, and in the turning and dodging, Slim found himself at 500 feet, almost stalled, and 'nearly spun!!!'

The 6th saw a day of intense fighting, with RAF claims for fifteen destroyed, five probables and seventeen damaged, for the loss of one Spitfire and seven damaged. Several Australians were among those who claimed: Eric Mahar damaged two 109s, and John Bisley shared a Savoia S84 with Flying Officer Donald Smith RAAF and Lieutenant Swales, of South Africa. Flying as Bisley's Number 2, Smith followed him through the fighter screen onto the bombers and both fired at the same one, and its destruction was later confirmed by radio intercept.[5]

Parkinson damaged a 109: 'Scrambled about 9 o'clock to 24 000 feet. Our section didn't see the bombers but saw the fighters. An Me109 swung in to attack a Spit but the Spit turned towards it; they then both went in opposite directions. I put my nose down and went after the 109 with everything pushed, got to within 150 yards and gave a long squirt with cannon and MG fire, allowed plenty for drop [bullet trajectory]. Saw strikes and black smoke pour out of the 109. He pulled up slightly and dived steeply. I kept on squirting until my cannon ran out of ammo.' He was attacked by another 109, but lost him by turning up into the sun, and dived away home.

Later that day he was hit in the port wing root by anti-aircraft shrapnel, and found that the pilot who slept opposite in the billet had his tail blown off by anti-aircraft fire, but managed to escape with only a bruise on his eyebrow. That night he again went to the shelter during a raid, and was annoyed by the loud prayers and chanting of the Rosary by the local people, led by 'one overfed Maltese.'[6] Eric Mahar found that he could not go into the air raid shelters, due to 'the fumes of garlic coming out!'

During the raid, another Australian began scoring over Malta, in a Beaufighter of 89 Squadron, when Mervyn Shipard destroyed a Ju88. His radar operator was Sergeant Doug Oxby, and they were on patrol when vectored onto the contact. On their three previous sorties since arriving on the island, their radar had gone unserviceable. On the first patrol on 3 July, they had five contacts but useless equipment made it impossible to engage. However, this night was to begin a string of successes for Shipard and Oxby, and Unteroffizier (Sergeant) Mellein and crew were lost in aircraft

118

M7+MH of KGr806. John Ross, a fellow Beaufighter pilot, described Shipard as, 'in my opinion, the keenest pilot I met during the war.'[7]

On 6 July, George Beurling was credited with two Macchi Mc202 and a Messerschmitt Bf109 destroyed, plus a Cant Z1007 damaged.

In the early days of July, Paul Brennan had been unsuccessful again, finding the German escort fighters well able to protect the small numbers of bombers sent over to attack the usual targets. After losses in the diving attacks, the Junkers contented themselves with level bombing from about 18 000 feet. By this time Brennan had nine confirmed victories, and was determined to get the tenth before leaving Malta.

Command of 249 Squadron had gone to Laddie Lucas, when Stan Grant was promoted Wing Commander. Brennan was now a section leader, and, aware that his time on Malta was to end soon, for some reason thought that he would be 'rested' from operations by being employed as a ferry pilot on the route from west Africa across the Sahara to Cairo. Laddie Lucas has clear memories of Paul's disgust, voiced in an Aussie accent, about 'the f----g Takoradi run'.

On 7 July, Paul was leading four Spitfires in Green Section; Raoul Daddo-Longlais was leading four in Blue Section, and Lucas had the other four. All twelve were to operate together, as a squadron. They took off, climbing east into the sun. At 15 000 feet, Blue Section was left to take the bombers if they dived, while the others climbed to 20 000. Lucas reported aircraft ahead, at the same level. Paul could see the 88s, but not any escort, then suddenly they came into focus and he saw fighters all around the six bombers. As he watched, some of the fighters swung to get up-sun.

He told Lucas that he would cut these off, and led Green Section in a head-on attack on the bombers. Smoke whipping back from the 88s' own machineguns made him think that for some strange reason they were all suddenly on fire, then realisation hit, he aimed at the extreme starboard Junkers and opened fire at 450 metres. At a closing speed of about 800 kmph, he had only seconds to fire and avoid a collision, holding course to the last moment then diving as the 88 pulled up.

The Messerschmitts were already after the Spitfires, and he

dived to gain speed, with three 109s following. With speed up, 'I whipped my aircraft out of their line of fire, turned slightly and skidded away to the left. Their leader shot past under my starboard wing. I slipped back on his tail, fifty metres behind him, and gave him three seconds. I saw my shells travel up the fuselage and hit the motor and cockpit. A streak of oil appeared on his port fuselage [side] and he went into a vicious spiral towards the sea. He was out of control, and crashed into the drink.'[8]

The other two Messerschmitts pulled up, Brennan followed about 200 metres behind, aimed at one and fired, saw three or four flashes as shells hit the starboard wing . . . and his port cannon jammed, skewing the Spitfire.

He decided it was time to go, called his section and told them to return to base when they had finished their own combats, and dived away. The aircraft was trimmed for the climb, and as his speed built up in the dive, aerodynamic forces caused the Spitfire to pull itself out of the dive, so violently that he blacked out, coming to soon after to find the nose pointing straight up. He recovered, went down to sea level, and passed over the white foam and disturbance in the water where the 109 had gone in.[9]

Part of Brennan's DFM citation had stated that 'This airman is a most determined and courageous pilot, an exceptional shot, and always presses home his attacks with vigour.'

At Takali, it was found Raoul Daddo-Longlais had been hit, and the Canadian Rob Middlemiss was missing. Paul and Flight Sergeant Delara found him sitting in his dinghy. Later in the day, three more Spitfire pilots ended up in the water, and the air-sea rescue launch was kept busy collecting them. Paul flew as escort to the launch.

It was his last operational flight over Malta. Soon after, he and Ray Hesslyn were told they were leaving the island, and had a few days' rest until they departed. The flight was postponed the first time, and the two discreetly took cover when an air raid developed. They had no intention of being killed or injured at that stage. At last, they looked down at the moonlit detail of the island passing behind and below as they flew west to Gibraltar and postings to units in the UK.[10]

During his time on the island, from 7 March, Paul had flown a total of 47 times. He had been in 22 combats, and another nineteen scrambles for which there had been no combat or result.

On seven flights, he had had to return due to unserviceability of the aircraft; his total flying hours on Malta were 35 and 5 minutes.[11]

About a week after Brennan's arrival in the UK, Laddie Lucas also returned from Malta, and the two young fighter-pilots enjoyed to the full the 'refreshment and all the comforting things' to be found at the Savoy suites kept with open door by Quentin Reynolds and Eric Baume. After what Lucas termed 'a brief spell of exceptional activity' during which Brennan made full use of the facilities, Paul went to 52 OTU. Later, he was to be posted to the first RAAF Spitfire squadron formed to fight the Japanese over New Guinea.

There were six attacks on Malta on 7 July, with many combats, resulting in five Spitfires lost, for claims of 24 enemy destroyed and 26 probables. R. H. Richardson RAAF, 126 Squadron, damaged a Ju88. In 185 Squadron, 'Slim' Yarra destroyed two Re2001s, and Eric Mahar a Bf109.

185 Squadron scrambled twelve Spitfires, led by Pilot Officer Broad, against a raid of 40-plus enemy. Yarra, in GL-W, was leading a section of four, the other three being Flight Sergeant Haggas as Yarra's No. 2, Sergeant Len Reid RAAF as No. 3, and Flight Sergeant Terry as No. 4. They found five Savoias with fighter escort, and Slim took his section on to the fighters, leaving the others to take the Italian bombers. The odds were six to one, and in the whirling action he shot down two Re2001s, but the Messerschmitts were there also. They shot away panels from his wings, and he went down for a crash landing. Sergeants Terry and Haggas were killed. The sortie lasted 35 minutes. Two bombers were claimed damaged.

'We could see the 109s up there,' Reid said, 'but Slim was trying to get altitude and was a few thousand feet below them. It was the old story, trying to get altitude; I had my speed down to about 120 mph and that's not much to have on the clock. We were sitting ducks. They came down and attacked, and it got all mixed up.'

Reid did not actually see either Haggas or Terry shot down. 'It was a general melee that went on, and I think we were attacked by two groups, one from one side, and it's the other group that comes in later that shoots you down, if you are not aware of them. It was quite a shaky do.'[12]

121

Referring to combats of this time, the other Australians who knew Slim Yarra recalled that 'he didn't know the odds. If there were 20 Messerschmitts and one Spitfire, he'd still go in. It was the sort of leadership we needed then.'

Next day, Pilot Officer Don Smith destroyed a 109. Smith was leading a section of three from 126 Squadron, when four 109s dived on them from 24 000 feet. Smith pulled up into them, fired, and the 109 he hit went down, later confirmed as destroyed. On the same day, 8 July, Beurling shot down a 109 and claimed another as a 'probable', then on the next day destroyed two more and a Macchi Mc202, followed on the 11th by three Macchis destroyed. He was awarded the DFM.

Colin Parkinson was awakened by the sound of aircraft and gunfire, so went up to the roof and saw Messerschmitt 109s 'all over the place, as low as 2000 feet in some cases.' He watched four 109s dive on four Spitfires, firing and hitting one, which dived but made a landing. Later he found that the pilot was another Australian, Johnson, who was unharmed, but the Spitfire had the gun-panels shot off, one aileron and the flaps made useless, hit in the glycol tank, and the tyres were punctured.

Parkinson noted in his diary for the day that Pilot Officer King had been killed, as had Hurst some days before, and Sergeant Gilbert, 22 years old, also had been killed, as well as Baxter having to make a belly-landing, while Flight Lieutenant Sanders had been shot down into the sea by two 109s, but survived. He wrote, 'I wonder whose turn it is next.'[13]

Sanders, RAF, had been fighting two 109s in a low level combat around the hills at Marsalforn Bay, on Gozo. Hit in the engine, he had to put the Spitfire into the sea, and it sank in five fathoms of water. There it sat for 31 years, visited only by divers and souvenir hunters from a holiday resort on the shore about 100 metres away, until it was salvaged in 1973 and the engine exhibited in the National War Museum.

At the end of the first week in July, the air-sea rescue launches and seaplane tenders had saved a total of 110 members of air-crews since the beginning of the war. Launch 108, operating from Kalafrana, had picked up 43, and Launch 107, from St Paul's Bay, had collected 39. In addition, the Germans and Italians had a flying-boat service which also operated in the rescue role.

On 9 July, R. H. Richardson RAAF, 126 Squadron, damaged a Ju88. Colin Parkinson destroyed a 109.

Parkinson, in 603 Squadron, had gone on readiness in the afternoon, having watched the Spitfires shoot down two 88s in the morning raid on Takali. With Dick Sherwood leading the formation, they scrambled and climbed over the island, diving to attack bombers below. Parkinson dived on one which already had black smoke streaming from the fuselage, closing to about ten metres before firing . . . the 88 tried to climb . . . flames flicked out . . . suddenly it exploded in a brilliant sky-filling flash right in front of him, and he flew through the fire and wreckage. The sight was engraved on his memory.

He broke up-sun, then saw a 109 weaving its way through a formation of Spitfires. It was about to fire on one when Parkinson shot at it first, and the German continued going west, with Parkinson close behind. 'It evidently saw me and started a dive. I gave a long squirt and followed it down through light cloud to about 700 feet above the water. The Me continued diving and crashed straight in.'[14]

The Luftwaffe gave Slim Yarra another rough return to base on that day, when he was 'bounced by 109s; bullet in glycol; could not bail out. Crash landed on aerodrome.' Again he was in GL-W.

On 10 July, Alan Yates, who had arrived two months before, and gone to 249 Squadron, damaged a 109, and Don Smith destroyed an 88 and damaged a 109. Smith was scrambled before breakfast, and they found a Ju88 at 1000 feet north-east of the island of Gozo. He attacked head-on, hitting the cockpit and starboard engine. The 88 turned back to Sicily, still with its bombs slung under the wings and one of the 109 escort sticking with it. Smith chased them for 35 miles before the Junkers went into the sea. The four 109s with the bomber had been scattered, and Smith claimed one as a probable.[15]

Colin Parkinson, forced to break away from a Ju88 because of cannon stoppages, could only claim it as damaged. Later in the day he flew to within a few metres of a 109, but this time the cannon did not fire at all.[16]

Next day, Yates shared a 109 with Warrant Officer C. B. Ramsay, and 'Slim' Yarra destroyed a yellow-nosed 109, his last victory over Malta. On his third scramble of the day, in GL-N, he joined another Spitfire to attack two 109s. He shot his down, but the other 109 pilot hit the second Spitfire, and Yarra had to escort him back to base. In his combats he had destroyed twelve, claimed two as probables, and damaged another six enemy, plus a few others not claimed as damaged.

He flew for his last time on Malta in GL-W on an air test on 16 July. His log book lists those killed in July: Moye, Terry, Haggas, Reid DFM RCAF, Kent, and Russell RCAF.

Colin Parkinson had it brought home to him that it could be quite dangerous on the receiving end of the attacks on the airfields, when he had to return to base after his radio failed on 12 July. He taxied into the pen, saw the crews running for the shelters, and a 'flock of Ju88s overhead'. He quickly evacuated the cockpit, and made what he thought would have been a world record for the 200-metre sprint, arriving ahead of a stick of bombs which fell along the dispersal pens, and punctured his Spitfire's wings.

He inspected the damage, walked back to the squadron office, and a delayed action bomb exploded 'with a roar, 20 metres from my kite—again. More holes, and a rock bashed the spinner. B Flight are left with six instead of twelve aircraft.' He also wrote that Pilot Officer Berkely-Hill was 'killed today, shot down by a 109 probably.'[17]

Don Smith also had an unusual flight, in BR383, when he dived from 26 000 feet, alone, on to nine enemy fighters. Then, at 390 mph, the Spitfire began to roll and he broke off the attack; the wings had warped.[18]

Mervyn Shipard, in Beaufighter X7642, took off for a night flying test, while an air raid was in progress. Unknown to him, the port wheel had been punctured, probably by shrapnel, just before the aircraft lifted off. He completed the test, but as they touched down, the heavy fighter slewed to port, and his first thought was that he had not pushed the hydraulic locking lever, 'so we spun around, going pretty fast, hit sideways, the port wheel fell off, the port wing fell off, we rolled over and the starboard wing fell off, and the rest of it rolled about 400 metres down the runway with Oxo and I inside it.' Amazingly, the only personal damage to either Shipard or Doug Oxby was a broken goggle-lens on Shipard's flying helmet. They flew next day, and were scrambled the day after that.

On 13 July, Don Smith, 126 Squadron, destroyed one Ju88 and damaged a 109, and Colin Parkinson claimed a 109, which flew through his sights, as a probable.

Next day, Ken Mitchell, 185 Squadron, shared inflicting damage on an 88, with two other pilots.

Colin Parkinson had been on readiness, and scrambled about 09.30, climbing to 24 000 feet, where the formation was bounced by 109s diving from out of the sun. The Spitfires scattered, and he joined two others who flew out to sea, then saw two 109s beneath, 'so we bounced them. I gave one a good squirt and saw bursts of cannon shell all over the fuselage and wings, the Me flew level for a few seconds, then did a slow dive down to the sea and right in.'[19]

That day, Pilot Officer Don Smith's flying career on Malta came to an end; he had begun on 1 July. At 11.00, he and three other 126 Squadron Spitfires scrambled to engage a formation of Ju88s and 109 escort. The 88s were at 15 000 feet, over the sea, positioning themselves to attack Luqa. Smith dived past four 109s on to the bombers, shooting off the port aileron of one, after which the port engine blew up, and it went into a spiral, going down into the water.

In Smith's log-book annotation, 'escort extremely savage after 88 went in', and they swung on to him. One hit the Spitfire eight times, damaging the radio and severing control wires, sending the Spitfire upwards, and wounding him in the ankle. He was alone, in a damaged aircraft, wounded, with a gaggle of 109s giving him their attention. Two went down to circle the bomber, and two others turned for Smith. He decided to fight his way back to Malta rather than bail out.

Waiting until the last moment, he whipped around in the tightest turn possible, coming on to the tail of the second 109 at 100 metres range, then found the airlines to his cannon had been severed. Gradually moving towards Malta, he edged across the 25 kilometres of sea to the cliffs, always trying to keep the Messerschmitts in front of him. But they managed to get on to his tail. All he could do was to skid sideways and down whenever they made a firing pass, until they turned away for Sicily. Smith landed without flaps, and collapsed unconscious as he tried to climb down from the cockpit.[20]

In the first two weeks of July, the fighters had flown 969

sorties, claiming 95 enemy destroyed, 23 probables and 98 damaged.

The reinforcements at Gibraltar had gone back aboard HMS *Eagle* on Monday 13 July, and next morning awoke to find the ship test-firing its guns before setting off into the eastern waters. There was a good breeze along the flight deck and the new pilots were more confident of a successful take-off in the morning.

Noel Pashen rose at 04.30 and went up to the flight-deck for take-off an hour later. He recalled that two pilots gave the watchers 'a sinking feeling', when one clipped off a wingtip on a 6-inch gun mount, and Knox-William 'tried to take-off without his petrol and ran into the bridge, the kite being pushed over the side after he pranged.' Pashen was last off, and watched the activities with interest.

The flight to Malta was uneventful, and they landed after some three hours flying. Pashen's first impressions were that the island was 'very white and bare and had been badly blitzed. Wal (Parkes) and I should get our first taste of battle tomorrow as we are due for a spot of readiness.' He was posted to B Flight 603 Squadron.

Next morning they were up early and went down to dispersal at 05.00, but were not called on. Noel wrote in his diary that the 'boys in the flight are a bloody good crowd and the flight commander a real man. We are going to be nursed along.'

Another day was to pass before he flew on operations, and he absorbed the tips passed on by the more experienced pilots. He also noted that 'no one has any doubt about taking shelter here. It's easily the safest thing to do as the island is so small.'[21]

On 15 July, R. H. Richardson RAAF, of 126 Squadron, damaged a 109. Len Reid claimed a Ju88 damaged on 16 July, when 185 Squadron scrambled six aircraft, with total claims being for one enemy destroyed and three damaged, but Flying Officer Stoop was shot down and later picked up by the air-sea rescue launch. Next day, Reid 'stooged over a Jerry in the sea' until the launch arrived. Noel Pashen, on his first Malta sortie, flew with McLeod as cover for the launch.

Human nature being what it is, a black market came into existence, not only for the luxuries, but what in other parts of the world were considered normal items of living. However, one particularly callous example of the thievery necessary for any black market was the removal of parachute silk from the seat packs which were left overnight in the Spitfires, and the packs refilled with paper. The perpetrators of this murderous act were not known to have been caught. Around the airfields, if caught, they would have been fortunate to have lived long enough to benefit from British justice.

The war raged on in the Mediterranean. Around the El Alamein positions, attack and counter-attack were made by both sides, with Rommel trying to break through and the Eighth Army resisting. A small but important unit was lost to Rommel in these actions, when the radio intercept company was attacked and annihilated by the Australians. From that time, he lost his ability to listen to the radio traffic of his enemies, a vital aspect of his appreciation of what they were doing, intending and how they were reacting to his moves.

In Russia, the Germans made further advances. It seemed that despite the terrible losses during the winter, they were even more dangerous and competent.

On Malta, despite the constant turnover of personnel, and the departure of the experienced pilots with a number of victories, others began to make their mark.

On 17 July, R. H. Richardson inflicted damage on a Bf109. Colin Parkinson had to turn back to base when his engine began pouring out clouds of glycol and oil smoke, and he had to force-land during the raid. 'Boy, did I burn the earth running for the shelter. No damage to myself; aircraft category two damage. Given another kite.'[22]

18 July was to have been X-Day for Operation *Hercules*, the Axis invasion of Malta. In the morning, the island was to have been covered with wave after wave of Luftwaffe and Regia Aeronautica aircraft battering the anti-aircraft defences while the paratroops and glider troops climbed into their aircraft on Sicily. The plan was for them to arrive over the island at 13.30, seizing and holding ground for the following sea-borne assault forces.

One surprised Aussie would have been Noel Pashen, 603 Squadron, who slept in and 'made my first blue as I was supposed to have been down [at the flight office] before dawn.' However they were not required to scramble before coming off readiness.[23]

On 18 July, Air Vice-Marshal Hugh Lloyd was replaced by Sir Keith Park, who had commanded 11 Fighter Group in the

Battle of Britain. During his fourteen months in command, Lloyd had slept at his office, so as to be always available if needed.

Some of the Australians preferred Lloyd, for his easy manner with the fighter pilots, whatever their rank, and his lack of formality when chatting with them to ask for their opinions and views. They thought Park, who would not deign to speak to NCO pilots, though highly spoken of for his part in the Battle of Britain, much more reserved and aloof.

But a couple of the colonials had a quiet sort of revenge. Park was also known for his habit of borrowing a fighter and flying around the island to see things for himself; if he could shoot someone down, so much the better. In 185 Squadron, Eric Mahar and Len Reid shared a Spitfire which was difficult to fly at the best of times let alone in action, and required considerable starboard stick pressure. Mahar was at dispersal one day when he was asked if there was a spare Spitfire, as the AOC wanted to get airborne.

Mahar flew the particular troublesome Spitfire to Takali, where the AOC waited, watched Park take off, and return, then deliver a lengthy list of complaints about the aircraft. 'It did him no harm,' said Mahar, 'to find out what we had to put up with.'[24]

The island Controllers always knew when Park was airborne, and discreetly placed a section of Spitfires between him and Sicily whenever he was flying.

Parkinson's series of close calls was not over, as he became separated from the formation during a break, dived to get away from the 109s in the area, and at about 600 kmph tried to pull out of the dive, 'but the stick was loose in my hands. Boy, did I get the twitch. However, by throttling back she lost speed and I gradually regained control.' He noted that Pilot Officer Lattimer 'was shot up, McLean also.'[25]

In the night skies, Mervyn Shipard, 89 Squadron, with Doug Oxby, destroyed a Ju88 on the 19th, seeing one parachute open as someone escaped the dying bomber, B3+PH of I/KG54, flown by Lt Siegfried Sack.[26] Again, on the 21st, he destroyed another Ju88, noting that two of the crew were seen to bale out. This loss has not been identified in detail.

Because of the shortage of petrol, the night fighters were held on the ground until the Controllers were sure that the enemy aircraft on radar really was heading for Malta, and not for Africa, Sardinia, Crete or somewhere similar. Of course, by this time the enemy was at about 21 000 feet and going flat out for its target. The Beaufighters were then scrambled, and would try to gain height in time to engage the enemy.

Shipard preferred to spend his time on readiness in the cockpit of the Beaufighter, with the seat back to a comfortable angle, often sleeping until someone came to tell him to scramble. The benefit of being outside the ready room was that 'as soon as I opened my eyes I had good night vision, and could just go.' He wondered how the Beaufighter's engines, Bristol Hercules, stood the strain. 'We would take off at full bore, engines at 2900 rpm, at 2000 feet pull the engines back to 2600 rpm, at 8000 feet go to high blower (supercharger), and get to 15 or 16 000 feet 50 kilometres out, and see the enemy going over our heads five to six thousand feet above, for Malta. No way could you get to them.'

Once the enemy aircraft had bombed, it really put its nose down and gained more speed in the dive back to Sicily. Sometimes Shipard could see the exhaust flames, 'the four little twinkles. I was about a mile away, and do you think I could catch him? I'd put the Beau down in a gentle dive, and when I got beneath him I'd be two to three thousand feet below. I'd ease back [up] and fall behind; this would go on all the way across to Sicily, when I'd have to call off the attack [as the radar was not allowed to go over the enemy coast.]'

Sometimes the raider made a simple mistake, and that made all the difference. 'I got one chap because he didn't fly straight. He was weaving from side to side. I could see his exhaust flames. I was just flying straight. You could see his exhausts appear, cross over, then reappear. When he started to come back across, I was flying alongside. If he was flying in a straight line, I couldn't have caught him.'

On one occasion, he and Oxby were doing the very basic test allowed by the petrol shortage. Both were dressed simply in shorts and desert boots, with Shipard warming the engines and Oxby operating the radar to see if a ground return was received, after which they would go away until time to go on readiness, properly dressed. Suddenly, a stick of bombs exploded across the field ahead of him, and Shipard looked up to see 'the place littered with Ju88s and Spits.'

He called to ask Oxby if his hatch was shut, got an affirmative, and 'gave it full bore, we went out and were airborne, I called and told Control and asked if there was anything I could do, and was told "20 000 feet as quick as you can". We sat there for an hour, in shorts, and then were told to go home. Gosh, it was cold!'

On another occasion, during a raid, he was told to take off, and was just about to push the throttles forward when the order was countermanded and he was told to return to the pen. The easiest way back was to go along the runway and enter the track system leading to the pens at the far end, so he began taxying along, peering ahead into the pitch black. Then he saw a dark shape on the runway ahead. He stopped and flashed on the landing lights. A tractor and petrol bowser were standing in the centre of the runway.

Shipard carefully taxied around, found his pen and parked, then walked back to the bowser. The engine was still warm, and he knew at once where the driver would be—in a nearby big shelter. He went there, asked for the driver, and a Maltese civilian came forward. Shipard asked where the bowser was, and received a voluble, gesticulating answer, 'I do not know! I do not know! The bombs were dropping!' Shipard was unimpressed, as he would have been travelling at 100 knots when he hit the full petrol bowser.[27]

Parkinson received a registered parcel which had come from Australia. It contained a hand-made woollen scarf, with his initials on it. While he appreciated the gift, he noted that 'I had hoped for a parcel of big eats—could do with them here. Beautiful moonlight night, ideal for bombing. Sirens went, so walked to the bastion to watch the fun. Saw an 88 go down in flames. Welcome sight.' He also noted further losses: 'Shorty Reid, who just received his DFM, was shot down, also Pilot Officer Paridise, and Flight Sergeant Russell. I knew all the pilots, trained both Reid and Russell in my old Squadron.'[28]

185 Squadron had scrambled six aircraft, led by the Canadian Reid, including the American Claud Weaver and Len Reid RAAF. In the combat, Weaver destroyed two 109s, Shorty Reid another, then he saw a Spitfire shot down and went to circle it, but was attacked and shot down himself, being killed.

Later in the day Eric Mahar was shot up, for the first of three times, but coaxed the Spitfire back for a landing. 'Half a Spitfire was better than none,' he recalled.

603 Squadron was scrambled, and as they went down the strip, Noel Pashen's motor 'conked, so I stayed on the deck.' Next day he was suffering from 'Malta dog, and felt crook all day with a nasty stomach ache and a lousy attack of diarrhoea.' It was the beginning of a series of attacks which combined with conjunctivitis to have him grounded medically and eventually sent to Cairo.

On 23 July Ken Mitchell, 185 Squadron, claimed a Mc202 as probably destroyed, and Weaver another two 109s destroyed. Len Reid had his own troubles, as his engine cut dead at the beginning of the combat, and he 'came gliding down past the enemy fighters. Almost baled out but eventually made base and landed safely.'

His Rolls Royce Merlin had simply cut dead, possibly because the diaphragm in the carburettor failed. He was sailing down, watching the enemy about 100 metres away, then decided to try the Ki-gas pump, 'and I managed to get the engine firing, kept it going until I got back to base. But it was pretty touchy, because I was gliding through these enemy aircraft, but probably they wouldn't have known I had engine trouble, the propeller would have been windmilling. They may have thought I was a decoy.'

Three enemy bombers, with escort, had come over, and all had been destroyed so rapidly by 249 Squadron that when ground control was telling the Spitfires to concentrate on the bombers, they were told that none were left.

On 24 July George Beurling continued his peerless shooting, destroying a Reggiani 2002, and three days later destroyed two Macchis and two Messerschmitts, with two more Messerschmitts damaged. He was awarded a bar to the DFM, and commissioned, despite not having applied and insisting he wanted to remain a Sergeant. One of the Macchi pilots killed in this day's combats is believed to have been Captain Furio Niclot-Doglio, 51st Stormo, who claimed six victories over Malta. On the same day, C. L. Baxter RAAF, who had gone from 249 to 1435 Squadron, claimed a 109 as probably destroyed, and Len Reid destroyed a Ju88.

Eight Spitfires from 185 Squadron had scrambled, Reid in AB526, and they intercepted Ju88s with a large escort formation. The Spitfires dived, Len Reid going 'straight down on one at a

45-degree angle, opened up with cannon at 500 metres, closing to 100, giving one long burst. Hit the top of the cockpit and starboard engine, which immediately gave off black smoke, and [it] went into a spin.'[29] 185 Squadron claimed two destroyed and two damaged, for no losses.

At night, Mervyn Shipard was vectored on to a contact, which he closed on and identified as a Ju87, the first he had seen, and not a type usually engaged by the nightfighters. The ground controller had vectored him on to the raider, and the Beaufighter descended from clear sky into haze. Then Oxby called a contact dead ahead, and Shipard looked up to see an aircraft. He saw it turning, and first identified it as a single-engined aircraft, thinking it would be a Spitfire which was often at that altitude to catch low-flying raiders. It was only about 30 metres away, turning through 180 degrees, so close that Shipard could clearly see two people under the canopy, and the distinctive Ju87 features, just as it rolled and dived so steeply that he lost sight of it and the radar could not find it again.

This was an Italian Ju87, flown by Tenente Remo Martini of 102 Gruppo Tuffatori, and who was hit in the tail. Martini jettisoned his canopy in case he had to bale out, but found he could control the Stuka and flew back to Gela.[30]

On one occasion, during a daylight raid, Shipard was at the aircraft pen, when a German landed by parachute about 200 metres away. Shipard began to walk across, then suddenly a dozen or so Maltese women appeared from the nearby fields. And they were armed with forks, spades and other heavy field tools. The German pulled a small pistol from his flying boot and pointed it at the menacing women. Shipard walked up behind him and quietly asked what he was doing, the German turned, recognised a serviceman, and surrendered the pistol, butt first.

Shipard waved it at the bunch of women, and ordered them to go away, which they did. The German was relieved, saying that they would have killed him.[31]

On 24 July, agreement had been reached among the Allies for the invasion of North Africa at the western end, to be called *Operation Torch*. This was to be in November, and was an illustration of the remarkable efforts in production and international co-operation between them.

On 26 July, Len Reid was one of three pilots who tested

Hurricanes, practising dive-bombing. Then, that night, he flew to Gela, to attack the Ju87s and Bf109s dispersed there. Wing Commander Dawson led, and Claud Weaver was the other pilot. As it was the first such operation, results were described by Reid as not as successful as they might have been.

'It was after midnight. We were waiting for the moon to come up. We were on radio silence, but I remember Weaver breaking radio silence one or twice, nothing of any importance, and Tiny Dawson told him to shut up. We went over at 15 000 to 20 000 feet. I thought the radar would have picked us up, and the night fighters would be on us, the flak would open up, but nothing happened at all!' The Hurricanes dived at about 45-degrees, released their bombs, and flew back to Malta. There were no signs of destruction behind them.[32]

Still suffering from 'Malta dog', Noel Pashen had flown several times with no combats. On 27 July, from the ground, he watched several interceptions, commenting that 'in later raids we got the drop on them, and in all, thirteen were destroyed. Parachutes were dropping in everywhere. I spent the afternoon over at Halfar and did not fly. Arrived back in the Mess at Mdina at 11 o'clock tired, hungry and unhappy! Highlight of the day was Screwball Beurling, who shot down three and probably four—he's a wizard.' Next day, from the ground again, he watched a raid at about 17.00, and saw four bombers go down, 'including two beaut flamers.'[33]

Alan Yates damaged a Ju88 on 28 July, and later that night Len Reid, Weaver and Wing Commander Turner again flew the Hurricanes to Gela, this time being 'quite successful. Little or no opposition. Obviously they knew we were there, but the bit of damage we could do would have been only nuisance value, so it was hardly worthwhile to scramble the night fighters.'

No results were seen, but Reid had a bomb hang up on the Hurricane, and no matter what he did, could not release it. The bomb, fitted with a long fuse that extended in front of the main body of explosive, was armed and dangerous. He was told to land in the distant part of the airfield, in case anything happened. 'I wasn't too happy coming back and landing, but came in cautiously, and the airmen came along and fixed it.'[34]

On 29 July, a Cant Z506 flying boat approached the island, narrowly avoiding being shot down by the fighters, and touched down in Kalafrana Bay, much to the surprise of all the watchers. It had been captured in flight by the crew of an RAF Beaufort bomber who had been shot down and were being flown from Sicily to Taranto. They had overpowered the Italian crew, and set course for Malta.

Mervyn Shipard was down at the coast with other members of 89 Squadron, and they were all alerted by the sight of a bunch of Spitfires wheeling and diving, shooting at something which was low on the water, watching in surprise as the Cant touched down on the water, a white singlet waving in surrender. Colin Parkinson was in one of the Spitfires, another interested observer.

On the same day, there was another indicator that the offensive use of Malta was being reactivated as soon as possible: the submarine base was re-opened.

Beurling added another 109 to his score, and Noel Pashen noted that 'no bombs were dropped on the island today—a happy change.'

In the USSR, on 30 July, Stalin ordered that not another step back be taken, but on the next day the Germans crossed the Don on a front of 250 kilometres.

Malta had food and fuel for three weeks.

None of this was known to the pilots such as Colin Parkinson, who scrambled at 08.00, climbing to 20 000 feet, where the squadron intercepted six 109s. At 22 000 feet, they were three miles (5 km) off Zonkor Point, when Parkinson, Red 3, saw two 109s 500 feet below flying in the opposite direction, south, then saw four more following the leaders. Parkinson broke right just as the 109s swung back to attack the Spitfires from behind, and was able to close to 50 metres astern and to the beam of one of the Messerschmitts.

Parkinson 'hit him in the engine with my first burst, followed him down to about 500 feet and gave a burst from astern at about 50 metres, his port wing fell off and he fell on the sea.' Sergeant Brough reported a stream of glycol pouring from the 109 all the way down from 15 000 feet. Parkinson flew again later, but they could not catch another formation of six 109s, and he came off readiness at 1300.[35]

Noel Pashen, in cannon-armed Spitfire X-C, was tangling with the 109s also. He turned after them, fired and believed he hit two, was turning onto another, gave a short burst and 'my seat collapsed and broke and I fell to the floor—blacked out and the

134

plane got completely out of control and dove towards the sea. I eventually managed to regain control at 500 feet and luckily flew back to the drome where I landed heavily. Thought my time had come. I was completely shaken up for quite a while. Boy, was I unhappy.' He did not put in a claim, but did see a 109 spin in. He flew again later, and shot at a Ju88 after two other pilots had hammered it, but did not put in any claim as the 88 was finished.

He was given the next day off, and spent it recovering from a sore back resulting from the stresses and pressures caused by the collapsed seat.[36]

Next day, as Oxo Red 2, Parkinson was one of four who took off, but two returned with engine trouble, leaving Parkinson and the Squadron CO, Bill Douglas. At 21 000 feet, Parkinson saw six enemy diving on them from out of the sun. Parkinson radioed repeatedly to Douglas, who did not hear him, so at the last second Parkinson broke up-sun and into the enemy. They were Macchi 202s, going so fast they flicked by both Spitfires and were out of range almost at once. Parkinson swung in dead astern of one, estimated range at 260 metres, fired 'a long burst and saw strikes but no other results.' He and Douglas returned to base.[37]

The intensity of operations is described in the official reports, and reflected in personal log-books. Len Reid's log-book mirrors that of Slim Yarra, listing the casualties to 185 Squadron: Moye, shot down and killed; Ferraby, baled out; Terry and Haggas killed; Stoop baled out; Kent killed taking off; Bruce and Livingston shot down; Weaver crash-landed. The squadron Operations Record Book reports the death of Moye, of Terry and Haggas, Ferraby baling out, Sergeant Dodd's crash-landing, Stoop bailing out, Sergeant Hartney crash-landing, Lambert baling out and Russell killed in action, the loss of Flight Sergeant 'Shorty' Reid DFM RCAF, Kent killed air-testing a Hurricane, Bruce and Livingstone [sic] baling out, interspersed with details of scrambles and contacts or return to base with no combat; day after day throughout the month.

The Luftwaffe and Regia Aeronautica had flown 3900 sorties over Malta, the defenders claiming 149-38-140, for a loss of 36 Spitfires. 550 tons of bombs had been dropped on the island, over 340 tons onto the airfields. There had been 55 night alerts, all of which contributed to the stress and tiredness afflicting

135

everyone on Malta. In the previous month, Malta-based aircraft had attacked 42 ships, but in July 52 sorties had resulted in attacks on only sixteen. In contrast, aircraft from Egypt had flown at least 63 sorties and attacked 36 ships. As the fighting moved east, so Axis shipping steamed further from Malta.

Meanwhile, another convoy was being assembled to punch through to Malta. This was to be *Operation Pedestal* and was to be an epic in convoy operations.

7

The Critical Week

Malta—August 1942

The August convoy was to be another great battle across the length of the Mediterranean, great resources of men and ships fighting their way to the tiny island so important to the Allied war effort. This was *Operation Pedestal*, launched when Malta had three weeks' supplies left. The formidable concentration of ships assembled to escort thirteen merchantmen and a tanker consisted of two battleships, four aircraft carriers, seven cruisers, twenty-four destroyers, four corvettes, two tow ships and two tankers. In addition, accompanying the fleet would be HMS *Furious* to launch more Spitfire reinforcements for Malta. She would be escorted by eight destroyers. As well, eight submarines from Malta would take station to engage the Italian fleet if it sortied.

Reinforcement crews for the torpedo bombers arrived on the island, as well as two squadrons of Beaufighters for use by day. However, the Spitfires allotted to the next batch of reinforcements from Gibraltar needed vital modification. When one of the Spitfires was test-flown from *Furious*, it was found that all of them would need a different type of propeller, which provided an extra 500 revolutions on take-off. The combination of the old ship's slow speed and the slower revving propellers which the Spitfires had fitted, made it improbable that the batch of fighters would be able to launch successfully. So, on the voyage from the United Kingdom, the propellers were changed by hard-working crews.

Poor security, at this stage of the war nothing less than a scandal, meant that the destination of the ships was widely known. Axis forces assembled to meet the convoy consisted of about 780

137

aircraft, six cruisers, eleven destroyers, two motor-torpedo boat squadrons and twenty-one submarines.

Against the backdrop of such large forces and strategic moves, the administrative events of individuals and single units seem tiny indeed. The Spitfire squadrons which flew in from the carriers were still without their ground staff. Those of 603 Squadron had ended up in Cyprus. The squadron was therefore disbanded as a single-engine fighter unit on Malta on 3 August, and reformed again in February 1943, as a Beaufighter squadron. The pilots on Malta were promptly absorbed into a reformed 229 Squadron, which had been disbanded on 29 April. (Presumably there were some bureaucratic machinations, as on 10 January 1945 229 was again disbanded and re-numbered 603.)

The relentless daily routine of scrambles and combats went on over the island. Len Reid, 185 Squadron, was flying on 2 August, when the formation was 'jumped by Me109Fs. P/O Guthrie and Sgt MacLeod shot down, killed.' In the combat, Claud Weaver, the American, claimed a 109 probable. Reid would fly such missions throughout the month, without claims until August was nearly gone. In all, he would fly 21 scrambles over eighteen days.

Noel Pashen's run of bad luck continued. In Spitfire X-O, his radio failed, and he found this out when he missed a call to 'break', so he returned to land. Next day, 4 August, he had another attack of stomach upset but scrambled with the rest of B Flight—until a tyre blew on take-off. 'I seem to be something of a Jonah,' he wrote. 'Hope my luck improves.' His illness increased, and on the 5th, he 'felt bloody awful this morning, the old influenza feeling.' He went to dispersal but was not called on to fly. Two others were sick, but had to fly.[1]

Colin Parkinson had two days leave, which he spent in Valletta. On 3 August, after having breakfast in bed, he emphasised the luxury with several exclamation marks in his diary: egg and tomato, tea with plenty of sugar. Lunch he noted was 'big eats again', before catching the bus back to the quarters at Rabat.

Next day, he saw a Spitfire destroyed, and watched it come down 'like a bat out of hell, on fire, pouring glycol. The pilot bailed out. It was the Baron Richardson, a friend of mine.' This was R. H. Richardson, 126 Squadron, who had come out to Malta in the same batch of reinforcements as Parkinson.[2]

Soon after, he noted in the diary that less food was served each day. A convoy was vital to survival.

Sergeant W. R. Irwin RAAF had arrived with 603 Squadron, but now was in 229. On 5 August, he was flying as Blue 3, led by Lieutenant Swales SAAF. At 20 000 feet 15 miles (24 km) west of Gozo at 14.00 hours, Blue 4 reported enemy, the section swung round to attack them, and Irwin estimated that there were about fifteen hostile aircraft.

Checking his tail, Irwin saw six 109s coming in from behind, called a warning, and the section broke right. Irwin climbed steeply, losing contact with the others, and became involved in a turning match with three or four of the Germans. Then three other enemy, possibly Re2001s, dived into the combat, one of them attacking Irwin.

He skidded sharply to port, and throttled back, letting the 2001 slip out in front, then swung back and fired a three-second burst from 250 metres. He saw strikes on the port wing, forward fuselage and tail; glycol and black smoke streamed back, and the 2001 flicked onto its back and fell away.

But the enemy wingman was there, firing, and an explosive shell hit Irwin's starboard magazine, detonating several shells in it, and throwing the Spitfire into a spin. Irwin was unable to recover until he was just above the sea, and went back to base. He was credited with a Re2001 probable.[3]

In Egypt, Prime Minister Churchill was touring the battle zone prepartory to making substantial changes in the higher echelons. There were a number of visits to units of all three Services, and one of these was to 89 Squadron, the Beaufighter unit formed and dispatched to the Middle East, which had men and aircraft detached to Malta. Charles Crombie RAAF, who was yet to go to Malta, was on parade in front of a part of the squadron, and was spoken to by Churchill, who asked what he did. Crombie replied that he was a pilot, and Churchill observed that he was not wearing pilot's wings over the left shirt pocket.

The PM asked why, and to the great amusement of the assembled airmen, joined by Churchill and the CO, Crombie replied that everyone around there knew he could fly.[4]

Noel Pashen flew on 6 August, but nearly passed out when airborne, and on landing was diagnosed as having 'sandfly fever'.

139

The medical officer could do little for him apart from giving him time off flying. The headaches persisted, and 'the blasted flies are nearly driving me crazy,' he wrote.

On 8 August George Beurling destroyed another 109. Pashen noted that 'old Beurling collected one more before he was shot down and crash-landed. His score is now 18.' Next day he recorded that 'Dicky Sherwood collected a 109 today,' adding that in all two were destroyed. Next day he was given another 24 hours off flying, watched a raid by 109 fighter-bombers and thought three were lost, then attended a briefing on the coming convoy. On the 10th, Moose Fumerton RCAF, 89 Squadron, was forced to ditch his Beaufighter, but he and his radar operator, Pilot Officer Byng, were seen by another 89 Squadron pilot, Nev Mitchell, and picked up.[5]

That day, the convoy passed Gibraltar, steaming east to Malta, and the battle was about to begin. At 17.00 hrs a French civil aircraft, en route from France to Algeria, passed overhead and broadcast in clear the size, composition, speed and course of the convoy. This could not be simple thoughtlessness on the part of the pilot or crew, as it would have been obvious which side in the conflict would have massed such a fleet. It should be remembered that apart from the Free French and the relatively few people in the Resistance of 1942, the overwhelming majority of 'heroes of the French Resistance' did not appear until after the Allied invasion of Normandy was seen to be a success. This information broadcast by the crew of the French airliner passing over the convoy confirmed for the waiting German and Italian forces the size and location of their opponent.

Next day, the aircraft carrier HMS *Eagle* was sunk by U-73, and *Furious* launched 33 Spitfires for Malta. The Spitfires were led by Wing Commander WM Churchill DSO DFC, a veteran of the Battles of France and Britain, with at least eight victories. Australians in the batch were Pilot Officer R. 'Bob' Park, Flight Sergeant E. T. Hiskens, Flight Sergeant John Sanderson and Sergeant Fred Clewley.

Fred Clewley was in his cockpit, saw *Eagle* tilt, and all the tiny planes on deck slide off into the sea. Another observer was Paddy O'Brien, a Glaswegian, who had already packed his kit into lots destined for Scotland, Gibraltar and Malta, and packed the rest into his Spitfire. He had then taken his camera to

140

photograph the first flights taking off. They all got off easily, and there was an air of confidence. The first two aircraft of the second flight had gone, when O'Brien glanced over and saw *Eagle* pouring smoke and listing to port. 'The panic was on. She'd been torpedoed and was sinking rapidly. I stood and watched her go right over and then she sank in about twelve minutes.'[6]

Eagle had been struck by four torpedoes in ten seconds, and sank with a loss of 131 lives; 929 officers and ratings were saved by the destroyer escort. She had escorted convoys, and also made nine aircraft ferrying sorties into the Mediterranean, sending over 180 fighters to Malta. This had been done with little publicity and reward, compared to the fanfare over the two ferry trips made by the USS *Wasp*.

Prudently, as *Furious* seemed to be a long way behind the convoy, O'Brien went below and put on his Mae West jacket. He was last to fly off, and had about ninety minutes to wait. Eventually he was in his cockpit, on deck, watching his flight leader, Rolls, fly off ahead. Then he taxied to the centre deck. 'There was a white line down the port side and we had to use it to keep straight. I had it between my cannon and the fuselage. I got the green flag OK and opened the throttle with brakes on, when I felt the plane starting to slip forward I released the brakes and slammed the throttle open. I went tearing off down the deck and before I realised it was airborne and away off the end. It was just too easy.'

He changed to the auxiliary tank, throttled back, retracted undercarriage while circling the carrier, formed up and headed for Malta. Off to the right was the coast of Africa, and in the distance the Atlas Mountains.

The flights arrived at Malta with no enemy interception, O'Brien landed and taxied to a revetment, noticing the ruins and that 'it was hellish dirty.' When he climbed out, 'very dirty, tired and hungry,' everyone asked him for chocolate, cigarettes and news of the *Eagle*. After checking into 185 Squadron, he went to bed, to find that he was sweating so much that sleep was difficult, then the sirens went, followed by the guns and bombs exploding. 'First night in Malta was no success!' he wrote.

On 12 August, according to plan, that part of the convoy escort designated as Force Z turned back. The battle continued unabated. Again the rolling thunder of sea battles could be heard on Malta, and faces turned to the north-west.

141

A crucial point in the *Pedestal* battles had been reached, and two Italian cruiser squadrons were moving to engage the convoy remnants. But the cumulative effect of a bluff by RAF search planes, calling in clear for the non-existent Liberator bombers to attack, the reluctance of the Luftwaffe to co-operate with the Italian Navy, and Mussolini's decision to recall the cruisers, averted what could have been total catastrophe. The remnants of the convoy steamed on.

As usual, information about the imminent arrival of the ships spread to the Maltese. Crowds gathered where they could see the entrance to Grand Harbour, and the boom was pulled aside. Through the gap appeared the damaged survivors of the merciless battles at sea. Hulls and decks torn and blackened by explosions and fire, *Melbourne Star*, then *Rochester Castle*, and finally *Port Chalmers* came through, to be greeted by an emotional population waving Union Jacks and the red-and-white colours of Malta. Children, and probably their elders also, burst into 'Rule Britannia'.

Nine of the precious merchant ships, selected for their modernity and speed, had been sunk. *Deucalion, Empire Hope, Clan Ferguson, Santa Elisa, Almeria Lykes, Wairangi, Glenorchy, Waimarama,* and *Dorset* were all gone, with the naval ships *Eagle, Foresight, Cairo* and *Manchester*, while *Victorious, Indomitable, Nigeria* and *Kenya* had been damaged.

The Italians had lost two submarines, and the cruisers *Bolzano* and *Muzio Attendolo* damaged.

Still making its painful way to Malta was the tanker *Ohio*, with its vital cargo of fuel, without which the island simply could not survive. Torpedoed, hit by bombs and by crashing Junkers, abandoned and re-boarded, lashed to destroyers to keep her afloat, under tow, with only about one metre of freeboard, constantly under air attack and menaced by any Italian ship which might appear, *Ohio* was dragged towards Malta.

There was another survivor, damaged, out of the convoy, but making her own way to harbour, dodging U-boats and Vichy French officials: *Brisbane Star*. After her own series of adventures, *Brisbane Star* made it, adding the undamaged part of her cargo to that already being unloaded at top speed in the new organisation on the wharves.

As individuals, RAAF pilots did not lodge claims during the first part of August, but on the 11th, two Australians in 248 Squadron, flying Beaufighters in attacks on the Axis airfields on

Sardinia destroyed and damaged Italian bombers. R. F. Hammond destroyed one Savoia S79 and damaged another, while P. J. O. Mueller destroyed one and damaged three.

Fred Clewley, who had flown in with the latest batch of reinforcements, had gone to 185 Squadron, with the other Aussies there. Eric Mahar had asked him if he wanted to do this, as Mahar, Clewley and Ken Mitchell had been together in 131 Squadron. Mahar then telephoned and fixed the transfer. On the 13th, Eric Mahar was leading a section of four, which included Fred Clewley, in a scramble at 18.10 hours.

It was Fred's first scramble on Malta, and there was one small but important point which was to be driven home. 'Our perspex hoods were so scratched that we tended to leave them open,' said Ken Mitchell, 'because with the sparkle on them you couldn't see enemy aircraft. Fred didn't know you had to keep right up, not like England where you could sit back in position. You had to sit right up along the other fellow, which is quite difficult, technically.'

When the scramble started, Eric pushed the throttle forward, the Spitfire leaped along the strip trailing a cloud of dust, with Fred coming along as his No. 2, but just that fraction of a second too late to keep in front of the dust from Mahar's aircraft. 'Fred got dust in his eyes,' said Ken Mitchell. Blinded, he lost direction, and has no memory of what happened next.

Mahar glanced in his mirror and was surprised to glimpse a Spitfire crossing behind him in the dust-cloud. Len Reid, not flying, was watching the scramble and realised that Clewley was in the dust cloud, blinded, but there was nothing to be done in the seconds of time remaining, and the Spitfire hit one of the stone walls, slewing sideways and crashing.

'Clew just got airborne, I could see it all plainly, and went slap-bang into a pen, hit it, probably, at 100 knots. I thought Fred had killed himself,' Reid said. Fred was taken to hospital with concussion and laceration of the chin. It was the end of his flying career on Malta, but not the end of his adventures in the Mediterranean.

On 13 August, George Beurling, the Canadian who was rapidly building up what was to be the top score over Malta, shared in the destruction of a Ju88. That day, an Australian in 1435 Squadron, R. A. Buntine, was killed in action; there is no record

143

of any claims made by him for enemy aircraft destroyed or damaged. Next day, E. T. Hiskens, 249 Squadron, damaged a 109.

Noel Pashen flew two convoy escort patrols, with no combat, but on the first his engine revolution counter failed. He was still sick, and wrote in his diary, 'Damn it all, I don't know what's wrong with me here.' That night he had violent stomach pains and attacks of vomiting, but all the medical officer could do was prescribe a dose of salts.

One of the other pilots, Hogarth, was attacked and 'didn't know what hit him and suddenly found his elevators shot away, but baled out successfully.'[7]

Colin Parkinson flew several sorties, but had no combats, though he listened to the radio chatter of others in action, and to Beurling's participation in the shared destruction of a Ju88. 'Too much natter,' Parkinson wrote in his diary. He noted the damaged ships below, and that 'Flight Sergeant Parkes was shot down again this morning. Bailed out and was picked up by a destroyer on the way to Gibraltar.' He added, 'Probably have big eats now.'

On 14 August, after several patrols over the 'lame duck' Ohio, and seeing lifeboats and the stern of a sunken ship, but no enemy aircraft, Parkinson returned to base to be told to prepare to go to Gibraltar. In collusion with Pilot Officer McElroy, who was also going, Parkinson cut off his Flight Sergeant's rank badges and entered the Luqa Officers' Mess, explaining to a couple of officers who knew him that at last his commission had come through. At 02.45, they took off as passengers in a Lockheed Hudson bound for Gibraltar, landing there at about 09.00.[8]

89 Squadron's Beaufighters were active, and though John Ross had to return with unserviceable VHF radio, Moose Fumerton, seemingly none the worse for his recent ditching, destroyed a Cant Z1007bis, as did Pilot Officer Reeves.

The Maltese were preparing for the Feast of Santa Maria on 15 August, and the convoy came to be known by them as 'the Santa Maria convoy'. Fittingly, for a people who had borne so much and clung to their religion in times of trial, Ohio did arrive on 15 August, after an epic voyage. The island forces had been reprieved; resistance and attack could continue.

Most of the wheat had been lost with Santa Elisa and Almeria Lykes, but at last four ships had arrived. The rations were still far below those in the United Kingdom, where it was 2800 calories a day. On Malta it was 1690 for men and 1500 for women.

The convoy battles had resulted in a tactical victory for the Axis attackers, but the strategic advantage lay with the Allies, as what supplies had got through enabled Malta to hang on for that much longer. The ability and daring of the Italian torpedo-bomber crews, and their submarine and torpedo-boat units, were in direct contrast with the actions and achievements of their larger surface units. Together, the Axis air and sea forces had inflicted heavy losses on *Pedestal* forces.

Eagle, Manchester, Cairo and *Foresight* had been lost, while the carrier *Indomitable*, two cruisers and three destroyers had been damaged, and would be non-operational for some time, plus nine of 14 modern merchant ships had been sunk.

The combats still went on overhead, and on the 15th Paddy O'Brien, not flying, watched a raid coming in. He and the others 'could hear and see some 109s mixing it at about 20 000 feet. Suddenly, some firing, a long burst and a few short ones, and the next thing we saw was a Spit coming down at a hell of a rate, making bags of noise and with glycol pouring from it. It flattened out over the sea, half-rolled and went straight down into the drink. "Poor bugger," or so we thought, but a few seconds after a parachute appeared. Thank God. The rescue launch darted out of the harbour and we all felt considerably better. We found out it was Tarbuck, one of the new chaps.'[9]

Also on 15 August, in a Beaufighter of 248 Squadron, R. F. Hammond claimed an S79 destroyed and a Ju88 damaged. A year before on that day, Noel Pashen had finished his flying training in Australia, and began preparing for the journey overseas. It led to England, to 53 OTU, to 242 Squadron and to Malta. Next day, he 'went down to dispersal full of daring and animal cunning, ready to do the dirt on Jerry. However nothing happened all day. Must have been the first day for months when there was no activity over the island.'[10]

Meanwhile, on Gibraltar, Colin Parkinson was enjoying a bountiful breakfast. He listed in his diary the 'bacon, eggs, toast, tea, grapefruit, sugar, butter, everything good to eat. We were all expecting to stay in Gib for about two weeks. To our great disappointment we were told to go aboard *Furious* at 5.30. Our job was to lead a section of new Spitfires to Malta.'

McElroy and Parkinson proceeded to buy as many cigarettes,

145

chocolates and sweets as possible before going aboard. Parkinson was still supposedly an officer, and noted the 'wonderful food and conditions' in the ward room. Learning of this escapade years later, Eric Mahar commented that he could well believe Parkinson enjoying the ward room, as 'he was always a law unto himself.'[11]

On 16 August, *Furious* put to sea, and the day was spent preparing the aircraft and briefing the pilots. Parkinson was storing his purchases in the various spaces of his Spitfire. He would lead the fourth flight of fighters, none of which had Hydromatic airscrews, which improved the rate of climb.

Next day, the Spitfires were launched. The first eight flew off safely, but one of the second flight swerved, stalled, knocked its tail off and swung over the side of the ship, falling inverted into the sea and sinking at once. Two others could not retract their wheels, so the pilots bailed out and were picked up. Parkinson's flight took off and made the passage safely, though one crashed on landing and the pilot was injured.

The jinx on Noel Pashen's flying continued, when his oxygen mask blew off and an earphone pulled out of the helmet during a scramble on 17 August. On the 20th, in the same aircraft, X-V, he passed out at 20 000 feet due to an oxygen leak from the hose, noting in his log-book 'shaky do!'[12]

On Malta, the exhilaration of the ships' arrival was countered by the knowledge of the heavy cost involved, and that there seemed to be no change in the situation in the Mediterranean. Rommel was still fighting close to Alexandria, and all convoys had been forced to fight through with heavy losses, or turn back. The future was still grim.

On 21 August, RAAF pilots in Beaufighter day-fighters again engaged, with R. F. Hammond claiming a Piaggio P32 destroyed and a Ju88 probable, while P. J. O. Mueller shared in the destruction of a Ju52 with Wing Commander J. M. N. Pike RAF.

Hammond was about 350 miles (560 km) from Malta, and at 16.18 saw a Ju88 1000 metres away, higher and flying north. He climbed on to its tail, opening fire at 600 metres, closing to about 150 metres. As he broke away, much white smoke was trailing from the 88's starboard engine. He swung back, firing from dead astern at 300 metres; flames were seen coming from the starboard engine, and hits seen on the fuselage and starboard wing as the Beaufighter surged in to 50 metres, with Hammond pulling up sharply about 30 metres above the sea. The 88 was diving, starboard wing down.

Hammond broke away, noticing a Piaggio P32 about 800 metres away, flying at 1000 feet. He attacked, firing from 400 metres, and hit the starboard engine, which burst into flames. Hammond turned to fire from the port quarter. He missed, and the Piaggio began to turn inside the Beaufighter.

Hammond throttled back, slid into position astern and fired again, shooting off the Italian's port tailfin. Large pieces flicked back, just missing the Beau, and more hits were seen sparking on the fuselage and starboard wing of the Italian, but oil streamed back onto the windscreen and leading edges of the Beaufighter. Hammond saw the Piaggio spinning out of control at less than 30 metres above the sea, and he set course for base. Enemy airfields were near, and it was not healthy to remain.[13]

'Lunch; food bloody lousy,' wrote Parkinson on the 23rd, before escorting a Hurricane fighter-bomber sweep to Sicily, 'led by two Wing Commanders who don't know the form yet. The whole thing was a mess-up. Disgusted.'

The food situation, constantly in everyone's mind, did have a few brighter spots for some people. The *Melbourne Star* and *Brisbane Star* had been on the UK-Australia run before the war, and included a number of Australians among the crews, particularly the officers. They soon found the RAAF on the island, and flights as passengers in aircraft such as the Beaufighter, which could carry more than one person, were repaid with meals and drink aboard the ships. Of course, the single-seat Spitfire was unable to take passengers, and it was only the night fighter or intruder pilots who could offer to smuggle a ship's officer on a flight.

Parkinson wrote of the loss of another friend on 25 August, when Reg Round, a New Zealander who had been with Parkinson in 19 Squadron, and who had come to Malta with him, was shot down and posted 'missing'. Later in the day, Micky Butler's aircraft crashed into the sea after suffering airscrew trouble. Then Parkes, another Aussie, crashed into an aircraft on take-off, but was unharmed.[14]

Parkes had collided with fellow Australian Noel Pashen, who had been taking off ahead of him. Pashen, in the same squadron, was told that Round, 249 Squadron, 'apparently peeled off and went straight in.' In the afternoon it was decided 229 Squadron would escort some Hurricanes on a bombing mission to Sicily, but that was cancelled and a normal sweep substituted. Pashen's jinx struck, blowing a tyre on take-off; he nearly collided with the flight leader, but stopped on the runway, only to have Parkes come speeding, through the dust, straight into his Spitfire. 'God knows how I got away with it,' Pashen wrote in his diary. 'Result— two aircraft written off, pilots unhurt.' Then, over Sicily, Butler's aircraft developed troubles, and he was last seen landing on the sea some sixteen kilometres off the coast.[15]

Mervyn Shipard, the night fighter pilot, was with other members of 89 Squadron enjoying a day at the seaside, when they noticed a man in a rubber aircrew dinghy paddling to shore. It turned out to be a Luftwaffe pilot, who was apparently disgruntled at his fate, and churlish enough to spit at the helper who extended a hand to lift him onto the rocks at St Paul's Bay. The hand turned into a fist, flopping the man back into the water, from where he was taken into custody by the Malta Police.

Shipard went aboard the *Brisbane Star* on invitation from a crew member, and had what he recalled as the best meal he had eaten, with fresh bread cooked in the ship's bakery.

On other days off, he sometimes went into the Operations Room, standing behind the Controller and watching the activity. On one occasion, Spitfires were being directed onto an enemy plot, but could not see them, so the Controller suggested they might be in cloud. He was smartly reminded of his parentage when the Spitfire leader abused him and said there was not a cloud in the sky. On another occasion, a Spitfire pilot called to say he was baling out, Control acknowledged, and then a few minutes later Shipard was amazed to hear him call the pilot, asking if he had baled out yet!

He had a personal anecdote concerning Controllers who seemed removed from reality. During a night chase he was pursuing a bandit across Malta when anti-aircraft fire began exploding all around him, though he was at least 4000 feet above the agreed-on height for such fire. In his experience, it always exploded behind the target. He called Control and informed him of the barrage, to be informed that it could not be so, as it was set to explode at 16 000 feet. Shipard heatedly told the man to come on up for a look, but was then reminded, 'Don't worry, it's friendly!'[16]

On 26 August, Photographic Reconnaissance Unit (PRU) had

detected flying boats on the slipway at Marsala, in western Sicily. So that night, Flight Lieutenant Edwards and John Ross, 89 Squadron, set off in their Beaufighters for the area. When they arrived, Ross noticed the flarepath on the harbour was alight, and an aircraft was taking off. He followed it and attacked, sending a Dornier Do 18 in flames into the town.[17]

On 27 August, Colin Parkinson, with 229 Squadron, and Len Reid, in 185 Squadron, claimed victories, Reid destroying a Ju88.

Parkinson had gone on readiness early, after a night disturbed by bombing, and further interrupted by barking dogs. Unable to do much about the Luftwaffe raiders, he decided to take action about the dogs, and fired his pistol 'in the general direction and they stopped.'

With the arrival of Air Vice-Marshal Keith Park, the Spitfires were tasked to go out over Sicily, looking for a fight, as the wings did over France. Group Captain Walter Churchill, as mentioned earlier, had been posted as Station Commander Takali and organised the first of these sweeps. Ken Mitchell, 185 Squadron, recalled him as 'this eccentric Group Captain, as we called him. He was sent out to shake us up, to take the war into enemy territory. While we were quite orientated to defend Malta, it was too hazardous, that hundred kilometres across to Sicily . . .'[18]

The pilots were briefed for a three-squadron attack on three airfields in Sicily. Parkinson was to fly as No. 3 to the leader, Group Captain Churchill. After take-off the formation flew at zero feet to Sicily.

'We went at dawn,' said Ken Mitchell. 'It was a very dangerous thing to do, because the Germans often used to get up at dawn and come across our way. If they'd been up they would have been able to attack us until we ran out of petrol. It was a beautiful morning, and as we came in I still remember there were fishermen and people on the beach, the fishermen looked at us in amazement, I saw one fellow fall out of his boat in amazement. We were right down on the deck, of course.'

Ten Spitfires of 185 Squadron, led by Major Swales, had attacked Comiso. Len Reid was among them, and as they crossed the Sicilian coast a gaggle of Ju88s was in process of forming up. They were promptly attacked.

'We were on the deck all the way, then saw five or six 88s in the circuit area,' said Reid. He fired a quick deflection shot

149

at one, broke away and chased another 'up and down a valley just over the tree tops. I was chasing him over the olive groves, in and out. He was doing everything possible to shake me off, but he didn't have flying speed. I had a lot of trouble catching him. Another 88 shot in front of me, going in the opposite direction—I think somebody else was chasing him. Finally I closed in and gave it two good bursts, saw big red flashes on the back and starboard engine. It immediately went steeply down,' and later was confirmed as destroyed. Leaving Sicily, he strafed a building and set out for Malta.[19]

229 Squadron was to attack the airfield at Biscari. As they approached, Colin Parkinson could see black smoke rising to starboard, and hear the radio chatter of the pilots attacking Comiso. He realised surprise had been lost, and his own formation had not reached their target, which was deepest in enemy territory.

Meanwhile, 185 Squadron claimed five destroyed, three probables and a damaged, losing Pilot Officer Woodger as a prisoner of war. Ken Mitchell had shared one of the probables with Wing Commander Thompson.

Ken Mitchell: 'We were very lucky. We caught them taking off and forming up. Just inside the coast were olive groves, and I can still see my cannon shells going through the 88 which was below me, and exploding on the harsh rocky terrain underneath.'

Meanwhile, 229 Squadron had been going on to their target. Biscari came into view, and Parkinson could see about six bombers parked close together, then Churchill was hit by flak, 'started to smoke, and then burst into flames, rolled on his back and crashed into the ground. Rather shook me.'

Speeding through the flak, Parkinson fired on the group of Ju88s, and set one on fire, strafed the right-hand hangar, then spent some time trying to dodge the ground fire which was coming at him from every direction. During the jinking he noticed a large column of black smoke coming from the target, then flew into a relatively quiet valley, snap-shot at a small train, flew out over the coast, among the gunfire of the aroused defenders.

Then 'I saw two 109s on the port and above. I looked to the other side and saw a 109 about to attack. I turned into the two, and continued to turn. The single 109 overshot, got in front of me, and I shot him down in flames. The other two nearly collided with one another and flew out of sight.'

Closer to Malta, he saw three Spitfires manoeuvring with two Macchis, and swung across to assist, but the Macchis broke away and escaped; Parkinson was out of ammunition anyway. He landed, and was afflicted with a bad attack of 'Malta dog', spending the afternoon and night in considerable discomfort.[20]

Flying in Wing Commander Tommy Thompson's section, Ken Mitchell had a close shave. 'Tommy was so excited that when we went back he led us right over the spires of Valletta cathedral, we were showing off, I was in the box [in the formation of four] and he nearly wiped me off on the spires!'[21]

The island fighters claimed 10-8-2 in the actions.

Eric Mahar led several 185 Squadron scrambles before the end of the month, with no combats, and the squadron itself did not make any more claims until September. But on 31 August, it was officially presumed that Squadron Leader Chaffe, missing since 22 February, was dead, and the body of Pilot Officer Ormrod DFC, missing since 22 April, was found at Cospicua and buried at the Cappuccini cemetery. During the month the squadron had lost Guthrie and MacLeod killed, Clewley injured taking off, Tarbuck and Stenborg shot down but baled out, and Woodger shot down, taken prisoner.

In 229 Squadron, Noel Pashen had recorded the loss of Dudley Newman, Dan Magruder and Francis injured after crash-landing, Hogarth shot down, but parachuted. Francis had attacked some Macchis, but developed airscrew trouble, Magruder went to his aid but was not seen again, presumably shot down by the Italians. Pashen thought Magruder 'one of the finest chaps I've met. A black show all round.' Noel, with others, flew searches for Magruder but nothing was found.

On 30 August, he flew two scrambles, continuing his run of bad luck when oil covered his windscreen. Next day he remembered that date a year before, when he plucked up courage to ask Ruth to marry him. He wrote in his diary that August 1942, 'has been my worst month in the RAAF and I hope my luck breaks.'[22]

A sense of humour still prevailed, and while the squadron Engineering Officer was pedalling his bike along, one of the Canadian pilots gave out a piercing whistle, which the cyclist took for a falling bomb, abandoned the bike and lost large areas of skin to the rocky ground, not to mention abrasions to his own sense of humour.

151

The RAF torpedo bombers had been active in the last two weeks of August, concentrating on the tankers so necessary to Rommel in North Africa. In ten days, they sank 23 000 tons, and none of the 5000 tons of fuel and ammunition promised to Rommel arrived.

The enemy had been able to mount heavy attacks against the convoys, and still send 3100 sorties over Malta. However only two bombing attacks were made on the island, and once the ships were in harbour there were no efforts to destroy them as had been done in March. Night bombing was greatly reduced, with eleven nights free of alerts. The Axis aircrews in bomber units were well aware of the toll paid in previous months. And the island still fought back.

8
The Lull

Malta—September 1942

Again activity slackened, and an element of boredom entered the life, or expectations, of some of the fighter pilots. Colin Parkinson began to write of the relative peace: 'Things are so quiet on the island now that it is not worth being here. The action was the only thing to compensate for being here. The sooner I go back to Australia the better I'll like it.' And a week later, 'Readiness 1 pm. No scrambles. Malta has gone to the dogs.'[1]

On 6 September, D. Partridge RAAF, 252 Squadron, attached to 227 Squadron, a Beaufighter pilot, was killed in action, with his RAF navigator, Sergeant A. W. Vivian. Mervyn Shipard, with Flight Sergeant Doug Oxby as radar operator, was also flying patrols, scrambles and night-intruder missions over Sicily with no success. During the month he attacked Gela airfield and Licata and Empedocle naval bases, and was sent after two enemy aircraft, with no result.

Noel Pashen, 229 Squadron, had flown several sorties, despite eye problems, and then the jinx re-appeared. On 8 September, on a sweep to Sicily at 16 000 feet, his seat collapsed again, and the Spitfire went down in a dive almost to sea level before Noel pulled it out. He had hit his left eye in the violent manoeuvre, leaving it quite sore. 'The solo attack on Sicily shook the boys,' he wrote, adding, 'Three times now I've got away with it. How long can it last?'[2]

On 11 September, Colin Parkinson noted that he 'had to get up during the night to fire my revolver at some barking dogs and nattering Maltese.' The lack of contact with the enemy continued to irritate some of the pilots, including Parkinson.

153

Despite flying sweeps over to Sicily, there were no combats. Len Reid recalled the sight of Mount Etna, the active volcano, always visible to the pilots during their flights over the island. When the Messerschmitts refused to come up and fight, the Spitfires continued going north and inland. Reid was commissioned as a Pilot Officer on 13 September.

On 14 September Parkinson was on readiness, but there were no scrambles, and he noted, 'Things are very slow. 249 mixed it with some Huns. My commission has come through at long last. Went to Officers' Mess to be welcomed by the new CO (Baker) and have a drink. Returned to the Sergeants' Mess with the old CO, Bill Douglas; had a very wet time on gin; CO was well oiled. Extra supper and then to bed.' Next day he moved to the Officers' Mess, noting that the food there was 'bloody awful', and Butch Baker 'a good type. Few drinks and then to bed. I'm drinking too much.'

While some people may have been missing combats, others were experiencing them, and on the 17th, he wrote that 'Peters was shot down, lost; Scott shot down, lost; Turner shot up but landed OK at Luqa.'[3]

The Spitfires had been directed onto eight Macchis, seen four and attacked, but the other Italians had pounced and the Spitfires had to fight their way out. Then two 109s got Peters, from 249 Squadron, over the island.

Many of the pilots and others sneered at the Italians, but some held them in higher regard. Len Reid said that the Messerschmitts would make one or two diving passes and be away. 'The 109s used to make these dive and zoom attacks and if you saw them coming you could normally evade them. But not the Macchi 202. Some Macchis would stay and mix it with you. You had to be a good pilot to shake them off. The Macchi 202 could turn with the Spit, and it didn't have much on the Macchi; it was about the same speed, I don't think we could out-climb it with the Spitfire Vb we had out there. Many Spits were shot down by Macchis. However, some of them, if you got on their tail, would more or less fly straight and level, and you'd just fly up behind them and shoot them down.'[4]

Still suffering from stomach illnesses, but flying some patrols and scrambles, Noel Pashen was greatly perturbed on 16

154

Above
185 SQN Spitfire V GL-A
BR375, Malta 1942 (*Paddy
O'Brien*)

Left
Dave, the army motorcyclist,
who ferried the pilots of 185
Squadron out to the Spitfires at
Hal Far (*Jim Yarra*)

Below left
Tony Boyd, RAAF 185
Squadron (*Boyd family*)

Below right
Noel Pashen, 229 Squadron
(*Ruth Pashen*)

Above left
Alan Yates, 185 Squadron (*Brian Cull*)

Above
Ken Mitchell, 185 Squadron (*Jim Yarra*)

Left
Ken 'Red' Gray, RAAF 89 Squadron, Malta 1942 (*Ken Gray*)

Below
Flight Sergeant Len Reid, RAAF 185 Squadron RAF, Malta 1942 (*L. S. Reid*)

Top
Scramble! Pilot in cockpit,
fitters in position

Middle
Hurricane landed after sortie
(*Jim Yarra*)

Left
Gordon Tweedale 'beating-up'
the airfield (*Jim Yarra*)

Above
Officers' Mess buildings, Hal Far, after bombing (*Jim Yarra*)

Left
Left to right: Howard Lester, RAAF, Philip Wigley, RAF, Ian McKay, RCAF, Hal Far (*Philip Wigley*)

Below left
Doug Oxby (*left*), Mervyn Shipard (*Mervyn Shipard*)

Below
Charles Crombie, RAAF, 89 Squadron RAF, Malta (*Mrs Betty Crombie*)

Above
'A' Flight 185 Squadron RAF, Hal Far, October 1942. Back row (*left to right*), F/Sgt 'Red' Walker RAF, Sgt Jim Tarbuck RAF, F/O Len Cheek RAF and Sgt Jim Gunstone RAF. Front row (*left to right*), F/O Paddy O'Brien RAF, W/C J. M. Thompson DSO DFC, RAF, Capt Keith Kuhlmann DFC SAAF and F/O Len Reid DFC, RAAF (*Paddy O'Brien*)

Middle
185 Squadron Spitfire after a landing by Danny Hartney (*Jim Yarra*)

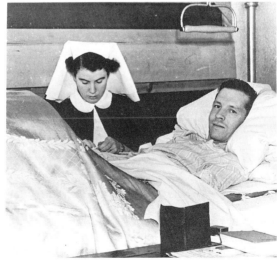

Right
Howard 'Chuck' Lester recuperating from wounds (*Mrs Ella Lester*)

Darwin Raid 55, 20 June 1943. A remarkable photo of the Japanese Nakajima Ki-48 'Lily' Bombers at just above tree-top height (*RAAF*)

Donald H. Smith RAAF (*AWM UK 1163*)

Eric Mahar RAAF. Note the unofficial, but widely worn, Maltese Cross on right breastpocket (*AWM UK 38*)

Jack 'Slim' Yarra (*Jim Yarra*)   Paul Brennan (*T. R. Brennan*)

Tim Goldsmith, in RAAF Spitfire V, 1943 (*Mrs Doris Goldsmith*)

John Ross, RAAF (*AWM UK 86*)

Mervyn Shipard, RAAF,
nightfighter pilot over Malta
(*AWM UK 810*)

Right
Gordon Tweedale's grave,
Malta (*AWM P54 5/171/15*)

September, when his CO spoke to him after lunch, and discreetly informed him that it was thought his nerves had gone, that he was not up to operational fighter flying. Pashen believed that he had done nothing to warrant this, and thought it was due to his run of bad luck in August, with burst tyres, collapsing seats, unserviceable radio and oxygen, and oily windscreen, plus several attacks of vomiting, diarrhoea and headaches.[5]

On 19 September, after an 8 hour 45 minute flight from Egypt to Luqa in a DC3, Flying Officer Charles Crombie arrived to join C Flight 89 Squadron. He had some 776 hours in his log book—an astronomical total compared with some of the Spitfire pilots. With him was Ken 'Red' Gray, the fourth Aussie pilot in 89. Art Spurgin was the fifth, but did not get to Malta, instead being quite successful over North Africa, where he destroyed five enemy.

Crombie, Gray, Ross and Spurgin had all joined the RAAF in May 1940, and were members of the first Empire Air Training Scheme intake. They had done their Elementary Flying Training at Narromine, New South Wales, then gone to Calgary, Alberta, receiving their wings on 24 December 1940. 'What a Christmas present!' said Red Gray. They then sailed on an unescorted ship, which sailed at about nine knots across the Atlantic, during which voyage the 400 or so aircrew aboard manned the sparse, ancient and varied collection of guns installed on it. Food, but not beer, was running out by the time they arrived in the UK.

With little money and awaiting posting to an OTU, the Aussies were given turns as Orderly Officer and Balloon Security Officer at RAF Uxbridge. However, one day they were taken to visit Windsor Castle, and had what was, for a batch of young Aussies far from home, an unforgettable experience: they were taken inside for afternoon tea with Queen Elizabeth and the Princesses Elizabeth and Margaret.

They moved on to the final stages of training, with Red Gray making his first night solo in a Beaufighter a year and three days after actually joining the RAAF on 25 May 1940. On 15 June 1941, with a total of 275 hours flying, he flew his first operational patrol with Sergeant Mervyn Mould RAF as his radar operator. Mould also flew with him from Malta, and later in India. Crombie and Gray had been together since enlisting, and, with the others,

155

had volunteered for 89 Squadron when it was formed for service in the Middle East. They had remained in Egypt when Shipard and Ross had gone to Malta.

John Ross had been on the island, with the 89 Squadron detachment, since 22 June. That night, 19 September, he flew to Gerbini with a 112-kg bomb under each wing. He duly dropped the bombs on the target, but as it was a bright moonlight night, he stayed over Sicily, looking for enemy, and then sighted a convoy of trucks. He attacked, setting some on fire with cannon and machinegun, and these were still burning an hour later when Pilot Officer Reeves flew by on another intruder sortie.

On 22 September, Red Gray flew his first sortie from Malta, an unsuccessful search for a downed aircraft. Next night he was off to Sicily on an intruder mission, strafed E-Boats in Trapani Harbour, dropped two 125-kg bombs on Gela airfield, and attacked two He111K bombers as they were landing at Gerbini, claiming them as damaged.

Intruder missions were flown to airfields on Sicily, Southern Italy, Pantelleria and as far as Tunisia, harassing the returning bombers and any other types of aircraft encountered. Captured German flare pistols and flares were used to confuse the Luftwaffe airfield controllers. In addition, trains, road convoys, shipping and port facilities were attacked. These operations continued as long as the squadron was in the theatre. For the day fighters, September passed with little action, the few enemy seen being too high and going too fast to engage.

After several days off flying because of illness and the saturated condition at Takali after rain, Noel Pashen scrambled again on 24 September, in X-V, but his undercarriage kept dropping, forcing him to leave the formation. 'I'm now regarded as the jinx of the squadron and I'm beginning to believe it.'[6]

On the 24th, Colin Parkinson and some of the pilots attended a supper party and dance given by Mr Pullichino, who had 'five very charming daughters. We had plenty of food and drink, which was eaten to the last crumb. Went through it like a plague of locusts. We danced in the open in the moonlight to a very good band. The adjutant got very drunk and drove the CO's car into the walls of three different houses; damaged the front of a very nice car.'

Of more immediate import to Colin Parkinson was that when

he went to breakfast that morning, after Pullichino's party, he found that someone had stolen his ration of jam, spurring him to write that it was a good thing officers were gentlemen by act of parliament, as it was the only way some of them would ever be so. His temper was not improved when he went to the cinema and could barely hear the sound track over the noise made by 'nattering, nut-chewing Maltese'.

But while the Spitfire pilots had been enjoying the Pullichino hospitality, Charles Crombie, in Beaufighter 5165, with Sergeant Moss, flew an intruder mission to Syracuse harbour, and destroyed a '3-engined seaplane'. Then on 25 September, while Parkinson was disgruntled about the missing jam and the talkative cinema audience, Beurling shot down two 109s.

Noel Pashen, testing X-E, found himself mixed up in a fighter sweep which tangled with fifteen or thirty Messerschmitts, and for once the jinx was elsewhere, as he fired at and hit a 109 on the port side, damaging it.[7]

Further away from the island, three Beaufighters of 227 Squadron were searching for a minesweeper off Kuriat Island, but found a Cant Z506B. This was flown by Maresciallo (Warrant Officer) Attilio Broccardo, 197d Squadriglia, and the three Beaufighters made short work of it. An Australian, Pilot Officer Robert Wills, was one of these pilots, in aircraft 'A'.[8]

Next morning, Parkinson went to Imtarfa Hospital to visit a friend. When he was there, the air-raid alarms sounded, and the anti-aircraft guns began to fire. Then, added to that was 'a hundred Maltese children making enough noise for 10 000. What with sirens howling, church bells clanging, guns and bombs going off, and Maltese yelling and shouting, it's a wonder I'm not a nervous wreck.'

His humour was not improved when lunch was poor, after a late arriving breakfast, and he had to fly a sweep over Sicily to help train some of the more inexperienced pilots to a standard at which they would be capable of leading the squadron. The section of four was directed over Gozo, and began gaining height, when they saw '25 Messerschmitts coming towards us heading back to Sicily. We broke into them but didn't do any good because they were a little too high and going much too fast. However they went like hell for home. Just imagine, they were six to one, and wouldn't play. If we had been doing another 120 kmph we'd have split them up and knocked a few down. Came back and landed, very "brassed".'9

Charles Crombie, with Sergeant Moss, again in Beaufighter 5165, had better luck on his second intruder mission to Sicily. He attacked and hit a He111 near Castelvetrano airfield, claiming it as a probable.

John Ross, the fourth Aussie in the Beaufighter night fighters of 89 Squadron on Malta, had flown back to Egypt on the 23rd after a depressing series of equipment failures. On ten scrambles his radar had failed, it burst into flames once, and on another his VHF radio failed. Ten contacts on the radar had been lost; his aircraft went unserviceable twice; he was bombed on one occasion when landing and on another when taking off; illuminated and fired on by the island anti-aircraft; scrambled too late on three occasions when the aircraft and radar did function properly.10

After another uneventful sweep over Sicily on 24 September, Colin Parkinson and a group went to the 'Monico' Bar, but on the way home were halted by the Maltese Police and nearly arrested for abusing the police and having the vehicle lights too bright. Similar activities followed on the remaining days and nights of September.

There was comparatively little combat, and it was noticed that it was necessary to go higher and higher. In July, the Spitfires had patrolled at 20 000 feet, gone to 22 000 in August, and by mid-September were at 28 000 feet in attempts to catch the enemy. In contrast, the Beaufighter intruder flights were at very low level as they attacked airfields and ports in Sicily.

By this time, Len Reid and Eric Mahar were leading sections of 185 Squadron on scrambles, but as for most others, there were no claims. Len had flown seventeen scrambles in thirteen days, but there had been only two combats in the period, despite sweeps over Sicily. Weaver had been shot down and taken prisoner, and Swain was killed spinning in after a practice dog-fight. It was a far cry from the hectic weeks of May, June and July.

Pressure on the enemy after sunset was maintained with night intruder sorties, and on 29 September the Beaufighters flew to the usual airfields on Sicily, but saw nothing. They had flown similar sorties on the 2nd, 11th and 14th, dropping 125-kg bombs, but not seeing any result. This time, as John Ross had already done on previous sortie, Mervyn Shipard decided to attack the enemy motor torpedo boats. Douggie Oxby recalls it as 'the night in the war when I was probably the most scared.

'We were coming from seaward to attack the E-boats, there were cliffs in front of us and Ship had to do a climbing turn away. As we were approaching the wharf along which the boats were moored, we were being fired at from the cliffs, downwards, and from the wharf, upwards. I thought we were bound to be hit, but, I'm happy to say, not a thing.' They dropped their two bombs and were away into the night.[11]

Indicative of the aggressive spirit Air Vice-Marshal Park encouraged, experiments were made dropping bombs from Spitfires, with rocky little Filfla the target. Despite an attack of diarrhoea, on 29 September, Noel Pashen made six direct hits out of eight bombs dropped, and was regarded as 229's 'bomber boy' for attacks on Sicily. 'A shaky show,' was his opinion of this.[12]

Attacks on land targets by bombers based on Malta had decreased from 87 in the month ending 16 June, to only thirty for the period 16 June to 8 September. There were to be none from then until 3 November. There had been 38 sorties against shipping from mid-June to 8 September, and there would be only five up to 3 November. The island was defending itself, but unable to put much pressure on the enemy. There were only 38 air raid alerts during September, and ten days passed without any alerts at all, while fourteen nights were peaceful. However, the island was still faced with the prospect of surrender through starvation, and what fuel and ammunition had arrived at such great cost in August was strictly rationed. The Axis forces had been held at the El Alamein position in Egypt, and a new General from England, B. L. Montgomery, had taken command of the army. Any resupply convoys to Malta would have to fight their way through like their predecessors.

159

9

Last Lightnings

Malta—October-November 1942

The beginning of October saw a continuation of the quiet period which had lasted through September, though October was later to bring a brief but intense renewal of Axis air attacks. Despite the island being close to starvation and reaching the absolute end of its precious petrol, the defences defeated these attacks.

The Beaufighters were crossing into Sicily, looking for targets, and on 1 and 2 October, Ken 'Red' Gray flew to Castelvetrano and Sciacca each night, bombing and strafing, meeting 'very active return fire' on the second sortie.

On 1 October, a bored Colin Parkinson wrote in his diary, 'Beginning of another month in this God-forsaken hole. I've been here just on four already.' After putting in eleven claims for destroyed or damaged enemy up to the end of July, only one in August and none in September, he was fed-up.[1]

Noel Pashen was employed as the 'bomber boy' of 229 Squadron, dropping two 125-kg bombs on Biscari during a daylight sweep over Sicily on 2 October, but no enemy aircraft were met.[2]

The days and nights passed with standing readiness, no combats, little flying anyway due to shortage of petrol, films, dances, and drinking. Others seemed to be meeting the Germans, and on 4 October he noted that 249 had lost two pilots shot down: 'One, Gass, was shot down straight into the sea; all they could find was his Mae West. Hogarth, a Canadian, was badly shot up, crashed into a house, not expected to live. Hiskens will have to go back to 249.'

Noel Pashen wrote of them that 'they were both damn good lads and I feel a personal loss at their deaths. Sort of puts a damper on otherwise good spirits.'

Meat continued to be scarce, and goats were being killed and passed off as sheep, giving rise to the name 'shoat', a play on 'sh' from sheep and 'oat' from goat. Parkinson noted that the carcase, when cleaned and skinned, was about the size of a starved Pomeranian dog. He returned to the bar, 'to drink, argue and listen to the bindings [grumblings] of other Mess members.'[3]

On 8 October, Parkinson wrote that the squadron thief had been caught red-handed in the captain's cabin of the merchant ship *Melbourne Star*, adding that it was 'a shameful affair', and the man was under close arrest. Then Jimmy Ballentyne arrived 'with the light of battle in his eyes', having just discovered his camera in a second hand shop. It had been sold by the same thief. Noel Pashen also noted the event, and that the thief was 'up the river a la housekow [sic]'.

The officers' dinner menu was questionable soup, bully-beef, cabbage, cheese and coffee. But three senior officers had entertained three women ('floozies' according to Parkinson), with a special dinner in private rooms, at which they consumed asparagus soup, fish, Scotch woodcock, fruit salad and cream, cheese savouries, coffee and cream, with champagne, sherry, gin and whisky.[4]

It was certain that no such supplies had arrived or remained in the ships' cargoes. The nightly trickle of transport and bomber aircraft were one source, and another was the nightfighters, which sometimes flew in to join 89 Squadron, but were searched at once. Any 'goodies' were confiscated, and it was believed that certain senior people, such as the party above, enjoyed the benefits of other people's enterprise. However, what was not discovered was the booty hidden in the wing compartments of the Beaufighters. Dinghys were supposed to be carried in the spaces, and no one in the searching parties thought the crews would be so silly as to leave their dinghys when making over-water flights.

Mervyn Shipard, with Flight Sergeant Doug Oxby as radar operator, had scrambled on 2 October, attempting to catch another of the fast high-flying raiders, but was unable to close with him. On the 5th, he had bombed the airfield at Castelvetrano. Pilot Officer Len Reid and Flight Sergeant Eric Mahar had each been leading patrols and sections of Spitfires as necessary in scrambles, though no contact was made with the enemy.

On 9 October, Parkinson, Wing Commander Arthur Donaldson, and 'Screwball' Beurling flew as a formation and individually over the ceremony for the presentation of the George Cross to the people of Malta. It was perhaps fitting that the presentation took place when it did, as the Luftwaffe was about to launch its final intense period of attacks.

Next morning, leading Blue Section, Parkinson had to return from an early morning scramble when his radio began operating intermittently. He stayed low, at about 1000 feet, listening to the interception. The remaining three aircraft were being directed by the ground controller, using callsign Gondar. Then Pashen's oxygen failed, and he returned, leaving Brough and Reynolds. Spitfire Vb X-V seemed to be a bad-luck aircraft and Noel Pashen had it.

Parkinson heard Brough report enemy aircraft, then Reynolds say they were Spitfires . . . then Reynolds again, calling 'Mayday', then silence. Both returned, though Reynolds had been shot up by a 109. In 185 Squadron, Roscoe had destroyed a Macchi and McElroy a 109, while other enemy were damaged so badly that it was believed they would not reach base. Ju88s had bombed Gozo, killing sixteen people there.[5]

None of the RAAF pilots claimed in the first week of the month, but on 10 October J. G. Sanderson, 249 Squadron, damaged a 109. In the early days of the month, Len Reid, 185 Squadron, had been in four scrambles, with no contact. But the Luftwaffe was gathering for a final series of attacks, and everyone was to be involved in combats. The series of raids began on 11 October, and though relatively large numbers of enemy aircraft attacked, the defences were now far more experienced, numerous and capable.

In day time combats on 11 October, of the RAAF pilots, Len Reid destroyed a 109, and Flying Officer Bob Park, 1435 Squadron, damaged an Re2001. The Spitfires had scrambled to engage 35-plus enemy, reaching 24 000 feet. Below them were a number of 109s. 185 Squadron dived onto them, Reid pulling up under the last two and giving one a single long burst. 'It broke up and crashed into the sea', he wrote in his log-book. Wing Commander Thompson, Sergeant Gore and Reid each claimed one destroyed. Ken Mitchell had scrambled, but been forced to turn back with radio-failure. Also in combat, Flight Sergeant William Knox-William, an Australian in 1435 Squadron, claimed a 109 as damaged.

Colin Parkinson had gone on readiness at 13.00, after ignoring three bombing raids during the night—'I didn't get up to watch'— and listening to another at 07.00, when six Ju88s attacked Takali; two Junkers were shot down.

The squadron was scrambled, but Parkinson's engine cut on take-off, and he had to take cover in the caves while Takali was bombed again. 'The whole air and sides of the shelter shook and vibrated. Went out to investigate when the raid was over. About five bombs had dropped on the drome; didn't make it unserviceable.'

After a second scramble, in which he did not damage any enemy, he took off for a third time at dusk, in a section of four, to intercept bombers. He saw one bomber go down in flames, and watched the display of anti-aircraft, searchlights, bombs and incendiaries, then decided to go and wait over Zonkor Point, to catch a departing bomber. 'I was lucky. I caught a glimpse of one at 10 000 feet, dived in to attack, was fired on by the rear gunner who I put out of action with my first burst. Made two more attacks and finally the Ju88 caught fire. Followed it down to about 1000 feet, lost sight of it while trying to manoeuvre for another attack. It probably dived into the sea.'[6]

Noel Pashen, returning from another test dropping 250-kg bombs, got mixed up with the 88s, but did not claim, though his morale was boosted.[7]

At night, of 89 Squadron, Ken Gray was again plagued by unserviceable radar, but Mervyn Shipard claimed a He111 as a probable on his first scramble, and a second as destroyed on the following sortie. The Heinkel may well have been 6N+HH of 7/KG100, lost at this time.

On 12 October, seven RAAF pilots claimed. E. T. Hiskens, 249 Squadron, destroyed a Ju88, claiming another as a probable but sharing it with Flight Sergeant L De L'ara, and also a 109 as a probable; Len Reid damaged a 109; J. G. Sanderson, 249 Squadron, damaged two 109s; Alan Yates, also 249 Squadron, damaged an 88 and a 109; Parkinson destroyed a 109, damaged a BR20 and shared a probably destroyed Ju88 with Pilot Officer H. T. Nash; Flight Sergeant Knox-William claimed a 109 as a probable and shared damaging a Ju88 with Pilot Officers Lattimer RNZAF and Stewart RAF, but Knox-William was shot down, baled out and was rescued by an air-sea rescue launch. At night, in a head-on contact, Mervyn Shipard destroyed a He111, probably 6N+AH of 5/KG100.

Ken Gray scrambled three times that night, made contact, but each time his radar was jammed and the quarry escaped.

Len Reid, with 185 Squadron, had flown three times during the day. On the first, a large formation of 109s was met at 23 000 feet, and he fired but with no observed result, and on the second flight protected the air-sea rescue launch which picked up three pilots—two Germans and one 'friendly', probably Knox-William. The third scramble was to engage 40-plus, and Ju88s were observed at 10 000 feet. The Spitfires attacked, Reid closed on one and fired, watching the strikes as his rounds and cannon shell struck, then it began smoking, but he could only claim it as damaged.

Sergeant Vinall RAF was missing after this combat, and Ken Mitchell took off alone to search for him, but was unsuccessful. Later Vinall's body was recovered, and buried in the Cappuccini Cemetery. 'We always used to have four aircraft out flying line abreast, or at least two [on a search]', recalled Mitchell, 'but we were so short of aircraft that day I did the flight myself. It was difficult, as you had to watch your tail as well as look. Dinghys were hard to see, and if the sea was choppy you could go right over one and not see it.'8

Parkinson had gone on readiness in the morning, but missed the first interception as his aircraft was unserviceable. When they next took off, he was flying with Wing Commander Arthur Donaldson, and the Wing intercepted a formation of Ju88s and Breda 205s about half way to Sicily. Parkinson dived on a Breda, aimed and fired, but the cannon were silent, only the machineguns working. 'Came back to drome disgusted,' he wrote in his diary.

At about 11.00 they took off to engage another raid, meeting eight Ju88s over the sea, and attacked head-on. 'Long before we were within range the bombers started to panic. I closed to within a few metres, firing head-on, could see shell bursts all over him. Put front gunner out of action, both engines were smoking, he went into a spiral dive. I was attacked by three 109s, one overshot me so I turned into him and gave him a burst, which hit the engine and pilot. The 109 went down in a series of wide barrel rolls, burning and smoking; crashed into the sea. Pilot Officer Nash saw my Junkers smoking like hell with his other engine unserviceable. Squadron Leader Stephen was shot down into the sea, but picked up by rescue launch OK.'

Parkinson noted that 229 and 249 Squadrons 'made a complete

rout of the enemy', adding that he doubted any 88s got back to base, and that the Spitfires had claimed 59 enemy in the past three days, despite enemy numerical superiority, and no Allied pilot had been killed. (He obviously did not know of the loss of Vinall, 185 Squadron.) However, on his flight the very next day, he was to see that the experienced Spitfire units also succumbed to confusion in the face of the enemy.

In a combat during the afternoon, Flight Lieutenant Roscoe was shot down, landing on fire at Takali. Parkinson listed his injuries: 'shot through the shoulder and weak from loss of blood; thrown out of the aircraft unconscious; broken shoulder, probably broken arm, cuts on face; otherwise OK.'[9]

In his diary, Paddy O'Brien RAF, in 185 Squadron, noted the four raids and the claims by the Spitfires for 24 destroyed and 41 damaged, commenting 'Bloody good'. Noel Pashen in 229 Squadron also noted these figures with approval.

The Beaufighter crews of 89 Squadron were quartered in a block of apartments at Sliema, on the northern side of Valletta Harbour. Crews who had been on duty during the night were supposed to sleep during the day, but this was not made easier by the flight path of the raiders, from Sicily to the airfields on Malta, over the top of the apartments. The anti-aircraft battery at nearby Spinola Point added to the din of bomber and fighter engines, cannon and machinegun fire and exploding bombs. Sometimes the bombs were jettisoned into the sea as the Luftwaffe pilots got rid of them early.

During an early morning attack, the crews went out onto the balconys to watch and cheer on the Spitfires. However, the Ju88s began to release their bombs well before reaching their targets, and it became obvious to the 89 Squadron audience that the bombs were going to arrive in their area. There was a general and rapid dispersal to cover, with Ken 'Red' Gray diving for the space under his bed, normally occupied by a large trunk, as bombs began to explode and shake the building.

When quiet returned, he found that he had been beaten into second place by Mervyn Shipard, snugly against the wall. It was this episode that earned Shipard the nickname of 'Slippery Ship'.

Charles Crombie, returning from a bully beef breakfast, had been caught at the door of the building, and with another crew member took cover under the staircase. The other man later reported that Crombie suddenly stood up, shook his fist at yet more falling bombs, shouted, 'You'll never get me on my guts again!' and proceeded to walk up the stairs.[10]

The Luftwaffe maintained pressure, and Hiskens destroyed a Mc202 while Eric Mahar, 185 Squadron, damaged a Ju88. Bill Knox-William, 1435 Squadron, apparently ignoring his dunking the day before, claimed damage to a Ju88. During the night, on an intruder mission to Catania airfield, Charles Crombie destroyed a He111. Ken Gray had gone to Gerbini, and attacked aircraft landing, claiming two He111 damaged, then dropped two 250-kg bombs on the runway.

A dusk raid on Luqa, using low scattered cloud as cover, was pressed home by the Luftwaffe. The Germans came in just as the old rickety bus had delivered the crews for 89 Squadron's Beaufighters. Charles Crombie and Ken Gray decided to go to the main dispersal shelter, but on arrival were delayed from entering by a crowd who wanted to stand around outside and watch the action. A Ju88 was passing overhead, trailing a stick of bombs, and Ken Gray saw the final bomb coming for them. He and Crombie were literally blown down the stairway to land on a heap of men and women who had all learned a lesson about curiosity. Fortunately, no one was injured seriously.[11]

Parkinson was promoted to Flight Lieutenant, and took command of A Flight 229 Squadron. There had been seven raids during the night, and the number of enemy planes claimed shot down since the beginning of hostilities over Malta reached 1000. In his diary, he noted that Pilot Officer Alan Yates had been shot down, crashing into the squadron armoury, but 'pilot OK', and 'Turner crash-landed, engine trouble, pilot OK'.

Parkinson scrambled at about 16.00, and the formation climbed to 20 000 feet, when they 'were all disorganised by someone screaming "Break!" Spits in odd pairs all over the sky. Never heard so much panic nattering and shouting in all my life. Said some extremely rude things to some pilot who kept shouting "Break". Nash shot 88 down; saw Squadron Leader Stephen shoot a fighter down; Dusty Miller had bullet through his wing; Ballantyne crash-landed, shot up by 109s, he was OK; Wingco crashlanded, shot up, he was OK; Squadron Leader Wicks is missing; 126 at Luqa has lost a number of pilots.'[12]

In an effort to get a little ahead of the Germans, it was decided that the Beaufighter crews would go to their aircraft earlier than had been done previously, so they could catch the dusk raiders when the Spitfires would normally be landing. But the Luftwaffe also came early, and the 89 Squadron crews were running to their aircraft as bombs were dropping. Red Gray was blast-assisted up the entrance ladder into his plane, and Mervyn Mould, his operator, went into a bomb crater, but managed to catch the Beau as it was taxying, complaining to Gray about having 'to jump onto a moving bus' as they raced off down the runway ahead of a stick of bombs. Gray was quite impressed by the determination of the attack on Luqa at that time.[13]

Mervyn Shipard destroyed a He111, possibly 6N+EH of 5/KG100, during the night. He had scrambled and chased a fast enemy back to Sicily, breaking off as the radar was not to be flown over enemy territory, and then noticed that the starboard engine instruments showed no oil pressure and the temperature 'was off the clock. I pulled that engine back, there was no feathering, and set course for Malta.'

Control called to say they had another bandit, and he replied that he was on one engine and returning to base. Suddenly, Oxby called, 'Skippy, I've got a contact, he's coming straight for you, about 4000 feet below!'

Shipard waited for Oxby to call at the moment to turn, and then rolled the big fighter almost on to its back, with both engines pulled back, and saw the enemy below. Even without engines the heavy Beaufighter was quickly speeding onto the raider, and Oxby called that they were going too fast, so Shipard dropped wheels and flaps and came 'screaming in to this chap, and when I was almost on him he started to climb and that's all I wanted, pulled back on the stick and opened fire. He blew up and we flew through the rubbish; all over the aeroplane. I opened up the other engine. Oxo yelled out that we were on fire. It was German petrol.'

Oxby had picked up the Heinkel at 15 000 feet, and seen Shipard close in to thirty metres, fire, and 'the thing blew up! That was the most exciting evening of the whole war, as far as I was concerned.'[14]

Also ignited was the oil and grease on the Beaufighter's exposed undercarriage, but it soon burned off, and Shipard retracted flaps and undercarriage and returned to base. Apart from a little

167

scorching, the only damage was a few panels of fabric burned from the rudder and elevators.

Ken Gray had scrambled three times during the night, on the first contacting a Ju87 which was spiralling down, but the Beaufighter radar fused at 1000 feet, which allowed the Stuka to escape. On the second sortie he and Sergeant Mould, his radar operator, made contact but the radar was jammed, and on the third scramble he was brought in twice for visual contact, but the enemy escaped, diving and successfully evading below them.

One of Gray's flights had started as a test flight, with a passenger, an Australian officer from one of the merchant ships. However, when the enemy appeared, the test became an interception, lasting 90 minutes, most of it at 17 000 feet, and the mariner was dressed only in simple short-sleeved shirt and shorts. Despite being blue with cold, he insisted to Gray that being bombed was nothing to standing in the unheated fuselage listening to the radio messages passing between Gray and the ground station. He invited 'Red' Gray back to the ship, and next night entertained him 'right royally'.[15]

Then, for the fourth successive day, the Luftwaffe and Regia Aeronautica returned. Colin Parkinson commented that the monotony had been broken by the new series of attacks, and again wrote that the Ju88s did not like head-on attacks, and had turned back several times. He estimated that about three of each Junkers formation of six or nine were shot down on each occasion. He also recorded that Messerschmitt 109s were being used as bombers.

The combats had not been one-sided, and the Germans had inflicted losses on the island defenders. They were no respecters of rank, and Wing Commander Arthur Donaldson, wing leader at Takali, was wounded on 14 October, losing three fingers from a hand and having wounds to his feet when a cannon shell exploded in the cockpit. Parkinson recorded this, then listed the casualties in the squadron: Pilot Officer Nash shot down, bailed out, broken jaw; Sergeant Bryden bailed out, broken leg; Sergeant Sandy bailed out, OK; Sergeant Miller bailed out. He was told that he had been recommended for the DFC, noting that he had twice been recommended for the DFM, but nothing had so far resulted. On 14 October, he claimed a Mc202 destroyed.[16]

The Pashen jinx returned, and Noel found his harness unfastened as they were attacking a bunch of Ju88s, a 'bad show.' He was unable to claim any hits, and X-V was hit in the tail.[17]

In the recent intense actions, 'Screwball' Beurling destroyed a Ju88 and damaged two 109s, but was himself shot down and wounded. They were his last victories over Malta, bringing his score of destroyed to 28. There is some disagreement over his exact score, figures varying between 29 and 31.33, including victories over France before and after his Malta tour.

During the day, Bill Knox-William had been shot down and killed. He was 26 years old.

Len Reid had flown twice, with combats each time. On the first scramble, the Spitfires were attacked by 109s, and in what he described as 'quite a do', he damaged a 109. On the second, the 109s again attacked the Spitfires, and 'after a hectic two or three minutes got ourselves sorted out. Saw three 109s diving on Spits below, gave the last one a good burst from a quarter-astern and it hit the sea. After breaking away, got in a good burst at a Ju88 from below; observed strikes under the belly.'

Later in the day, in an eight-aircraft scramble led by Major Swales SAAF, Eric Mahar destroyed a Ju88 in an attack from astern. The citation for his DFM mentioned this action in particular, plus general reference to his other victories and activity in the squadron.

On 15 October, E. T. Hiskens was killed in action, while Eric Mahar destroyed a Mc202, and J. G. Sanderson an 88 as a probable, while Alan Yates, with Pilot Officer A. B. Stead, shared yet another 88 as a probable.

Len Reid scrambled, the enemy reported as 60-plus, and again the Spitfires were attacked by the 109s, 'before we could get at the 88s. After bags of action we got ourselves sorted out. [I had] no luck.'

Noel Pashen, collecting X-V from the repair shop, got into the action, claiming hits on an Re2001. He scrambled again later, but his old eye troubles returned, and though he fired at three separate 109s could not claim any hits.[18]

Next day, Len Reid claimed another Ju88 probably destroyed, when flying as Bullet Red 3, in EP343 'X', to Wing Commander Thompson. Seventy-plus enemy were reported, and the squadron managed to get above them, to 21 000 feet. Below, at 17 000 were the Ju88s, and the whole squadron half-rolled and dived on them. Speed built up quickly, and Reid was going so fast that he was unable to see the results of his first burst, then the 88s swung left, and he almost rammed one, but swung around on to the tail of another, and began firing at 200 metres dead astern, closing to less than 15 metres, watching the cannon and machinegun strikes flicker along the top of the bomber. 'When I left [it] was smoking badly and rapidly losing height about 8 km from Grand Harbour.'[19]

Colin Parkinson, 229 Squadron, had not been on readiness during the morning of the 16th, and observed several raids during which he saw or was told that some 88s and 109s were destroyed. He noted in his diary that Pilot Officer Reynolds was badly shot up but managed to land with wheels down, and that Sergeant Lundy had to bail out but was picked up OK. He added that 'We shall need reinforcements soon; very short of pilots.'

When he did scramble, leading Blue Section, the Squadron leader's radio failed, so Parkinson assumed command of the wing formation. 'We made head-on attacks at about seven Ju88s. I very nearly collided with one on my right side, saw strikes along [its] wings, both engines and cockpit, starboard engine cowling came off.' While this had been going on, bomb-carrying Messerschmitt 109s had attacked the airfield, scoring some hits. For the second time, 'Dusty' Miller was shot up.[20]

Len Reid also flew three more scrambles that day, but the bombers did not come on across the waters, and the 109s which were seen could not be engaged. That night Charles Crombie destroyed a Ju88 on the ground while strafing the airfield at Catania. Mervyn Shipard was scrambled, but the aircraft became unserviceable.

As well as being active in the air, Parkinson had been busy in the Squadron Mess life. He had been elected Messing Officer, and decided to use his position to investigate various illegal activities involving food and cigarettes from the airmen's and officers' messes. He wrote that food 'in the Mess has improved 100%. I have been sticking my nose into the Messing affairs and the bar, much to various people's annoyance.'

He was on dawn readiness on 17 October, and they took off for an unsuccessful interception at 08.00. When the next scramble was ordered, the Squadron commander's aircraft was unserviceable, so Parkinson led the formation. He would later recall the morning and the sight of the approaching enemy as one of his most vivid memories of the Malta campaign. The sky was clear and still, the air clear, and the formations seemed to hang peacefully suspended in the sunlight. It was almost possible to forget the warlike purpose of attack and defence. Then in an instant it was shattered as the combat began.

The cumulative pressure of the day-after-day combats was beginning to tell, and some of the pilots were tired and nervous. Parkinson noted that some of them had 'the twitch, and I had a hard job to keep them together. Someone spoilt my interception of Ju88s by breaking down across the squadron. Managed to get them all together again and dive to attack. 109s shadowed us all the way in. Attacked bombers and fighter escort. I shot a 109 down; pilot bailed out. Hell of a mix up for a minute or two; sky was full of blokes who had bailed out. Saw various aircraft in flames and diving into the sea.'

As he was preparing to land, with wheels and flaps down, bombs began to explode near the airfield, and he looked up to see 'three 109s going like bats out of hell.' He retracted wheels and flaps and chased them out to sea but could not catch them.

Then he saw Dusty Miller in his parachute, so circled him, but three 109s swung in for an attack on the lone Spitfire. Parkinson turned into the 109s, fired and missed, and they kept on going. Miller descended into the sea, Parkinson guided an air-sea rescue launch to him, then escorted the launch until he had to return to land. He finished the mission with ten gallons [45 litres] of petrol in his tanks.[21]

Later he found that the pilot under the parachute had not been Miller, but a German; Miller was missing. In other actions, Len Reid, 185 Squadron, claimed a 109 probable, and Bob Park claimed two Ju88s and a Bf109 all as damaged.

On the night of 18 October, Ken Gray, with Sergeant Moss as his operator, scrambled twice. They first obtained a visual sighting of a Ju88, which was nose down for home and going too fast for them. Then they found a He111 which successfully evaded them. On the second scramble, the enemy was too high, and they had to give up the chase when actually over Sicily.[22]

Mervyn Shipard, with Flight Sergeant Oxby, in X7777, was scrambled and directed on to a bandit, but soon found he had no hope of catching it, as the enemy sped away at a true air speed of 480 knots, going flat out for Sicily. This was Shipard's last interception over Malta. He had flown a total of 102 times, of which 41 were scrambles or other operational sorties. On nine of these he had suffered unserviceable equipment of one sort or another. He had destroyed six enemy bombers confirmed, and probably destroyed one other.

Basically, he had been satisfied with his time on the island. 'Malta was a good spot,' he recalled. 'I enjoyed it.' He had one bad memory. 'The food. Jesus, I got sick of bully beef three times a day, but apart from that it was a good life. There was always something to do.'[23]

Douggie Oxby later went on to become the most successful radar operator of the Allied air forces, receiving a DSO, DFC, DFM and Bar. Of the Australians who flew with him in 89 Squadron, Oxby later said, they were 'competent, proud to be Australian, loyal to Britain and to the squadron. They used to talk about Australians as undisciplined. They were wild, yes, undisciplined, no. Ship, I felt safe flying with him. Red Gray was very kind. John Ross was known as the local bad boy, I can't recall any reason, but he was. Chico Crombie was the salt of the earth, very loyal, very proud of his country and proud of the job he had to do.'[24]

Everyone on the islands at the time suffered from lack of food, but some recollections are coloured by the situation. Eric Mahar had scrambled one day before the food was brought around, and so had missed it. He was really hungry as the day drew on, there was nothing to eat, so he asked one of the ground crew to find something. The airman came back with two ration biscuits which had a slice of bully beef between them, and Mahar recalled it as 'the best meal I ever had.'[25]

The food, or lack of it, also remained in other people's memories. John Ross and other members of the squadron detachment returned to Egypt on 23 September, were given leave, and set off to get the biggest meal obtainable. But after one course, no one could eat any more. Their stomachs had shrunk after a diet of bully beef and one slice of bread three times a day. Ross had lost eight kilos in weight. He felt compassion for the Maltese population, who were also starving, and suffering the effects of the bombing campaign.

Cigarettes were in great demand, and Ross was able to get

some from a friend. He met a Czech pilot he had been on the same squadron with in England; the Czech was now doing a mail run to Gibraltar and back. He asked Ross if there was anything he could bring back for him, and got the immediate reply, 'Yes, cigarettes.'

Two nights later, the Czech appeared at the dispersal hut, saying, 'Johnny, I bring you 15,000 cigarettes.' Ross recalled that within half an hour it was nearly impossible to see inside the hut for smoke.[26]

On 18 October, 185 Squadron scrambled, and again were jumped by 109s. Len Reid, in EP343 'X', broke left and came in behind and above one of the fleet Messerschmitts, fired 'a good squirt' and saw strikes and flashes over the cockpit canopy and engine. He claimed the 109 as probably destroyed; it was his last combat, as in his final four scrambles to 25 October the fast bomb-carrying 109s could not be caught.[27]

The Axis units had been unable to absorb the recent losses for such small results, and the intensity of their attacks slackened. Parkinson noted the lack of Ju88s, and their replacement with fleet bomb-carrying 109s, who made five or six attacks each day. In addition, the night bombing had lessened. People were posted out of the squadrons, and replacements arrived. Paddy O'Brien noted the losses to 185 Squadron in his diary: Bruce, shot down, paddled home; McLeod, killed; Tarbuck, baled out, died of injuries; Vinall, killed; Lindsay, killed. The squadron daily log also reported that Sergeant Garvey crashed on landing, after being damaged in combat, and was admitted to hospital with light injuries; Sergeant Saunders, killed in action.[28]

On 19 October, Charles Crombie was writing a letter to his wife, when the alarm went. He did not stop writing, but described the raid as he witnessed it: 'I believe the Huns are coming after this drome—our AA has just started. Two of our chaps are up. I am having a spell today. I wrecked my plane last night. Taking off in an air raid I ran into a bomb hole. No one hurt but we had to leave the plane in the hole all sort of broken up and walk back to dispersal with bombs and things all over the place. Awful noise.

'Here come the Huns now. A screen of Me109s. Our Spits are with them, but nothing much has happened yet. Here are all the bombers now. Eight Junkers 88, as far as I can see, in close formation about 15 000 feet, 109s all around them. Think there were 40 or 50 109s, perhaps more, there seem to be planes everywhere. The 88s are still in formation and are just starting to open up and dive on the drome now. One has been hit, a Spit got him and one engine is on fire. Two of the crew have bailed out. Christ, here are the bombs also. I think they will miss.

'They did, fell on the other end of the drome. The 88 that was hit has just hit the ground and blown up about a mile from here. Three of the crew are coming down in parachutes. No sign of the other one. Still planes everywhere. A fighter coming down now. Spinning like hell, a Spit. The bombers have split up now and are coming back to attack singly. Another fighter has been hit and blown up in the air. Another bomber coming down burning like hell. He's blown up. Will finish this later.

'Sorry, I couldn't take it, got down into a hole. An air raid is really worth watching if the bombs don't come too close. I'm not sure what the Hun lost or what we lost, but none of our squadron planes were damaged on the drome. A bomb set alight to a plane next to one of ours, but a couple of us got ours taxied away in time.'

Later in that letter he added, 'Sorry there is nothing really interesting to write about, but I'm afraid we live an awfully groovie sort of life. This would be an awful dump if there were no work.'[29]

Heavy rain accomplished what the Luftwaffe could not, putting Takali out of commission on 20 and 21 October.

On the 21st, Noel Pashen was stood down from flying for medical reasons. He had made 47 flights from Malta, and his flying hours were now 284, some 38 more than on arrival. He would remain on Malta until 6 December, flying a PRU Spitfire to Egypt before reporting for further medical treatment. In 1943 he went to 601 Squadron and flew with it for a year in the North African, Sicilian and Italian campaigns.[30]

J. G. Sanderson destroyed a Mc202 on 22 October. The same day, Mervyn Shipard, Beaufighter pilot in 89 Squadron, left Malta for Egypt. He would finish the war with a score of thirteen enemy destroyed. Going to Gibraltar were Ken Mitchell and Eric Mahar. With two other pilots, they were to lead more reinforcement flights from Gibraltar, on HMS *Furious*. On 29 October, they each led sections which made the flight from the carrier deck to Malta independently of each other.

As Mahar and Mitchell were leaving the island, rain began to fall. 'It was the first rain we'd seen,' recalled Mitchell. 'We were short of drinking water, as the underground water reservoirs had been damaged in the bombing.'

The members of the flight had collected what money was available, and the two were to bring back from Gibraltar all the cigarettes, chocolate and similar that they could acquire. This was to be packed into the ammunition boxes in the wings. The supply situation on the island was still precarious, and events such as the fly-in of a batch of fighters was used to cram a few items in demand into the few suitable places in a Spitfire. (Len Reid expressed surprise that tobacco had taken precedence over ammunition in a combat zone, remarking righteously that he was always a non-smoker. Mahar and Clewley remained unmoved.)

They enjoyed their week away from Malta, duly bought up all the luxuries they could, and stacked them in the wing boxes of a Spitfire flown by a pilot who would accompany them. The fighters were prepared on the carrier deck, and they began to fly-off.

When running up the engines before take-off, Mahar found that one magneto was losing revs. The organisers immediately ordered another pilot out of his Spitfire, and Eric into that cockpit. There was not time to transfer the personal kit and other items Mahar had put into his Spitfire. 'I had to *go*, change aircraft and *go*'.

When flying to Malta in May, from the USS *Wasp*, the flights had not been allowed to cut across Tunisia, but this time they did so, turning at Sfax. Despite recent events in the war, the situation was still serious, and 'the enemy had control of the Mediterranean, apart from where we were.' They flew back without interception, in what Ken Mitchell described as a routine flight. But when they arrived over the island, they were astounded. 'When we came back, it was like having a schizophrenic nightmare. The island we knew so well had turned green. From a chalk, dry, stony, barren island to a green island.'

But the replacement pilot in the Spitfire packed with good things had somehow managed to land at another airfield, and 'we lost all the valuable booty . . .'[31]

Noel Pashen watched two Bf109 fighter-bomber raids on Takali on 25 October, and saw a 109 lose a wing, spin into the ground

175

and burn. 'It was rather gruesome seeing the pilot roasted, but one gets used to death.'[32]

On that day, in 229 Squadron, Colin Parkinson's Section was bounced, but did not suffer damage, and the 109s sped on their way. Other people were not so fortunate, and Parkinson noted that Milligan was in hospital with leg wounds, Goodyear had been hit in the wing, and Reynolds from 126 Squadron was shot down and missing. Parkinson damaged a 109 (or Mc202), and later bounced another formation who successfully evaded the attack.

He had begun remarking on his hoped-for imminent return to England, but continued to record his impressions of daily life on Malta. Quick raids by the 109s continued, and scrambles were ordered to catch them, with engagements and losses to both sides. On 29 October, Sergeant Walter Parkes, RAAF, in 229 Squadron with Parkinson, was killed when his wingtip clipped the steam-roller and the Spitfire—EP329—flicked sideways into a nearby aircraft revetment.

Noel Pashen and Parkes had been good friends through training, the flight to Malta and in 229 Squadron, and had been in the same flight for a time. 'I was told that Wally had pranged on take-off and was in hospital,' wrote Pashen. 'It was worse than that. He did not regain consciousness and died only an hour or so later. That broke me up, for the Kid and I had been together right through this and his loss, as far as I am concerned, is very great. He was a good flyer and well thought of by everyone.'[33]

Soon after, Pilot Officer Giddings crashed after hitting a truck, breaking his arm and wrist; two Maltese were killed. Then the 109 was shot down, crashed near the eastern dispersal area, and burned. Parkinson commented that the pilot was quite young.

On 31 October, Colin Parkinson farewelled the contingent of wounded flying out to Gibraltar. 'Wingco Donaldson with his arm in a sling and minus three fingers, a stick in his other hand, shot in the foot. "Screwball" Beurling on crutches with his foot and leg in plaster. Roscoe looking very pale with his arm in a sling and a scar on his forehead. The sight of all these blokes and cripples ought to shake some of the reinforcement pilots in Gib. Bryden is still in hospital with his leg in a bad way. A cannon shell hit it and exploded inside. Will be very lucky if he doesn't lose it. Milligan has a badly shot-up leg also. Giddings has a shattered wrist and arm.'[34]

Along with the wounded were several women and children, and six Australians; Fred Clewley, Eric Mahar, Ken Mitchell, Len Reid, Richardson and Alan Yates. Altogether, there were some forty passengers and crew in the hull of the big bomber, and they made themselves comfortable wherever possible. Left behind, and somewhat disgruntled, were a number of Army officers who had been displaced to make room for the tour-expired fighter pilots.

November 1942

The month began with tragic news: the Liberator taking the wounded and other evacuees to Gibraltar had crashed, killing some of the passengers. Arriving at Gibraltar in a thunderstorm, short of fuel, the pilot touched down on the runway too far along to either halt the big aircraft or make a take-off. He pulled it into the air to avoid the fence, and stalled.

Ken Mitchell: 'At Gibraltar the strip ran across the causeway, and they'd extended both ends but packed the sides with aircraft for the North African landing, and they were fully laden with fuel. The whole thing was a time bomb ready to go off if anyone crashed. When the pilot found he'd overshot there was no nonsense such as ground-looping; he tried to take off again and stalled off the runway, crashed into the sea beyond.'

The passengers were not strapped in, but sitting anywhere comfortable. They were thrown forward, along with their belongings, as the bomber sank to the seabed. Only twenty of the 34 passengers survived, among them Arthur Donaldson and Beurling. The Canadian is said to have had a premonition of disaster, and had deliberately picked a place near the escape hatch, through which he left the bomber. In the darkness, people clambered or swam out of the wreckage. The fuselage, as usual with B24 ditchings, had broken at the bomb-bay, and some of those nearby were able to escape through this gap; others went out of the side hatches.

Eric Mahar went out through the bottom, the bomb-bay, then scrambled up onto the starboard wing and began helping people up onto it. Someone threw him a doll, which he briefly wondered at, then realised it was a dead baby. He had suffered compressed

177

vertebrae, a fractured ankle, concussion and bruises. Alan Yates had damaged his tongue, which swelled so that he could hardly talk intelligibly when the survivors met later.

Mahar saw Len Reid looking out the gap in the fractured fuselage, and watched him come out from there, joining him on the wing. Fred Clewley also went out through the bomb-bay, saw Ken Mitchell in the water, and they swam together, then decided to swim ashore. Boats were coming out to the crash to assist the people there.

Len Reid had only a small cut on the arm. Working from the starboard wing, the survivors pulled up Eddie Glazebrook RAF, who was already dead.

The Australians were lucky; they all survived with small or minor injuries, such as a cut arm, or compressed vertebrae; they all went back to flying status. All their kit was lost, and this later retarded their careers in the RAAF, as log-books and endorsements were gone. Len Reid was the fortunate exception. He normally carried his log-book and photo album in a small haversack, which floated ashore, all being returned to him in the UK some three months later.

Among those killed was Williams, 'Willy the Kid', who had flown with Tim Goldsmith and the others, and survived the fiercest days of the siege, only to die at the very threshold of safety. The Army officers who had so resented being left off the flight were naturally quite pleased to have been removed from the list, and rejoiced at their luck.

'After the crash,' said Ken Mitchell, 'I was in the same [hospital] room as the Liberator pilot. I had an injured knee and he had minor injuries; we were talking away. [The authorities at Malta] said it was up to him if he accepted the manifest. They said, "you are overloaded, they are the wives of British artillerymen who were there and they'd been having a hard time, with the children; if you want to put them off here, where their lives are at stake, that's your business." He accepted them.

'One of the girls killed was the daughter of a parliamentarian, who wanted to bring it up in Parliament, to get some sort of retribution or revenge. He advertised for people to contact him, but none of us pilots did, as we did not consider it was the pilot's fault.'

Ken Mitchell and Len Reid flew back to the UK in a C47,

fellow passengers with several Royal Navy Admirals. Arriving with nothing but the clothes they stood in, Mitchell and Reid were looked after by Lady Bruce, wife of the Australian High Commissioner, who was in charge of the Comforts Fund. She knitted a pair of socks for Len Reid, despite the calls on her time.

Fred Clewley found himself in hospital again, along with George Beurling. When they recovered, they were passengers on the same aircraft to England. Fred had now two crashes in succession, and awaited the landing on this third flight with some interest. Beurling took a direct interest in the matter, and as the aircraft approached the airfield, pulled out his pistol and called to the pilot, 'If I don't like your approach . . .'[35]

From Sicily, the Luftwaffe continued to send Messerschmitt 109 fighter-bombers, with other 109s as escorts, to attack Malta. The defences sent the fighters up, but few engagements were made. The only Australian to add to his score was Charles Crombie, with four claims: 7—8 November, on an intruder mission to Castelvetrano, a Ju88 destroyed; 26 November, a scramble resulted in a claim for a Ju88 probable; 17—18 December, again over Castelvetrano, two Ju52 destroyed.

But not all Crombie's engagements were with the Axis. On 15 October, after a scramble, while being guided on to the enemy at 20 000 feet, his Beaufighter was hit by the Malta anti-aircraft fire. Then, on a convoy patrol on 28 December he 'was shot at and hit by the Royal Navy. Most impressive.' On 3 December he flew from Malta to Heliopolis, ending his detachment on the island. He had flown 160 hours since his arrival in September.[36]

Ken Gray was maintaining his maritime contacts, and when some of the officers from the destroyer HMS *Javelin* visited Luqa, he found that the First Lieutenant was an Australian. Again, a flight in a Beaufighter was exchanged for an invitation to visit the ship, moored in Sliema Creek, Valletta. The dinner and party in the wardroom was unforgettable for Gray, particularly as the Navy arranged for him to remain aboard that night. When time came to retire, he was led up and down ladders, around corners, through hatches, to test his ability to navigate after a Royal Navy party. Next morning he found his cabin was only ten paces around the corner from the Wardroom.

On another occasion, he was asked to attend the Luqa Officers' Mess, and on arrival was surprised to be told that whatever he drank would be 'on the Mess', an unheard of event in any mess on Malta at the time. However, he was to earn this largesse by entertaining a captured Ju88 pilot, whose unit had recently moved to the Mediterranean from the Russian Front; Intelligence was eager for the background to this move. It was hoped that after a few drinks with a fellow pilot, the German would become talkative. The party, Gray recalled, was a roaring success from the point of view of two pilots, but seemed to have little value as an Intelligence exercise. The ability of pilots, of either side, to establish rapport and respect despite the war impressed the Intelligence officers, who even agreed that the bar bill was worth it![37]

Noel Pashen was still waiting to leave the island, and noted the casualties in 229 Squadron: 15 November, Sergeant Roberts killed; 21st, Kid Lindy killed when spinning off an upward roll; 23rd, Sergeant Wallace baled out, seen getting into his dinghy but not found again; 28th, Flight Sergeant Edwards lost, flying the reciprocal course of his homing; 30th, Sergeant Wendt killed over Sicily; 1st December, Pilot Officer Mowbray lost near Sicily. By 2 December, seven of the twelve who flew to Malta with him in a formation group had been killed; of the 32 in the batch of reinforcements only four were still flying, all the others having been killed or posted.[38]

While in hindsight it is obvious that the Axis air attacks had been held, and the Luftwaffe and Regia Aeronautica could no longer accept the losses inflicted by the island defences, this was by no means clear to all on Malta then. It was known that many enemy had been shot down and damaged, but this had happened before, and who was to know that there would not be another onslaught.

Losses attacking the island were one thing, and the successful passage of convoys with food, fuel and munitions was another. All convoys in 1942 had been attacked with ferocity, and shipping losses had been extremely heavy. The island was still in desperate straits as far as rationing was concerned. On 10 November, Colin Parkinson noted that rations had been cut and now were 9 oz bread, 6 oz of other food, 2 oz fried fish, 'and about four dog biscuits.'[39]

There was little day contact, but the nightfighters were active, flying out to the routes used by the enemy in the hours of darkness to airlift supplies from Italy to North Africa, where the El Alamein battles were raging. On 12 November, Parkinson noted that the Beaufighters shot down six 'Hun troop carriers off Linosa', and on the 13th wrote that the Beaufighters had 'bumped about 60 Hun aircraft of different types. They shot down seven, probably destroyed four more and damaged ten others.'

Soon afterwards, Colin Parkinson left Malta, having lodged 22 claims, for nine enemy destroyed, three probables, eight damaged, and sharing in the confirmed destruction and probable destruction of two others.[40]

As noted by Parkinson, the Beaufighters had another successful day on 13 November, when 227 Squadron intercepted sixteen Ju52s and thirty S81s. Robert Wills RAAF was hit in the ankle by return fire, and had to break off, with his navigator flying back to Malta, where Wills made a safe landing. He was later evacuated to the UK.

Flying Officer Bob Park RAAF was killed on 19 November in a flying accident. He baled out over the sea, but was drowned before he could be picked up by a destroyer. His friends thought he was safe, and were deeply saddened by the news. Along with other young Australians from the Gallipoli campaign, and aircrew from 1941-42, he was buried on Malta. Tony Boyd, Gordon Tweedale, and Walter Parkes also rest there. The tragedy of Bob Park's death was felt particularly by his mother, as he was the last of that branch of the family. His father and sister had died just before the war. After the war, Mrs Park travelled to Malta to visit her son's grave, and to make a donation of several thousand pounds to assist in reconstruction on the island. Having done that, and seen the island Bob Park had died defending, with little money remaining, Mrs Park returned to Australia.

The intruders continued to range far afield, and on 5 December, Red Gray was tasked to attack Regio de Calabria in southern Italy, after photo reconnaissance had detected a concentration of Ju52s there. Obviously the aircraft were to be used that night to fly men and materials to Africa. To assist him, a Fleet Air Arm Swordfish was to drop flares while Red made his attacks across the parked Junkers. Along with Mervyn Mould as radar operator, Corporal Harris went along for the ride. Harris was an artist, and stood behind Gray during the attacks, sketching his impressions for later paintings. Gray went on to other airfields near Mount Etna, but the defences were waiting. The flak and other ground fire made the sky light enough to read by, and it was obvious that the attack on Regio de Calabria had alerted the other bases.[41]

On 17 December, Charles Crombie flew an intruder mission to western Sicily and came upon Ju52s taking off from Castelvetrano. He destroyed two which were taking off, putting a temporary halt to reinforcement operations for Rommel. After returning to Malta, he flew to Tunisia, to harass the railway at Tunis.

That night, Red Gray had flown three times, two scrambles and an intruder to Pantelleria and Sicily, with no result. The third sortie, a scramble to intercept low-flying Ju52s, was unsuccessful as the targets were too low. Red left Malta for Egypt on 24 December 1942, two years after receiving his wings in Canada. He had flown a total of 37 operational sorties, totalling 77.5 operational hours during the detachment to Malta.[42]

At the end of December, the 89 Squadron detachment left Malta, having seen the entire character of the air war change from defensive interceptions to an active seeking out of the enemy wherever he might be within range of the Beaufighters. During its time on Malta, the detachment destroyed 59 enemy aircraft, probably destroyed seven and damaged another eight. The RAAF pilots had contributed 13-3-2 of these.

(On 10 January, 89 Squadron despatched crews to India, to counter the Japanese raids there. On 19 January Crombie, still with Moss as his radar operator, engaged a formation of four Japanese bombers flying in bright moonlight. The Japanese gunners shot out one of Crombie's engines, and the Beaufighter caught fire, but he went into the attack, shooting down two, and possibly three, before baling out when the wingtank exploded. He had told Moss to bale out after the first Japanese was destroyed. They both survived and were decorated, Crombie receiving an immediate DSO. Red Gray was also airborne, and witnessed the action. Four nights earlier, he had witnessed Flight Sergeant Pring engage and destroy three Japanese bombers. There were no further such attacks.)

Gradually the RAAF fighter pilots left the island as the normal service rotation of personnel continued. Some returned to Australia and a variety of flying or staff jobs there, while others remained

182

in the European theatre. Their time on Malta would be indelibly engraved on their memories.

The Axis forces were now forced to fight on two fronts along the North African shore, in the west against the US-British invasion and in the east against Montgomery's 8th Army. Resupply to both fronts became a deadly burden, and the campaign ended on 8 May 1943, with the complete surrender of German and Italian forces in Africa.

Malta was used as an offensive base during these operations, but perhaps its greatest moment came when, after the invasion of Sicily and Italy, and the capitulation of the Fascist regime, the Italian fleet sailed into Grand Harbour in September 1943 and surrendered. The long siege was over.

As a base for collection of priceless signals intelligence and for attacks on Axis naval and merchant ships, Malta had played a pivotal role in the Mediterranean campaigns, and by standing firm during the crucial months of 1942, had tilted the balance in favour of Allied victory.

The RAF fighter squadrons on Malta had made a peerless contribution to that victory by flying, and continuing to fly, against all odds.

10

Australia

While the Australians in the United Kingdom and the Mediterranean were engaged in the campaigns and battles of 1942, in the South West Pacific the Japanese had only narrowly been defeated in several crucial actions north of Australia. Several Australian towns and locations were attacked by Japanese aircraft, with Darwin receiving most attention. After some pressure was applied from Australia, it was agreed by Prime Minister Winston Churchill that Spitfires would be provided for the defence of Darwin. As well as RAF personnel, experienced Australian pilots from the UK would be posted to this force. Several of the RAAF fighter pilots who had served on Malta would be involved in further combats over Darwin, and so this account of those actions is included in this book. Most of the Malta veterans described previously went to 452 Squadron at Darwin.

452 Squadron, Darwin

The squadrons of Spitfires deployed to the Darwin area to counter the Japanese attacks found operating conditions difficult. The airfield construction programme had begun only since the war began, and accommodation for men and machines was primitive. The major urban centres with the network of businesses and organisations so necessary to modern warfare were over 3500 km away to the south and east, with a poorly developed patchwork of towns, roads and some railways between those cities and Darwin. Everything was in short supply, including spare engines, which were soon to be needed because of the dusty environment.

Popularly called the 'Churchill Wing', the Spitfires formed No. 1 (Fighter) Wing RAAF, and were supported by 44 Radar Wing and 61 Works Wing. After disbandment in the UK, the squadrons were re-formed in January 1943, and moved from the 'civilised' south east region to the north west.

The Wing comprised 54 Squadron RAF, which already claimed over 130 enemy aircraft destroyed during the war, 452 Squadron RAAF, which had been formed in the UK and had seen service in Europe, and 457 Squadron RAAF. 457 had seen comparatively little operational activity in Europe, compared with the other two squadrons. Among the 95 pilots in the Wing were several aces, and 37 with operational experience of varying degrees.

In January 1943, 452 Squadron recorded the arrival of Goldsmith, Bisley, Mathews, Ferguson and Hutchinson, with brief details of their training and operational careers. Goldsmith was credited with 12.25 enemy destroyed and seven damaged, Bisley with six and one damaged.

After the settling-in period, there was some boredom as the Japanese made few appearances, though on 6 February Flight Lieutenant Bob Foster, 54 Squadron, destroyed a Mitsubishi Ki-46 'Dinah' reconnaissance aircraft. The Ki-46 Dinah was one of the outstanding reconnaissance aircraft of its time, the Model II having a speed of 375 mph at 19 000 feet (604 km/h at 5800 metres) and a range of 1540 miles (2474 km). However, the Japanese were about to begin a bombing campaign against the Darwin area, using both Army and Navy units.

7 Repair and Salvage Squadron, under Fying Officer Campbell, was formed specifically for operations in the Darwin area with the Spitfires. The squadron sailed by Liberty ship to Darwin and settled into Pell Strip, which it shared with 4 RSU. As well as establishing a camp in the virgin bush, the squadron had to cope with the task of Spitfire serviceability, which was 'a real problem.' Flight Lieutenant S. O'Connor was an Engineering Officer, and recalled that many parts were not available in Australia, but this problem was partly solved by the old methods of salvage and swapping items from one aircraft to another.

As flying training and operations increased, 7 RSU was 'out on salvage jobs day and night, 60 per cent of our serviceability being provided from parts we could grab from wrecked kites.'

On 2 March, sixteen Japanese bombers, with fighter escort, attacked the airfield at Coomalie. Seven Spitfires engaged, destroying three and damaging one of the raiders, for no loss. Then on 7 March, a Dinah was destroyed by Flight Lieutenant

MacLean and Sergeant McDowell of 457 Squadron, the unit's first victory in the campaign.

Raid 53 on Darwin, 15 March

Raid 53 was made on 15 March. Coincidentally, Squadron Leader Thorold-Smith, Flight Lieutenant Ted Hall and Flying Officer Tim Goldsmith had just taken off from Darwin, returning to Strauss after night flying. They were informed of the raid, and became White Section of the Squadron. Red, Blue and Yellow Sections took off and steered as directed by ground control. White Section climbed to 20 000 feet and saw the Japanese formation approaching Darwin from the north, went on up to 23 000 feet, and on command from Thorold-Smith dived to attack the Japanese from the port quarter.

Ted Hall saw the Zeke fighter escort, slightly above and between the Spitfires and the bombers, and warned Thorold-Smith, who dived for the bombers anyway. A section of Zekes followed, closed in behind, and fired on the leading Spitfire, hitting it. Thorold-Smith bailed out over Picnic Cove.

Ted Hall also dived, to attack the starboard flank of the bomber formation. Five Zekes intercepted, forcing him to engage them instead. Hall manoeuvred on to the tail of one, and at a range of 100 yards (91 m) fired three one-second bursts, seeing hits on the top of the engine cowling. The Zeke started smoking badly and spun down towards the sea, five miles (8 km) north-east of Point Charles. Hall was credited with the Zeke as a 'damaged'.

But Hall was alone amid the Japanese. He saw another Zeke close behind, firing, tracer coming close but missing, and turned the Spitfire as tightly as possible, to make a head-on attack. The Zeke broke left, and another above rolled over on to its back, dived and shot at Hall, but missed him. He fought briefly with two others, who climbed steeply, hoping to come down behind his Spitfire as it passed, but Hall was not caught by this, and broke away from the Zekes, going after the bombers.

One of the Zekes was flown by Petty Officer Tsugio Sakamoto, who had come to combat flying after a time as a flying instructor, and was a little more proficient than the usual Japanese pilot. Sakamoto believed that P40s had intercepted the raid. (This misidentification was probably caused by the change to the appearance of the Spitfire made by the large Vokes tropical filter, which deepened the outline of the nose.[1])

An enthusiastic, but misguided, Spitfire made several attacks on Ted Hall, forcing him to dive for 5000 feet. He got away, then chased after the bombers for 115 kilometres, and was able to watch Tim Goldsmith make his attack.

Like Ted Hall, Goldsmith had been forced to break off his attack on the bombers to deal with Zekes which had intervened. Two approached from starboard, one diving in front of him, as a decoy, while the other lagged behind, waiting to get onto Goldlsmith's tail.

Goldsmith was aware of the trap, but decided to attack the leading Japanese. At 350 metres range he fired his machineguns, saw strikes, and three or four panels flew off the starboard wing, then the Zeke broke sharply left, pouring black smoke. The second Zeke fired, at a range of 200 yards (183 m), hitting the Spitfire, but not affecting the aircraft's performance. Goldsmith rolled away from the attack, dived east, and lost the Zeke.

Ground control directed him towards the bombers, who were flying out to sea on a bearing of 200 degrees. Goldsmith climbed up-sun, 5000 feet above the bombers and went after them. One hundred and thirty kilometres west of Port Patterson, Goldsmith saw a Zeke closing in from port, weaving and watching him. When the Japanese turned away, Goldsmith put the Spitfire into a dive towards the bombers.

He saw a Zeke ahead, trying to take advantage of his dive, and switched his attack onto the fighter. He gave it a 1½ second burst of machinegun, which had an immediate effect—the Zeke flicked over, smoking and spinning fast towards the sea. Goldsmith watched it fall to about 8000 feet, lost it, then saw a large splash. From the distance, Ted Hall had seen the action and watched the Zeke fall all the way to the ocean.

The bombers had moved into a series of crescent-shaped formations, six to a unit, each aircraft only about 20 metres from its neighbour. This allowed effective defensive cross-fire. Goldsmith was now at 24 000 feet, and again started for the bombers in a shallow dive, which he later realised was too fast for easy firing. With his ASI showing 350 mph (560 kmph), he opened fire with cannon and machinegun in a six-second burst from fine rear quarter, at 300 yards (274 m) range, closing to 150 yards (136 m). He saw strikes on the starboard wing and fuselage side,

187

then, dodging red tracer from the top turret, broke starboard. He whipped around in a climbing turn and attacked the bomber again. His starboard cannon stopped after firing ninety rounds. Goldsmith identified the bombers as Mitsubishi Bettys, and noticed their dark green camouflage paint, whereas the Zekes seemed to be a glossy golden brown on which the hinomaru stood out clearly.

The Mitsubishi had fallen out of its position on the tip of the crescent-shaped formation, lagging some 60 metres. Diving below it, Goldsmith pulled up and fired a six-second burst, hitting it from one wingtip across to the fuselage and back to the tail. It fell even further behind the formation, and Goldsmith last saw it losing height, but then had to avoid another gaggle of Zekes which were closing on him from behind.

Red Section, comprising Flying Officers Lloyd, Gould and Williams, had attacked the bombers but had been engaged from behind by Zekes. Lloyd was shot down but bailed out and survived. Gould and Williams engaged several other fighters, with no visible results. Lloyd's engine and mainplane were hit, the cockpit filled with fumes and he baled out, landing six kilometres inland. He walked towards the coast, came upon a road which he followed to Picnic Cove, and was picked up there by a launch.

Blue and Yellow Sections did not engage. Thorold-Smith had been killed, as had two of 54 Squadron, Flight Sergeant Varney and Sergeant Cooper. Goldsmith landed BR526 with fourteen litres of petrol left. The limited fuel capacity of the Spitfire was to take its toll in the next big clash. Tim Goldsmith now had 319 hours on Spitfires, including 110 operational hours.

Further to the north-west, Tsugio Sakamoto and his comrades were landing after the long flight back to base. They gathered around and made a verbal report to the commander, in the normal fashion. Claims were based on the word of the pilot. If an enemy was seen to be hit hard, and thought not able to survive, then it was claimed as destroyed; if hit to a lesser degree, it was claimed as a probable. On this raid, Sakamoto thought all the Japanese had returned safely.[2]

At the end of March, 452 Squadron Record book noted that the general health of its members had been good, despite a relatively large number of scorpion bites, 'none of which have produced serious effects. Insect pests generally, and particularly mosquitoes and sandflies, have been greatly diminished in number and ferocity by the burning off of the grass in the camp area.'

The Squadron's health at the end of April was again reported to be good, with only seven airmen sufficiently ill to be incapacitated, though there were fourteen cases of external ear infection from the local water supply, picked up both in showers and swimming holes. The Record book contained the comment that 'Cricketophilia is reaching serious proportions and some of the senior officers of the Squadron have been infected; it is estimated that at least one in every three persons in the camp exhibits this physchopathological reaction. There were no flying accidents during the month.'

Squadron strength was:
Flying personnel:—33
Non-flying personnel:—7 Officers and 329 Other Ranks.

2 May 1943: Raid 54 on Darwin

Early in the morning, to the north-west, Japanese bombers and fighters began taking off for Darwin. One of the fighter pilots was Petty Officer Tsugio Sakamoto. In what he described as the usual way, the pilots were told the barest details of the mission, and took off. They paired off indiscriminately, as part of the larger formation. Radios were only used by formation leaders, if then. The Japanese fighter pilots tried to emulate the traditions and standards of the samurai.[3]

452 Squadron was led by Wing Commander Caldwell, and scrambled at 09.45, the eleven pilots being Caldwell, MacDonald, Hall, Goldsmith, Fox, Nichterlein, McNab, Makin, Evans, Stagg and Mawer. Only five returned. Goldsmith, Fox, Nichterlein, McNab, Makin and Stagg were either shot down or force-landed, with McNab listed as 'missing', the others as 'pilot safe'.

452 had rendezvoused with 54 and 547 Squadrons at 10 000 feet over Hughes. 452 was in the centre, 54 to port and 457 to starboard. Caldwell was informed that a formation was approaching from the west-north-west some hundred kilometres from Point Charles, at 20 000 feet. Climbing towards them, he was then told that an estimated twenty bombers and the same number of fighters were between 22 000 and 27 000 feet, so Caldwell ordered the formation to go to 30 000 feet.

At 10.10, after twenty-five minutes of climbing, the Spitfires

189

saw the Japanese. Eighteen Mitsubishi Bettys and 27 Zekes of 202 Kokkutai, 23 Koku Sentai, were to port, sixteen kilometres west of Darwin, crossing the harbour at 27 000 feet. Some of the Zekes were in front of and behind the bombers, at the same level, and some in vics of three were higher, up to 31 000 feet. Caldwell continued the climb, turning port, to get up-sun and above, intending to attack in a series of squadron masses against the bomber formation.

Caldwell radioed the height of the enemy for the benefit of the anti-aircraft guns. They fired, but the rounds exploded slightly behind or to one side of the bombers. The Spitfires continued to gain height, while the bombers attacked RAAF base Darwin, with about a hundred bombs. These exploded across the south-eastern part of the airfield and into the scrub, slightly damaging two buildings, cutting electricity and telephone lines, and killing one soldier.

By now, Caldwell had the Wing in position, waiting for the Japanese to turn left off the target, when the Spitfires would have attacked from above, head-on, out of the sun. But the bombers turned right and began to dive away out to sea.

At 32 500 feet, at an indicated airspeed of 185 mph (296 kmph), Caldwell positioned the Wing in the sun and gave his orders: 54 to attack the Zekes; 457 to attack the bombers from out of the sun, breaking starboard and climbing back into the glare after their passes; 452 to wait to cover 457's withdrawal in case of interception by Zekes, or if the Zekes were sufficiently scattered, to follow up with an attack on the bombers. By this time, the enemy formation was sixty-five kilometres out of Darwin, at 22 000 feet.

Squadron Leader Gibbs led the RAF Squadron down on to the fighters, and combats began. Forming line astern, 457 dived on to the bombers, at an angle of about 70 degress, reaching 400 mph (640 kmph). This was considered to be too steep and too fast to allow accurate shooting at the bombers. But the Zekes rallied, and some turned into 457, disrupting their attack so that only four got through to the Bettys.

Caldwell led 452 down into the combat, but the Zekes managed to protect their charges, and only one bomber was shot down. The limited fuel capacity of the Spitfire had to be taken into consideration, and Caldwell warned the pilots to watch their fuel, and return to base if necessary.

Tim Goldsmith had been flying as White 3, with McNab as his Number 4. Goldsmith's Spitfire could not keep up with the others, so he and McNab attacked alone. Below them, the Bettys were strung out, roughly in line abreast, with the extreme starboard machine some 50 metres ahead of the others. This one was selected by Goldsmith.

At 250 metres, IAS 400 mph (640 kmph), he opened fire with cannon and machineguns. After two seconds, the port cannon stopped and he fired on with the starboard, closing to 50 metres. Tim later reported that 'many strikes were seen in the vicinity of the cockpit and wing root. When I broke away the registration numbers could be seen on the rear of the fuselage.' He broke to port, but could not go down because of the line of Bettys, so flew along them, just a little higher, which made it difficult for the gunners to traverse quickly enough to fire effectively. 'I had just reached the end of the line when I saw a Zero coming up at me on the left hand side, so I rolled over and went down in a spiral dive.'

Goldsmith broke down in an aileron turn, followed by the Zeke, who was firing. As they dived, at a height he later recalled as 'below 10 000 feet', the Spitfire was hit. Rounds hit the canopy, and 'part of the cover fell in on me. Then the controls were shot away and the stick went loose in my hand. The plane was completely out of control, and I thought the game was up. I was going at 400 miles an hour [640 kmph] straight into the sea.'

The Spitfire went into a bunt [an outside loop] which forced Goldsmith out through the hood as the structure began to break up. He has suffered a 'red-out', blindness from blood vessels ruptured by the centrifugal force of the manoeuvre. 'When I went through the hood I lost my vision and I could see nothing for the next quarter of an hour. I knew I was falling so I felt for the ripcord and pulled it.' While under the parachute, though blind, he thought the Zeke made some attacks on him. (This was often done by the Japanese.)

Overhead, the combats went on. 'I could hear the planes zooming and blazing away above me. I was wondering how far I was from the water, when I went into it face forward with my mouth open. The parachute came down on top of me, and I had a hard job disengaging myself from the shroud lines. I felt around and got the dinghy free and blown up, and after getting rid of the parachute, got into the dinghy.'

The Japanese force was still going fast out to sea, and gradually the noise of combat died away. Goldsmith was alone, blind, in the sun, in a dinghy just big enough for one person. Only the slapping of the wavelets against the rubber sides of the dinghy broke the silence.

The Spitfires were now facing the enemy of fuel exhaustion. The climbing and combat had burnt petrol at a great rate, and the pilots were wondering if they could get back to an airfield. In addition, they had to fly into strong headwinds.

Later, the Wing claimed 6-4-8, for the loss of five Spitfires destroyed in action and three others during forced landings because of engine troubles or lack of fuel; two pilots had been killed; three others were sitting in their rubber dinghies, while Flight Sergeant Stagg had bailed out over the mainland, and was not recovered for some sixteen days.

Dissatisfaction was expressed by some of those involved, mainly about the long time taken to get into an attacking position, and not doing so until the bombers were on the way home. However, in his combat report, Tim Goldsmith wrote that Caldwell's commanding of the interception was '100 per cent perfect', adding that the height and sun were 'absolutely in our favour, and the fact that the interception was not a smashing success seems to me to be entirely due to individual pilots' lack of initiative and to armament failures.' (However, that was in the future, and when the squadron returned to base, he was one of those listed as missing.)

In the dinghy, Goldsmith realised that his sight was returning, and he was able to read the face of his watch, if held close to his eyes. It was 10.55. As his vision cleared, he saw that there was no land in sight, nothing all around him except the sea, choppy waves splashing.

He drifted wherever the current took him. Then, at about 16.00, a Hudson appeared, flew to him and circled. Goldsmith presumed it was fixing his position, and was happier. 'That cheered me up, but it was getting dark. I could not see a plane or ship. I was looking out when I saw a long yellow sea snake with brown stripes swimming around me. I was pretty scared, and splashed the water hard until it disappeared.

'I lay down in the dinghy and tried to sleep, but my neck was hurting where it had been cut by the parachute cord, and my eyes were giving a lot of pain. During the night I felt something scraping along the bottom of the raft, I suppose it was a shark, and it gave me another fright. Then, just as it was getting light, I heard a hissing noise and thought the dinghy was going down. I looked over the side, and there was a big turtle, on the surface, blowing. I beat it off with the paddles.'

At about 08.00, Goldsmith was having breakfast—a fruit drop—when he saw a ship, about sixteen kilometres away. He stood up in the dinghy and waved, but the ship kept on steaming, moving away over the horizon. The disappointment was intense. 'I had just about given up hope, lay down again and went to sleep, not caring much what happened.'

Then the noise of engines woke him, he looked up and saw a motor boat and a naval ship almost alongside the dinghy. It was 11.00, and the ship was HMAS *Inverell*, a Bathurst Class Australian-built corvette, commanded by Lieutenant Suffren RANR (S).

Inverell had searched further out to sea, and a little longer than the other ships, but it was ML805 which actually picked up Goldsmith, then transferred him to the corvette. R. H. Ware was a telegraphist on the ship, and saw Goldsmith come aboard, noting the cuts and bruises on the pilot's face, then heard Tim describe how he was shot down by a Zero which he did not realise was so close until the cockpit canopy burst around him. Goldsmith told the crew that he had seen the ship earlier, but when it turned away from him he felt all chance of rescue was gone.

A Walrus amphibian aircraft arrived to collect Goldsmith and allow *Inverell* to continue searching. The ship's whaler was lowered and the oarsmen enthusiastically pulled across to the waiting Walrus. There was an air of excitement, and Ware was concerned that the keen rowers would collide with the aircraft instead of merely coming alongside. Sure enough, the plane's fuselage was stove in.

However, the ship had a very wide roll of 'Elastoplast', and this was used to mend the hole in the aircraft's aluminium hull, so that it could take off. Tim was trundled back to the mainland in the patched Walrus and delivered to medical attention. Three days later, after a time in hospital, he was back with 452 Squadron.

Raid 55, 20 June 1943

On 17 June, at 28 000 feet, a Dinah reconnaissance aircraft flew over Darwin, Hughes, Batchelor and Coomalie. It was untouched by anti-aircraft fire, and because of its height evaded the 42 Spitfires which took off in pursuit. Two days later, enemy radio traffic indicated the arrival of many aircraft at Koepang. Little else was needed to alert the fighter squadrons to probable combat next day, and the ground crews worked on the Spitfires to prepare them for the expected action.

Radar detected the approaching formations at 09.45, and 46 Spitfires took off to intercept. Again mechanical difficulties plagued them; Wing Commander Caldwell's radio failed, and when Squadron Leader Gibbs RAF was ordered to assume command, his engine failed and he was forced to return. So the squadrons attacked independently.

Squadron Leader MacDonald led 452, Flight Lieutenant Watson 457, and Flight Lieutenant Foster 54 Squadron. Foster and 54 Squadron saw the enemy first, at 27 000 feet over Bathurst Island. With 452, they attacked soon after the Japanese crossed the coast on to the mainland. The Spitfires dropped auxiliary tanks and engaged, with 54 Squadron dividing to take on both bombers and the fighter escort.

The RAF pilots shot down four 'Bettys' and a Zeke, with two of the bombers claimed by Flying Officer Hughes and another by Foster. In fact, the bombers were Nakajima Ki-49 'Helens', from 61 Sentai, an Army formation, escorted by Navy Mitsubishi A6M Zekes.[4]

John Bisley was flying as Blue 1, with Flight Sergeant A Ruskin-Rowe as his No. 2. After Red Section went into the attack, Bisley prepared to follow. Then two Zekes were seen below, and Blue 3 asked permission to take Blue 4 and 5 to attack them, so Bisley and Rowe attacked the bombers alone, as the last in the squadron to do so.

There were twenty bombers in the formation, and Bisley closed to 50 metres, opening fire on the beam at 300 metres and swinging in to dead astern. His port cannon stopped after forty rounds, then the starboard after sixty. Bisley closed in, noting the bomber's starboard engine burning, then saw tracer from a Japanese fighter passing close to the canopy of his Spitfire.

As he evaded the Zekes, Bisley saw a bomber—which he thought was a Betty, but was a Helen—on fire, with both wings snapped off outboard of the engines, spin into the water about eight kilometres off shore at Adan Bay. Bisley found that Rowe was no longer with him, and later surmised he had been shot down by the Zekes. Later, Rowe was found, dead, in his Spitfire, with camera-gun evidence of two Zekes destroyed before falling himself.

Over Darwin again this day was Petty Officer Tsugio Sakamoto, in a formation of 25 Zekes. They were determined to engage the Spitfires.[5]

Bisley was not impressed with the anti-aircraft fire, which he described as 'most inaccurate', the first salvo being 10 000 feet low and behind, the second being behind and 500 feet above the bombers.

While climbing again, Bisley saw the bombers above, and radioed their position to 457 Squadron. He watched the Spitfires diving to attack, and after 457 had passed, Bisley saw another bomber spin into the sea off Cox's Peninsula. Bisley kept on in the climb, counting twelve bombers and noticing three Zekes well above and behind them at 20 000 feet.

61 Sentai had reached their target, and at 10.45 bombed Winellie, scattering forty 'daisy-cutters' across the air force and army camps, killing three and wounding eleven Australians, destroying two huts, a railway wagon loaded with oil drums and cutting the railway line in three places.

As the Japanese bombers flew out over Darwin, Caldwell and Group Captain Walters attacked. However, they were engaged by the fighter escort, and each shot down one Zeke.

Then, ten minutes after the bomb-run at Winellie, another ten bombers attacked at tree-top level, going for Darwin airfield and Winellie again. These were from the Japanese Army 75 Bomber Sentai, and had made the entire flight from Lautem below 1000 feet, dropping to 50 feet when about 200 km north of Darwin. It had been intended that both formations of bombers were to arrive over the target almost together, with 75 Sentai's Kawasaki Ki-48 Lilys bombing immediately after 61 Sentai, but from only

50 feet. The crews of both bomber units were buoyed up by the knowledge that they were the first Army air formations to attack Australia itself.[6]

As they sped over the tree tops, the 75 Sentai crews peered ahead and above for the signs of 61 Sentai's passing, and for the smoke and dust of the bomb bursts. But they saw nothing. Later, they realised that 61 Sentai had been over the target at least five minutes before them. They dropped thirty-six 100-kg bombs set with 15-second delay fuses, aiming for the runway, and believed they had been successful as they swung off the target and began the flight back. Actually, their bombs and cannon-fire destroyed one building and damaged the Sergeants' Mess.

The bomber crews thought they were under 'heavy AA and machinegun fire throughout the bombing run', and then were engaged by what they believed was two Hurricanes and four Spitfires. One Spitfire dived in from 7 o'clock, pressing on to about forty metres from the Lilys, and all the gunners fired on him, then watched the fighter go into 'a half roll and plunge smoking into the sea.' A Japanese pilot in the formation believed all of them returned successfully, though one Lily crashed at Lautem when the undercarriage failed. He also thought that three others had an engine hit, but returned on the other, and that the only personnel casualty was one pilot, who suffered two wounds in a cheek of his buttock. However, 54 Squadron did destroy one Lily.[7]

As Bisley reached the high-flying bombers and manoeuvred to attack, he passed out from lack of oxygen, and spun down to 10 000 feet. Recovering, he could hear on his radio reports of the low-level bombing below. He tried to learn the position of the low-level raiders, but there was so much radio chatter that nothing could be gained, and after searching unsuccessfully, Bisley returned to Strauss.

In his combat report, he said he considered the attack as initiated by Red Leader, 'well conceived and excellently timed'. He saw three bombers—at this stage thought to be Bettys—crash after 452 Squadron's attack. Nine bombers and five fighters had been destroyed, with another ten enemy damaged, and General Douglas MacArthur, Allied commander in the South West Pacific theatre, was sufficiently impressed to send his congratulations. However, Pilot Officers Nichterlein and Ruskin-Rowe, of 452 Squadron, were killed.

When the wreckage of the Japanese bombers was examined, the references to 'Bettys' in the combat reports were questioned, identification charts and photos were examined, and it was decided the attack had been made by Nakajima Helens. Bisley's victim had its tail fin removed, and this was made into the squadron scoreboard.

Back at his own base, Tsugio Sakamoto claimed two Spitfires destroyed. He had three machinegun bullet holes in the tail of his Zeke. He thought that only one bomber had been shot down, for ten Spitfires destroyed. The pilot with 75 Sentai heard that four escort fighters were shot down and another crashed into the sea due to engine problems on the approach.[8]

Raid 62, 7 September 1943

The Spitfires had been quite successful against the high-flying Dinah reconnaissance aircraft, having shot down four in the first two weeks of August alone.

The Japanese then decided to send a strong fighter escort with the reconnaissance plane, and 25 Zekes were ordered to protect the Army Dinahs. Tsugio Sakamoto was one of the Navy pilots who flew this mission, ordered to protect the Army Dinahs.[9]

At 08.30, when the enemy were only 290 kilometres from Darwin, radar detected the approaching formation. 457 Squadron was sent to various exit points which had been used by the Japanese, but when it became obvious that there was a larger force than usual, all three squadrons, totalling 48 Spitfires, were launched. 452 Squadron took off at 09.25, Tim Goldsmith flying as White 1, in Spitfire 'Y', and Bisley as Blue 1.

The Spitfire squadrons met over Sattler and climbed east to 8000 feet, then turned west towards the enemy. Bisley believed this to be wrong, and later wrote that 'the leadership was extremely poor, as we were climbing down sun and still well below the reported height of the enemy, at the same time climbing straight into the enemy force.' 452 was in what Bisley described as 'a long straggling line astern formation.'

Interception was made at 09.50, 23 000 feet, nineteen kilometres west of Strauss. The Japanese had the advantage. Bisley identified the enemy fighters as Oscars (radial-engined Army fighters), while Goldsmith believed them to be both Tonys (in-line engined Army fighters) and 'radial-engined fighters'.

197

In one of the 25 Zekes above was Sakamoto, who counted about 40 Spitfires climbing to intercept. The Japanese began to dive to the attack.[10]

As he saw three Oscars turning to come down from the sun on to the Spitfires, Bisley called a warning, and the squadron swung around to starboard, but another twelve enemy dived from port. He called a break, but no one reacted, so he began an aileron turn, meanwhile watching the Spitfire on his right hit and the pieces falling from it, then finally his wing-waggling alerted his section to the bounce.

Tim Goldsmith saw a 'Tony' attacking from above, rolled over using aileron and saw Japanese tracer flicking by. He dived 600 feet and saw a 'Tony' attacking head-on from below. Goldsmith fired back, opening at 200 metres and closing to 50, later writing in his combat report, 'when last seen the enemy aircraft was disintegrating.' Two other enemy fighters were probably destroyed in this part of the combat.

Three Spitfires were lost, with Flying Officer Hinds of 54 Squadron killed, and MacDonald and Pilot Officer Tully of 452 baling out. A cannon shell exploded in MacDonald's cockpit, inflicting serious burns on him before he managed to get out of the aircraft. He was found and flown back to medical attention in a Tiger Moth piloted by Squadron Leader Fenton, who had been a 'flying doctor' in the Northern Territory before the war.

However, 457 Squadron had arrived with the advantage of height, and attacked, destroying four Zekes and damaging others. Flight Lieutenants Watson and MacLean, and Flying Officer Smithson got one each, while Flying Officer Gregory and Flight Sergeant White shared one.

From the Japanese side, Sakamoto believed that only one Japanese was shot down, while thirteen Spitfires were claimed destroyed.[11]

This was Tim Goldsmith's final victory. At the end of September he had a total of 545 hours flying, with 404 on Spitfires. None of the other Malta pilots claimed victories after this combat, though some of them flew further tours of operations until the end of the war.

11

Paul Brennan—
79 Squadron RAAF 1943

While the Japanese effort north-west of Australia from late 1942 was confined to air attacks, the major threat posed by them was further east, in New Guinea and the neighbouring Solomon Islands. By early 1943, the Japanese had been held, but the Australian and US forces had only begun to advance.

Fighters were needed to combat the Japanese on the ground and in the air, and General Kenney, commander of the US 5th Air Force and responsible for directing Allied air operations, could never get enough of the correct types. Early in 1943, he began asking for a Spitfire squadron for operations in New Guinea, though the Spitfire Wing was employed in defence of Darwin. Sufficient aircraft were available for another squadron, and it was formed.

Alan Rawlinson was a Squadron Leader on Air Staff in RAAF HQ in Melbourne, and was well aware of Kenney's repeated requests for Spitfires in New Guinea. One day in April 1943, the Deputy Chief of Air Staff, Group Captain McCauley, appeared in his doorway. Rawlinson at once realised that something unusual was about to occur, as normally one went to the office of DCAS, not the reverse. McCauley said that a squadron of Spitfires was to be raised for service in New Guinea, and asked if Rawlinson wanted to command it. The answer was an immediate yes.

Rawlinson had already done two tours of operations on fighters, in the Middle East. A 1938 graduate of Point Cook RAAF Academy, he went overseas with 3 Squadron and had flown Gladiators, Gauntlets and Kittyhawks, which were markedly inferior to the opposing Italian and German fighters, both in numbers and quality.

He had analysed the details in his logbooks, and found that on average the Commonwealth fighters were outnumbered by at least three to one in every combat, and on occasion by six or more. When the Luftwaffe arrived with its Messerschmitt Bf109s, the Germans made good use of their advantages in height and speed, making life miserable for the pilots of the Hurricanes and Kittyhawks. The first Spitfires to operate outside the UK were not deployed until March 1942, and then it was by aircraft carrier to Malta.

Rawlinson had survived two tours and was credited with six victories. After return to Australia he had flown on the staff of, or commanded, operational training units, and was being 'rested' in Melbourne. Then came the offer of a Spitfire squadron. His reply to McCauley was a definite affirmative. For Rawlinson, it 'would be the first chance of fighting in a very good aircraft.'

Accordingly, on 26 April 1943 he was posted to command 79 Squadron, which formed at Woolloomanata Homestead, at Lara, near Geelong, Victoria. The squadron lived at the homestead, and personnel and aircraft began to arrive. Officially, the squadron came under the auspices of the RAAF base at Laverton, near Melbourne. Rawlinson was pleased with the standard of pilot assigned to him, describing them as 'a good mix of experienced and inexperienced pilots. The Flight Commanders were Vanderfield, who had flown Buffaloes in Malaya, and Max Bott, who had flown P40s in New Guinea.

'Paul Brennan was posted in about 14 days before we left for New Guinea. I was delighted to have such an experienced Spitfire pilot with us. He had an easy nature, and he fitted in with the rest of the chaps. He was still strained, a bit taut. I had the feeling he was marshalling his reserves for the tour he was about to undertake; a bit tired.'

Paul Brennan passed on his operational experiences, describing the Malta combats and life on the island. The others heard of the incessant shortages of everything, the constant lack of food, drink and tobacco; the unrelenting deadliness of the situation where every flight was operational; no test flying, no sector reconnaissance, no breaking-in; all flights short, but many of them, his experiences crammed into 40 or 50 hours of flying over Malta.

He was not beyond relating yarns about himself, and Rawlinson recalls Brennan telling of the meteorological briefings when on 64 Squadron in the UK, and the reference to 'the odd bit of precip'. It was not until Brennan left the UK that he found it meant rain.

79 Squadron was given an initial issue of twelve Spitfires, and told to be ready to move to New Guinea in 28 days. Alan Rawlinson managed to fit in seven flights in the new fighters before they began the long journey north. The total flying hours for the squadron in May had been 203 hours 25 minutes, all by day. The original dozen Spitfires were flown to Laverton to be fitted with 90-gallon (490-litre) slipper tanks, and another twelve aircraft were collected by pilots. There was no testing; that had already been done by Air Depot pilots. The squadron had to move on.

Rawlinson was disturbed enough to demand a navigational escort, as none of the Spitfires had been brought to operational standards, and compasses were unswung. Accompanied by a Lodestar, the squadron flew north, via Richmond and Amberley, to Garbutt, at Townsville, arriving there on 13 June. The last leg had been 4.5 hours. Alan Rawlinson recalls that 'we were landing in stream, Paul was running towards the south end of the strip, and the aircraft behind him, tail down, did not see Brennan's Spitfire in front and overran it, cutting it to pieces half way down the runway. I was parked in a dispersal about 70 metres away and saw the whole thing. I was so cramped after 4½ hours in the cockpit that I couldn't move, couldn't walk, let alone run.'

The squadron record book describes it succinctly: 'F/O Brennan EE 954 and Sgt Gardner JG 897 came into collision on landing at Townsville. EE 954 burst into flames and was completely destroyed and JG 897 was so extensively damaged it was written off.'

Flying Officer Paul Brennan DFC DFM died of his injuries on the way to hospital.

Appendix 1

Afterwards

Tim Goldsmith died suddenly on 25 March 1961, at the age of 39. He left his wife, Doris, son Timothy and daughter Janet. In accordance with his last wishes, his remains were cremated, and the ashes were scattered from an RAAF Dakota over the Timor Sea, at 13 degrees 30 minutes south, 126 degrees 0 minutes east, at 10.30 am on 12 February 1963.

James Hamilton Ballantyne RCAF, who flew with Colin Parkinson, left Malta with a score of 7.75 victories and a DFM. He was commissioned, began a second tour of operations over Europe, and was killed by flak on 8 March 1944.

John Bisley is, at time of writing, still quite active in business in Sydney.

Eric Broad RAF, friend of Tim Goldsmith and Slim Yarra, survived the war with seven victories and a DFC and Bar.

Fred Clewley, who survived his own crash on take-off on 13 August 1942, and the Liberator crash at Gibraltar, returned to Australia, and to flying Spitfires. After the war he went into his own business, is now retired and lives on the coast south of Melbourne.

Charles Crombie, Beaufighter pilot in 89 Squadron, was killed in a crash at 5 OTU, Williamtown, Australia, on 26 August 1945. Pilots who knew him in other theatres and Australia refer to the shock with which they heard of his death, and his qualities as a person and Australian are remembered some 45 years later. 'A chapter in my life closed with that news,' said Red Gray, 'and I have never experienced a sense of loss like that before or since. Five years is a long time in wartime to be serving with some one, especially over three tours of operations.'

Edward 'Jumbo' Gracie, who led the Spitfires in March 1942 from the aircraft carrier *Eagle* to Malta, commanded several other squadrons after leaving Malta. He was killed in action on 15 February 1944, with a score of 11.33 victories.

Ken 'Red' Gray, 89 Squadron, flew to India with the rest of the squadron, and later went to staff and OTU postings, returning to Australia in June 1944. In September he again met Charles Crombie, at 5 OTU, converted to Mosquitos and went to 87 Sqn RAAF (PRU) near Darwin. In February 1945, one engine failed over Java and he landed in the sea, spent two days in a dinghy, was blown ashore by a cyclone, walked for four days and was found by natives. In June he flew with two other aircraft to Cocos Island for a secret photographic mission to Singapore. In July he completed his operational tour, and returned to Sydney, moving to Narromine as Commandant. Five years earlier, he had completed his Elementary Flying Training there. 685 Squadron RAF was intended to drop mines from Mosquitos into Tokyo Harbour, and Gray was to participate in this, but the war ended. In November he was discharged as a Squadron Leader, with 1200 hours flying time, having flown three tours of operations in North Africa, Malta, India and the Pacific. At time of writing, Red Gray lives in the UK.

Stan Grant, 249 Squadron on Malta, survived the war with a score of 10 victories, DFC and Bar.

Ted Hall, who flew with Tim Goldsmith over Darwin, is retired, at 'Tangmere', Junee, NSW.

Ray Hesslyn died in 1965. After returning to the UK, he went back on operations, achieving a total of 21.5 victories, but was shot down and captured. He received an MBE for his activity as a prisoner.

Tim Johnston, Tim Goldsmith's Flight Commander in 126 Squadron, returned to the UK, returning to operations for the D-Day and Normandy campaigns. After the war he returned to the Colonial Service, but died in 1967.

Howard Lester was flown to the UK for medical treatment after being shot down into the sea off Malta. The aircraft from Gibraltar was attacked by the Luftwaffe but reached England safely. While in hospital in Torquay, Lester survived a deliberate attack on the building by the Luftwaffe, though a wall beside his bed was blown away. Treatment for his wounds continued to the end of the war and beyond, though Lester arrived back in Australia on VJ-Day. It was not until 1950 that he was able to begin civilian employment, with the Post Office, but this was ended in 1972 on direct orders from his doctor. Gradually his condition worsened, but Howard Lester never admitted it or sought sympathy. Encouraged and supported by his wife, Ella, he became quite active in lawn bowls, eventually playing in a special wheelchair. While demonstrating his techniques as a one-armed wheelchair-borne bowler, Lester was stricken by a serious stroke and spent his final years in a nursing home. This brave man bore the unfortunate results of his war service with no complaints, and perhaps exemplifies the spirit of those young Australians who volunteered for aircrew service.

Laddie Lucas survived the war, becoming a Member of Parliament and a golfer of international status. Due to lack of records on Malta, his score is uncertain, but is at least six and may be as high as twelve enemy destroyed.

Eric Mahar returned to Australia, and, like many others from the European Theatre, was treated poorly by some RAAF members who had remained in Australia. As his log-book had been lost in the Liberator crash at Gibraltar, any operational experience was officially non-existent and he was angered then, and still is today, at the attitude adopted by those who remained in Australia. He is retired and lives now in Bendigo, Victoria.

Robert 'Buck' McNair, 249 Squadron on Malta, returned to the UK and to operations, but as a result of injuries had to retire from operations in March 1944, with a score of 16 victories. He died of leukemia after the war, displaying to the end the courage already shown as a fighter pilot.

Gerhard Michalski claimed 26 RAF aircraft over Malta, ending the war with a total of 73 victories, was awarded the Knight's Cross with Oak Leaves, but was killed in a car accident on 22 February 1946. He had been shot down six times during the war.

Ken Mitchell, one of the Aussies in 185 Squadron, returned to Australia and became a doctor after the war. At time of writing he lives and practises in Brisbane.

Edward Mortimer-Rose, 185 Squadron on Malta, met again by Tim Goldsmith soon after Goldsmith's arrival on the island, was killed in an air collision in North Africa in late 1942.

Colin Parkinson, 603 and 229 Squadrons on Malta, survived the war with a score of ten victories. At time of writing, he was living in Sydney, still appreciative of good food and drink, and when circumstances permit—out in the country—driving at high speed, resulting in repeated meetings with the constabulary.

Jimmy Peck, who had flown with Tim Goldsmith, was killed in the UK in a P38 Lockheed Lightning crash, on 12 April 1944.

Alexander Rabagliati, 'Ragbags', Goldsmith's CO on arrival, was killed by flak on 6 July 1943 while leading a Typhoon wing. He had a score of seven victories, a DFC and Bar.

Len Reid survived the war, after returning to Australia and commanding 79 and 452 Squadrons. At time of writing, he lives near Melbourne, devoting much of his time to aid projects in India and Pakistan.

John Ross, 89 Squadron, also survived the war, and at time of writing was living north of Sydney.

Donald Smith, wounded and crash-landed on 8 July 1942, returned to operations in the UK, went back to Australia, then back again to the UK, as CO 453 Squadron RAAF. Bringing his score to five, he returned to Australia as a Wing Commander.

Mervyn Shipard, Beaufighter pilot, flew from North Africa as well as Malta, reaching a score of 13, with DFC and Bar. At time of writing he was retired and living in Sydney.

Alan Yates became a manager for a large removals firm, living for many years in both Canberra and Sydney, and died in the early 1980s.

*   *   *

In January 1941, Gordon Tweedale wrote the following, which is reproduced with permission of his family.

An Airman's Dream

Oh, I'm lonely for the mountains
And fed up with the towns
I'm longing for those stony spurs
O'er the rolling blue grass downs
As I'm lying here a'thinking
I can see the wattle shine
For way out in the mountains
It's right in wildflower time

And I'm thinking of a valley
Where the bally weaners feed
And I see old Nelson grazing
As good as any steed
And now I find I'm riding
Down that valley rich and green
The grass smells rich as lucerne
Where the summer rains have been

And the sun is hot at midday
While the music of the bees
Is harmonised by rustling winds
That filter through the trees
And all the while the wallabies
Sit lazing in the shade
Just prick their ears and watch
As I amble past their glade

At last I reach the plainlands
Where the windwaves gently flow
Through the miles of gold-topped bluegrass
Interspersed with brigalow
And following the creekbed
With its water azure blue
I pass by clumps of cottonbush
With their flowers bright and new

And beneath a stately bluegum
By the creek so short and steep
I lie amid the gumsticks
And soon am fast asleep
And that's where I would be right now
If this cold world were sane
If men would live in peace and quiet
And shoulder no-one's blame

So when this war is over
And the fight's been lost and won
I'll head my horse along that creek
To that tall and grand bluegum

And with the wind a'rustling
The leaves around my feet
And the bees agently buzzing
In the noonday heat I'll sleep.

A 16-year-old girl, June Ulcoq, wrote the following after Gordon Tweedale's death. Now Mrs George Robertson, she gave permission for it to be included here.

Answer to An Airman's Dream
Oh, I'm sitting neath a gumtree
And I'm thinking lad of you
Of your love for this dear country
And your dream that won't come true

How you longed for the open spaces
But your honour bade you go
Perhaps you saw the old bush places
Ruled by a cruel and ruthless foe.

The bush is just as silent
The creek is running by
The mountains in the distance
Still seem to touch the sky.

The gumtrees are as stately
The waters azure blue
I wonder do they ever mourn
For one who loved them true.

The world will never change lad
There'll still be land and sea
But thanks to you and comrades
This land will always be
Australia for Australians
And they will still be free.

John 'Slim' Yarra, posted without a rest to be a Flight Commander in 453 Squadron RAAF in England, was killed on operations off Flushing on 10 December 1942. His brother Bob also went to 453 Squadron and was killed in a dive-bombing attack on a V1 site in France on 14 April 1944. While on Malta, Slim wrote the following letter, reproduced with permission of his brother and sisters.

My Dear Mother,

By the time you receive this letter you will have officially been informed of my death. This is just to let you know that I am quite satisfied with my life and the way it has ended.

I entered this war with the knowledge that I had a rather small chance of coming out of it alive. I was under no false impressions— I knew I had to kill—and perhaps be killed. Since I commenced flying I have spent probably the happiest time of my life. I loved flying more than most things, and, if I had come through the war alive, I should probably have killed myself in civil flying. I am not just being fatalistic—I honestly think I would rather have ten years of action and thrills than 50 years of security in some stuffy office.

Since I've been in the Service I have met more real friends than I could ever hope to meet in a lifetime of peace. Not just self-styled friends who talk platitudes to one's face, and, when it is conducive to their own well-being are quite prepared to disown your friendship; but men who daily risk their lives to save yours. There is nothing like the element of danger to seal a friendship.

I have seen a lot of men killed and have often wondered how I managed to escape alive from some shows, but I know that when the time comes I am quite prepared to face it.

Do not grieve too much, Mother. My life was not wasted. To date I have destroyed 11 enemy aircraft, which squares the account to the nation for my training. I am not sorry it happened this way. If I could live my life over again I would certainly have made a lot of changes, but I should still have flown in the war, and tried to accomplish what I have. What better way to die than fighting against odds in the service of one's country.

Above all, Mother dear, I have proved to my satisfaction that I was, at least, a man.

God Bless you
John

Appendix 2

Statistics

Malta's first air raid occurred on 11 June 1940, and the last alert was on 28 August 1944. In between, there had been 3340 alerts. In 1940, there had been 211; in 1941, 963; in 1942, 2031; in 1943, 127; and in 1944, 8.

1484 Maltese had been killed and 54 were missing, while 3778 had been wounded. Considering the high number of raids, the casualty figures, though heavy for such a community, were relatively light, and can be attributed to the ready availability of shelters, or the ease of excavating them from the island rock.

The RAF claimed 1252-383-1050, while the guns claimed 241-49-161.

RAF losses were 547 destroyed in the air, and 541 damaged, with another 160 destroyed on the ground and 231 damaged.

The German Luftwaffe and Regia Aeronautica flew some 26 000 sorties over the islands of Malta.

Appendix 3

Roll of Honour

RAAF fighter pilots killed on active service from Malta 1942 are listed below. There are many others from the reconnaissance, bomber and torpedo-bomber squadrons.

Rank	Number	Name	Squadron	Date
P O	404548	JL Boyd	185	14-5-42
P O	408000	GM Briggs	601	10-5-42
Sgt	403554	RA Buntine	185, 1435	13-8-42
F O	403136	JJ Guerin	249	21-3-42
FSgt	400888	CGD Hains	249	11-12-42
W O	404677	ET Hiskens	249, 229	15-10-42
W O	400585	RF Hammond	248	1-12-42
Sgt	403087	WB Knox-William	1435	14-10-42
P O	402150	JM Mayall	126	10-3-42
P O	400152	HR Murray	249	10-3-42
F O	4049981	RB Park	229	19-11-42
FSgt	403476	W Parkes	229	29-10-42
F O	402878	D Partridge	252, 227	6-9-42
FLt	402260	RHC Sly	—	9-5-42
P O	404269	GR Tweedale	185	9-5-42

Appendix 4

RAAF fighter pilots known to have flown from Malta 1941-42

402335 W/O	Adams	DG		185 Sqn
400771 Sgt	Baxter	CL		249, 1435
402720 P/O	Bisley	JHE		126
404548 P/O	Boyd	JL	KIA 14/5/42	242,126,185
404692 P/O	Brennan	VP	KIFA 13/6/43	249
408000 P/O	Briggs	GM	KIA 10/5/42	601
403554 Sgt	Buntine	RA	KIA 13/8/42	185,1435
400599 Sgt	Clewley	FW		185
404093 F/L	Crombie	CA	KIFA 26/8/45	89
404240 Sgt	Freeman	HT	KIA 20/4/43*	249
402500 P/O	Goldsmith	AP	died 25/3/61	126,185,126
402119 S/L	Gray	KJ		89
403136 P/O	Guerin	JJ	KIA 21/3/42	249
404677 W/O	Hiskens	ET	KIA 15/10/42	249,229
402054 F/O	Haley	A	KIA 1/1/43*	126
400585 W/O	Hammond	RF	KIA 1/12/42	248
404447 Sgt	Irwin	WR		603,229
402518 P/O	Johnson	ER		229
403087 Sgt	Knox-William	W	KIA 14/10/42	1435
400147 Sgt	Lester	HC		185
33231 P/O	Mahar	EL		126,185
400140 P/O	Mayall	JM	KIA 10/3/42	126
402523 Sgt	McBurnie	DH		229
404928 F/O	Mitchell	KR		126,185
400480 W/O	Mueller	PJO	KIA 1/12/42	248
400152 P/O	Murray	KM		249
404981 P/O	Park	RB	KIA 20/11/42	185
402877 P/O	Parkinson	CH		603,229

211

403476 Sgt	Parkes	W	KIFA 29/10/42	229
402878 F/O	Partridge	D	KIA 6/9/42	252/227
406261 Sgt	Pauley	JB		229
404984 F/O	Pashen	NL		603,229
400735 F/O	Reid	LS		185
404185 P/O	Richardson	A		126
402138 F/Lt	Ross	JMcK		89
407835 F/O	Sanderson	JG		249
402041 P/O	Scott	TW		601
403823 Sgt	Simms	RJ		249
407071 Sgt	Shepherd	FG		185
402257 F/L	Shipard	MC		89
402260 F/L	Sly	RHC	KIA 9/5/42	—
407256 P/O	Smith	DH		126
404269 P/O	Tweedale	GR	KIA 9/5/42	185
406375 Sgt	White	CA		?
400666 F/Lt	Wills	RA		227
402823 P/O	Yarra	JW	KIA 10/12/42	249,185
403392 F/O	Yates	AS		249

Other pilots, believed to have been Australians but not members of the RAAF, nor able to be identified as such in RAAF personnel records at 15 February 1988:

Mitchell	RA	603,249
Pain	JF	261

* in Burma.

Appendix 5

Aircraft numbers and squadron letters flown by some of the pilots in preceding chapters. The following detail for each pilot is taken from his log-book, or from squadron records.

The list and its detail are incomplete, as little or no records could be located for some pilots. Those records kept by the pilot, or his family, and the squadron records reflect the hectic nature of the times, with some detail missing and probably not recorded. In addition, some pilots or their families could not be traced. Several are known to have died in the intervening years. Much detail was provided by Brian Cull; my personal thanks for making it available.

Squadron codes were:

126 Squadron	TD
185	GL
229	HB or X
249	GN or T
601	UF
603	XT
1435	V or individual letter

*   *   *

Tony Boyd
242 Squadron

11 Nov 41	Hurricane IIb	BG711	carrier to Malta
Jan 42	Hurricane IIb	BG745	scrambles, patrols
		BG765	
		O 741	
		'A'	
22 Jan 42	Hurricane IIb	'P'	one Ju88 probable
25 Jan	Hurricane IIb	K 711	jumped by 109s five Hurricanes lost

Feb 42	Hurricanes	GN-A, HA-E, LE-E, LE-W, LE-Y, UP-N, LE-O, LE-D, LE-P, UP-E	
11 Feb	Hurricane IIa	GL-K	Bf109F damaged; claim not sustained
23 Feb	Hurricane IIb	LE-P	Bf109F destroyed White 5, 10/JG53
Mar 42	Hurricanes	'J', 'K', 'A', HA-K	
5 Mar 42	Hurricane IIb	LE-P	two Ju88 damaged
9 Mar	Hurricane IIb	GL-K	combat, no claim
10 Mar	Hurricane IIb	HA-F	one-third Ju88 destroyed
13 Mar	Hurricane IIb	LE-D	combat, no claim
15 Mar	Hurricane IIb	HA-H	combat, no claim

185 Squadron

April 42	Hurricanes	HB-B, HA-S, HB-Z	
1 Apr	Hurricane IIa	GL-M	combat, no claim
5 Apr	Hurricane IIa	GL-L	combat, no claim
8 Apr	Hurricane IIa	HA-S	one Ju88 probable; one Ju88 damaged
8 Apr	Hurricane IIa	HA-S	one Ju88 probable
9 Apr	Hurricane II		marking unintelligible, claim one Ju88 damaged
10 Apr	Hurricane IIa	GL-C	combat, no claim
20 Apr	Hurricane IIa	GL-L	one Ju88 damaged
24 Apr	Hurricane IIa	GL-L	two Bf109 damaged
25 Apr	Hurricane IIc	2481	combat, cannon jam
28 Apr	Hurricane IIc	GL-A	combat, no claim
29 Apr	Hurricane IIc	GL-A	one Ju88 damaged
7 May 42	Hurricane IIa	GL-Y	combat, no claim
8 May	Hurricane IIa	GL-Y	one Ju88 destroyed
9 May	Spitfire Vc	3-J	three combats, no claims
10 May	Spitfire Vc	3-J	three sorties, one Ju88 probable, one Ju88 damaged
13 May	Spitfire Vc	3-C	two combats, no claims
14 May	Spitfire Vc	3-C	two combats, one Bf109 destroyed; killed second sortie by Macchi 202

Tony Boyd made a total of 88 flights from Malta, 70 of them

being scrambles or other operational flights. He was involved in 42 combats, and made 18 claims. He had 208 hours 45 minutes flying time when he arrived, and 273 hours twenty minutes when killed (log-book analysis).

*　　　*　　　*

Paul Brennan
249 Squadron

7 Mar 42	Spitfire Vb	AB344 (249 Sqn)	carrier to Malta
17 Mar	Spitfire Vb	GN-R	1 Bf109 destroyed
26 Mar	Spitfire Vb	GN-F	1 Ju88 damaged
20 Apr 42	Spitfire Vc	W-2	1 Bf109 destroyed
			1 Ju88 destroyed
21 Apr	Spitfire Vc	U-2	1 Ju88 probable
25 Apr	Spitfire Vc	E-2	1 Bf109 destroyed
			1 Ju88 destroyed
4 May 42	Spitfire Vc	A-2	1 Bf109 destroyed
10 May	Spitfire Vc	U-3	1 Ju87 destroyed
			1 Ju87 damaged
11 May	Spitfire Vc	U-3	2 Bf109 destroyed
18 May	Spitfire Vc	C-25 BR176	1 Re2001 destroyed
25 May	Spitfire Vc	C-25	1 Re2001 damaged
7 Jul 42	Spitfire Vc	37	1 Bf109 destroyed

(also this day flew BR562 X-R; maybe on this sortie)

　　　　　　　　　　　　　　　　1 Bf109 damaged

79 Squadron RAAF, Australia
13 Jun 43　Spitfire V EE954 'J'　　killed

Paul Brennan made a total of 47 flights from Malta, 42 of them as operational. He was involved in 22 combats and made 17 claims (log-book analysis).

*　　　*　　　*

Charles Crombie
89 Squadron

24 Sep 42	Beaufighter	5165	1 seaplane destroyed
26 Sep	Beaufighter	5165	1 He111 probable

13 Oct 42	Beaufighter	5161	1 He111 destroyed
17 Oct	Beaufighter	5161	1 Ju88 destroyed
7 Nov 42	Beaufighter	5165	1 Ju88 destroyed
26 Nov	Beaufighter	7777	1 Ju88 probable
17 Dec 42	Beaufighter	8158	2 Ju52 destroyed
26 Aug 45	Beaufighter	A19-198	crash; killed

*   *   *

Tim Goldsmith
185 Squadron

26 Mar 42	Hurricane II	GL-X	1 Ju87 damaged

126 Squadron

21 Apr 42	Spitfire Vc	964 XI	1 Bf109F destroyed
			1 Bf109F damaged
9 May 42	Spitfire Vc	BP 871	3 Bf109F destroyed
			1 Cant Z1007 destroyed
			1 Ju88 damaged
13 May	Spitfire Vc	BR 244	1 Mc202 damaged
14 May	Spitfire Vc	BR 290	1 Bf109F destroyed
			1 Ju88 destroyed
25 May	Spitfire Vc	'H'	1 Cant Z1007 damaged
			1 Reggiani damaged
30 May	Spitfire Vc	'C'	1 Reggiani destroyed
			BR20 shared
15 Jun 42	Spitfire Vc	'J'	1 Cant Z506 destroyed
			1 BR20 destroyed
			1 Mc200 destroyed
16 Jun	Spitfire Vc	'DI'	1 Bf109F destroyed
17 Jun	Spitfire Vc	—	1 Bf109F damaged
30 Jun	Spitfire Vc	—	1 BR20 destroyed

452 Squadron (Darwin, Australia)

15 Mar 43	Spitfire Vb	BR526	1 Betty destroyed
			1 Hamp destroyed
2 May 43	Spitfire Vb (destroyed)	BR526	1 Betty destroyed
7 Sep 43	——	——	1 Tony destroyed

*   *   *

E. T. Hiskens
249 Squadron

14 Aug 42	Spitfire V	T-L EP706	1 Bf109 damaged
12 Oct 42	Spitfire V	T-Z BR135	1 Ju88 destroyed 1 Bf109 probable 1 Ju88 probable (shared)
13 Oct	Spitfire V	T-Z	1 Mc202 destroyed
15 Oct	Spitfire V	T-M EP340	killed

*　　　　*　　　　*

W. Knox-William
1435 Squadron

11 Oct 42	Spitfire V	O EN978	1 Bf109 damaged
12 Oct	Spitfire V (destroyed) (baled out)	O EN978	1 Ju88 probable 1 Bf109 probable
13 Oct	Spitfire V	T EP714	1 Ju88 damaged
14 Oct	Spitfire V (destroyed)	Q AR470	killed

*　　　　*　　　　*

Eric Mahar
185 Squadron

1 Jul 42	Spitfire V		1 Mc202 damaged
6 Jul	Spitfire V		2 Bf109 damaged
7 Jul	Spitfire V	BR292	1 Bf109 destroyed
22 Jul	Spitfire V	BR109	shot up by 2 109s (fateful number!)
13 Oct 42	Spitfire V	EP696	1 Ju88 damaged
14 Oct	Spitfire V	EP722	1 Ju88 destroyed
15 Oct	Spitfire V	EP722	1 Mc202 destroyed
31 Oct	passenger in Liberator which crashed on landing at Gibraltar; hospitalised.		

217

Ken Mitchell
185 Squadron

14 Jul 42	Spitfire V	BR109	1 Ju88 damaged (shared)
23 Jul	Spitfire V	BR292	1 Mc202 destroyed
24 Jul	Spitfire V	BR292	5 Ju88 damaged
27 Aug	Spitfire V	EP553	1 Ju88 probable (shared)
31 Oct			passenger in Liberator which crashed at Gibraltar; hospitalised.

      *   *   *

Colin Parkinson
603 Squadron

9 Jun 42	Spitfire Vc	376	HMS *Eagle* to Malta
23 Jun	Spitfire Vc	X-N	1 Mc202 destroyed
1 Jul 42	Spitfire Vc	W-C	1 Re2001 destroyed
2 Jul	Spitfire Vc	X-S	1 Re2001 damaged
6 Jul	Spitfire Vc	UF-N	1 Bf109F damaged
9 Jul	Spitfire Vc	X-S	1 Bf109F destroyed 1 Ju88 finished
10 Jul	Spitfire Vc	X-S	1 Ju88 damaged
11 Jul	Spitfire Vc	X-S	destroyed on ground
12 Jul	Spitfire Vc	L-2	hit on ground; bomb
13 Jul	Spitfire Vb	GL-T	1 Bf109F probable
29 Jul	Spitfire Vc	N-4	saw captured Cant
30 Jul	Spitfire Vc	N-4	1 Bf109F destroyed
31 Jul	Spitfire Vb	A-1	1 Mc202 damaged

229 Squadron

13 Aug 42	Spitfire Vc	X-J	patrol over 'Ohio'
17 Aug	Spitfire Vb	A	HMS *Furious*—Malta
27 Aug	Spitfire Vc	X-N	sweep to Sicily— 1 Ju88 destroyed on ground 1 Bf109F destroyed
Sep 42	Spitfire Vb		(no claims for month)
		X-E	flown twice

		X-J	flown ten times
		X-Y	flown three times
11 Oct 42	Spitfire Vb	X-A	1 Ju88 probable head-on, night
12 Oct	Spitfire Vb	X-O	one Breda 205 dam machineguns
	Spitfire Vb	X-A	1 Bf109F destroyed
13 Oct	Spitfire Vb	X-V	1 Ju88 probable head-on
14 Oct	Spitfire Vb	X-V	1 Mc202 destroyed
16 Oct	Spitfire Vb	X-V	1 Ju88 damaged head-on
17 Oct	Spitfire Vb	X-V	1 Bf109F destroyed
25 Oct	Spitfire Vc	D-M	1 Mc202 damaged

Colin Parkinson made a total of 114 flights from Malta, 98 being operational. He was involved in 28 combats and made 20 claims. On arrival, he had a total of 449 hours 45 minutes flying time, and on departure this had increased to 570 hours and five minutes (log-book analysis).

*   *   *

Noel Pashen
603 Squadron

15 Jul 42	Spitfire Vb	EN972	HMS *Eagle* to Malta
30 Jul	Spitfire Vc	X-C	seat collapsed

229 Squadron

17 Aug 42	Spitfire Vb	X-V	oxygen/earphone
20 Aug	Spitfire Vb	X-V	oxygen; passed out
8 Sep 42	Spitfire Vb	X-V	seat collapsed
25 Sep	Spitfire Vb	X-E	1 Bf109 damaged
29 Sep	Spitfire Vc	W-S	6 hits bombing
2 Oct 42	Spitfire Vb	X-N	2x125-kg on Biscari
14 Oct	Spitfire Vb	X-V	harness loose
15 Oct	Spitfire Vb	X-V	1 Re2001 damaged
7 Dec 42	Spitfire Vb	BP910	Malta-Egypt

Other Spitfires flown were: X-L, B-3, A-2, UF-R, T-R, X-O, X-G, X-Y, X-U, X-A, X-F, X-M, X-S, BR293.

Noel Pashen flew 47 times, 26 of them being operational flights. He was involved in nine combats, and made two claims. He had 243 hours 15 minutes flying time when he arrived, and 284 hours and five minutes on departure (log-book).

Len Reid
185 Squadron

3 Jun 42	Spitfire	BR230	HMS *Eagle* to Malta; combat en route, 3 Spitfires lost
Jun 42	nine Spitfires flown on 12 scrambles and two tests: BR315, AB500, AB264, BR112, BR163, BR292, BR109, BR876, BR321; no claims; no squadron letters		
2 Jul 42	Spitfire	BR166	1 Bf109 damaged
7 Jul	Spitfire	AB264	scramble with Slim Yarra; Terry and Haggas lost, no claim by Reid
16 Jul	Spitfire	BR376	1 Ju88 damaged
23 Jul	Spitfire	BR315	engine cut, glided back past enemy
24 Jul	Spitfire	AB526	1 Ju88 destroyed
26 Jul	Hurricane	E408	night divebombing of Gela, Sicily
28 Jul	Hurricane	E408	night divebombing of Gela, Sicily

Other Spitfires flown on scrambles and patrols in July were:
BR166, AB264, BR109, BR368, EP137, BR376, BR387, BR379.

27 Aug 42	Spitfire	BR380	1 Ju88 destroyed

No other claims in August; other Spitfires flown were: BR387,
AB264, BR375, EP122, EP200, BR376, EP139, EP695, EP553.

September 1942: no claims, but Spitfires flown were: BR380,
EP471, EP186.

11 Oct 42	Spitfire	EP186	1 BF109 destroyed
12 Oct	Spitfire	EP186	1 Ju88 damaged
14 Oct	Spitfire	EP521	1 Bf109 damaged
		EP722	1 Bf109 destroyed 1 Ju88 damaged
16 Oct	Spitfire X	EP343	1 Ju88 probable
18 Oct	Spitfire X	EP343	1 Bf109 probable

Other Spitfire flown in October was: EP584.

31 Oct	Liberator to Gibraltar, passenger in crash, survived.

During his tour, Len Reid had flown 110 times, including

scrambles, air tests and patrols, ending October 1942 with 358 hours, almost exactly 100 more than on arrival from the aircraft carrier on 3 June. He had engaged the enemy on 31 occasions, though only claimed as in the list above (log-book).

*   *   *

J. G. Sanderson
249 Squadron

Date	Aircraft	Code	Claim
10 Oct 42	Spitfire V	T-N BR373	1 Bf109 damaged
12 Oct	Spitfire V	T-Z BP869	1 Bf109 damaged
		T-M EP340	1 Bf109 probable
15 Oct	Spitfire V	T-F EP448	1 Ju88 probable
22 Oct	Spitfire V	T-K EP199	1 Mc202 destroyed

*   *   *

Mervyn Shipard
89 Squadron

Date	Aircraft	Code	Claim
22 Jun 42	Beaufighter	X7702	LG 16 to Malta
7 Jul	Beaufighter	X7642	1 Ju88 destroyed
12 Jul	Beaufighter	X7642	written off; crash
19 Jul	Beaufighter	X7702	1 Ju88 destroyed
21 Jul	Beaufighter	X7695	1 Ju88 destroyed
11 Oct 42	Beaufighter	V8219	1 He111 probable
			1 He111 destroyed (6N+HH of 7/KG100)
12 Oct	Beaufighter	X7840	1 He111 destroyed (6N+AH of 5/KG100)
14 Oct	Beaufighter	V8219	1 He111 destroyed (6N+EH of 5/KG100)

Mervyn Shipard made a total of 109 flights from Malta, of which 37 were operational flights. He was involved in ten combats, and made seven claims, though there were another ten contacts lost through faulty equipment. He had 494 hours 55 minutes flying time when he arrived, and 627 hours 15 minutes on departure (log-book).

*   *   *

Donald H. Smith
126 Squadron

6 Jul 42	Spitfire Vc	BP873	1 Cant shared
8 Jul	Spitfire Vc	BR122	1 Bf109 destroyed
10 Jul	Spitfire Vc	BR366	1 Ju88 destroyed
			1 Bf109 probable
14 Jul	Spitfire Vc	BP992	1 Ju88 destroyed
			(wounded in ankle)

*   *   *

Alan Yates

6 Jul 42	Spitfire V	T-J	shot up, crashland
		BR246	Takali
11 Jul	Spitfire V	UF-S	1 Bf109 destroyed
		BR301	(shared, W/O Ramsay)
28 Jul	Spitfire V	T-T	1 Ju88 damaged
		BP975	
12 Oct	Spitfire V	T-K	1 Bf109 damaged
		EP199	1 Ju88 damaged
15 Oct	Spitfire V	T-S	.5 Ju88 probable
		EP488	

*   *   *

Jack 'Slim' Yarra
185 Squadron

25 Mar 42	Spitfire Vb	AB333	carrier to Malta
		(249 Sqn)	
1 May 42	Hurricane II	H-3	1 Ju88 probable
		(185 Sqn)	
12 May	Spitfire Vc	GL-K	1 Bf109 destroyed
15 May	Spitfire Vc	GL-K	2 Mc202 destroyed
			1 Bf109 damaged

222

18 May	Spitfire Vc	K-3	2 Bf109 destroyed
			(awarded DFM)
1 Jun 42	Spitfire Vc	GL-K	1 Bf109 destroyed
7 Jun	Spitfire Vc	GL-N	2 Re2001 damaged
16 Jun	Spitfire Vc	GL-J	1 Bf109 damaged
21 Jun	Spitfire Vc	GL-W	2 Bf109 destroyed
			1 Ju88 damaged
4 Jul 42	Spitfire Vc	GL-W	1 Ju88 destroyed
		BR387	1 Bf109 probable
			1 Bf109 damaged
7 Jul	Spitfire Vc	GL-W	2 Re2001 destroyed
11 Jul	Spitfire Vc	GL-N	1 Bf109 destroyed
		BR305	

453 Squadron RAAF (United Kingdom)
10 Dec 42   Spitfire Vb   FU-U   killed in action

Slim Yarra made a total of 101 flights from Malta, including 84 operational flights. He was involved in 54 combats, and made 20 claims. He had 227 hours flying time on arrival, and 299 on departure.

*   *   *

Victory claims for leading Luftwaffe fighter pilots have been the subject of discussion by Allied pilots and historians since 1945. Reactions range from disbelief to blind acceptance. Factors affecting a pilot gaining a high score are generally agreed to be individual ability; experience; a suitable aircraft with effective armament; opportunities for combat; and operations over or close to friendly airfields or territory.

Those factors applied to the RAF fighter pilots over Malta in 1942, and their scores, reflect the situation. If Beurling's 28 victories in four months are extrapolated over the remaining three years of the war, he conceivably could have amassed 100-120 victories—if the above factors persisted. Similarly, Paul Brennan, Tim Goldsmith and Slim Yarra may have achieved scores of 80 or 90 victories.

The same (theoretical) results may be arrived at for some of the Battle of Britain pilots who amassed respectable scores in two or three months with the above factors applying. Even allowing for over-claiming, some of the Luftwaffe victory seem to be possible.

*   *   *

Appendix 6

Claims by RAAF pilots, Malta 1942

Tony Boyd
242 and 185 Squadrons

22 Jan 42	1 Ju88 probable
23 Feb 42	2 Bf109 (doubtful)
5 Mar 42	1 Ju88 probable, 2 Ju88 damaged
10 Mar	1 Ju88 destroyed (shared)
1 Apr 42	1 Ju88, 1 Ju87 damaged
8 Apr	1 Ju88, 1 Ju88 probable, 1 Ju88 damaged
9 Apr	1 Ju88 damaged
20 Apr	1 Ju88 (shared), 3 Ju88 damaged
22 Apr	2 Bf109 damaged
29 Apr	1 Ju88 probable, 1 Ju88 damaged
8 May 42	1 Ju88
10 May	1 Ju88 probable, 1 Ju88 damaged
14 May	1 Bf109, then 1 KIA

*   *   *

Paul Brennan
249 Squadron

17 Mar 42	1 Bf109
26 Mar	1 Ju88 shared, 1 Ju88 damaged
21 Apr 42	1 Bf109, 1 Ju88, 1 Ju88 damaged
22 Apr	1 Ju88 damaged
25 Apr	1 Bf109, 1 Ju88
4 May 42	1 Bf109
10 May	1 Ju87, 1 Ju87 damaged
11 May	1 Bf109, 1 Bf109 damaged
18 May	1 Re2001
25 May	1 Re2001 damaged

7 Jul 42   1 Bf109, 1 Bf109 damaged, 1 Ju88 damaged

             *   *   *

John Bisley
126 Squadron
5 Apr 42   1 Ju88, 1 Ju87
9 May 42   1 Mc202
18 May   1 Bf109
11 Jun 42   1 Bf109, 1 Bf109 probable
6 Jul 42   1 S84 (shared)

             *   *   *

G. M. Briggs
601 Squadron
22 Apr 42   1 Ju88 (shared)
9 May 42   1 Bf109
10 May   1 KIA

             *   *   *

C. L. Baxter
249 and 1435 Squadrons
23 Jun 42   1 Re2001 damaged
24 Jul 42   1 Bf109 damaged

             *   *   *

Tim Goldsmith
185 and 126 Squadrons
26 Mar 42   1 Ju87 damaged
21 Apr 42   1 Bf109, 1 Bf109 damaged
9 May 42   1 Z1007, 1 Ju88 damaged
10 May   2 Bf109
13 May   1 Mc202 damaged
14 May   1 Bf109, 1 Ju88
25 May   1 Z1007, 1 Re2001 damaged
30 May   1 Re2001, 1 BR20 (shared)
15 Jun 42   1 Z506B, 1 Mc200, 1 BR20

16 Jun   1 Bf109
27 Jun   1 Bf109 damaged

          *   *   *

E. T. Hiskens
229 and 249 Squadrons
14 Aug 42 1 Bf109 damaged
12 Oct 42 1 Ju88, 1 Bf109 probable, 1 Ju88 probable (shared)
13 Oct   1 Mc202
15 Oct   1 KIA

          *   *   *

W. R. Irwin
603 and 229 Squadrons
15 May 42 1 Bf109 probable
26 Jun 42 1 Bf109 damaged
6 Jul 42 1 Ju88 (shared), 1 Bf109 damaged
13 Jul   1 Ju88
20 Jul   1 Bf109 probable, 1 Bf109 damaged
5 Aug 42 1 Re2001 probable
17 Sep 42 1 Bf109 probable, 1 Mc202 probable, 1 Mc202
            damaged

          *   *   *

W. B. Knox-William
1435 Squadron
11 Oct 42 1 Bf109 damaged
12 Oct   1 Bf109 probable, 1 Ju88 damaged (shared), shot
            down, baled out, rescued
13 Oct   1 Ju88 damaged
14 Oct   1 KIA

          *   *   *

H. C. Lester
605 Squadron
12 Feb 42 1 Bf109 damaged

1   Mar 42   1 Bf109
18 Mar   shot down, wounded

*   *   *

Eric Mahar
185 Squadron
1   Jul 42   1 Mc202 damaged
6   Jul   2 Bf109 damaged
7   Jul   1 Bf109
13 Oct 42   1 Ju88 damaged
14 Oct   1 Ju88
15 Oct   1 Mc202

*   *   *

Jack Mayall
126 Squadron
19 Jan 42   1 Ju88 damaged (shared)
26 Feb 42   shot down, killed, by Hptmn Krahl of II/JG3

*   *   *

Ken Mitchell
185 Squadron
14 Jul 42   1 Ju88 damaged (shared)
23 Jul   1 Mc202 damaged
27 Aug 42   1 Ju88 probable (shared)

*   *   *

Colin Parkinson
603 and 229 Squadrons
23 Jun 42   1 Mc202 (shared)
1   Jul 42   1 Re2001
2   Jul   1 Re2001 damaged
6   Jul   1 Bf109 damaged
7   Jul   1 Ju88 damaged
9   Jul   1 Bf109
10 Jul   1 Mc202 damaged

227

13 Jul	1 Bf109 probable
14 Jul	1 Bf109
27 Jul	1 Bf109 plus 1 Ju88 on ground, Sicily
30 Jul	1 Bf109
31 Aug	1 Mc202 damaged
11 Oct 42	1 Ju88 probable
12 Oct	1 Bf109, Ju88 probable (shared), 1 Br20 damaged
13 Oct	1 Bf109 probable
14 Oct	1 Mc202
16 Oct	1 Ju88 damaged
17 Oct	1 Bf109
25 Oct	1 Mc202 damaged

*　　　　　*　　　　　*

Jack Pauley
229 Squadron

1 Apr 42	1 Ju87 probable, 1 Ju87 damaged
2 Apr	1 Ju88 damaged (shared)
9 Apr	shot down by Oblt Belser or Ltn Neuhoff JG53, parachuted, picked up by ASR launch, injured

*　　　　　*　　　　　*

Len Reid
185 Squadron

24 Jul 42	1 Ju88
27 Aug 42	1 Ju88 over Sicily
11 Oct 42	1 Bf109
12 Oct	1 Bf109 damaged
14 Oct	1 Bf109, 1 Bf109 damaged, 1 Ju88 damaged
15 Oct	1 Ju88 probable
16 Oct	1 Ju88 probable
17 Oct	1 Bf109 probable

*　　　　　*　　　　　*

R. H. Richardson
126 Squadron

| 7 Jul 42 | 1 Ju88 damaged |

228

9 Sep	1 Ju88 damaged
15 Sep	1 Bf109 damaged
17 Sep	1 Bf109 damaged

* * *

J. G. Sanderson
249 Squadron

10 Oct 42	1 Bf109 damaged
12 Oct	2 Bf109 damaged
15 Oct	1 Ju88 probable
22 Oct	1 Mc202

* * *

Donald H. Smith
126 Squadron

6 Jul 42	1 S84 (shared)
8 Jul	1 Bf109
10 Jul	1 Ju88, 1 Bf109 damaged
13 Jul	1 Ju88, 1 Bf109 damaged
14 Jul	1 Ju88, shot in ankle, crash-landed on Malta

* * *

Gordon Tweedale
242 and 185 Squadrons

9 Mar 42	1 Ju88 damaged
10 Mar	1 Ju88
2 Apr 42	1 Ju88 probable
14 Apr	1 Bf109 damaged
20 Apr	2 Ju88
21 Apr	1 Ju88
23 Apr	1 Ju87
25 Apr	1 Bf109
7 May 42	1 Bf109
8 May	1 Ju88, 1 Bf109, 1 Bf109 probable
9 May	shot down, KIA

* * *

Alan Yates
249 Squadron
10 Jul 42   1 Bf109 damaged
11 Jul   1 Bf109 (shared)
28 Jul   1 Ju88 damaged
12 Oct 42   1 Ju88 damaged, 1 Bf109 damaged
15 Oct   1 Ju88 probable (shared)

        *   *   *

Jack 'Slim' Yarra
185 Squadron
1   May 42   1 Ju88 probable, night
12 May   1 Bf109
15 May   2 Mc202, 1 Bf109 damaged
18 May   1 Bf109, 1 Bf109 damaged
1   Jun 42   1 Bf109
7   Jun   2 Re2001 damaged
16 Jun   1 Bf109
21 Jun   2 Bf109, 1 Ju88 damaged
5   Jul 42   1 Ju88, 1 Bf109 probable, 1 Bf109 damaged
7   Jul   2 Re2001
11 Jul   1 Bf109

        *   *   *

Beaufighter pilots
Charles Crombie
89 Squadron nightfighters
24 Sep 42   1 3-engine seaplane
26 Sep   1 He111 probable
13 Oct 42   1 Ju88 on ground, Sicily
8   Nov 42   1 Ju88
26 Nov   1 Ju88 probable
27 Nov   1 Ju88
17 Dec 42   2 Ju52

        *   *   *

Mervyn Shipard
89 Squadron

```
7  Jul 42    1 Ju88
19 Jul       1 Ju88
21 Jul       1 Ju88
11 Oct 42    1 He111 of 7/KG100, 1 He111 probable
12 Oct       1 He11 of 7/KG100
14 Oct       1 He111 of 7/KG100
```

*   *   *

```
John Ross
89 Squadron
1  Jul 42    1 Ju88 probable
26 Aug 42    1 Do18 Catania, Sicily
```

*   *   *

```
R. F. Hammond
248 Squadron dayfighters
11 Aug 42    1 S79, 1 S79 damaged on ground, Sardinia
15 Aug       1 S79, 1 Ju88 damaged
21 Aug       1 P32, 1 Ju88 probable
1  Dec 42    1 KIA
```

*   *   *

```
P. J. O. Mueller
248 Squadron
11 Aug 42    1 S79, 3 S79 damaged on ground, Sardinia
21 Aug       1 Ju52 (shared)
1  Dec 42    1 KIA
```

*   *   *

RAAF pilots in the various RAF Squadrons claimed a total of 102 enemy destroyed, 34 probably destroyed and 77 damaged. Of these, the eight highest-scoring pilots claimed 69-13-29. If the two leading nightfighter scores are deleted, it will be seen that the six leading dayfighter pilots claimed 58-10-29, over half the total claimed by those 27 pilots who did claim-out of the

47 RAAF pilots who are known to have flown from Malta in 1942.

Almost all the leading dayfighter pilots were Sergeants, products of the EAS, who arrived on Malta with a total of about 200 hours flying time.

*   *   *

Acknowledgements

The following people assisted by providing material, putting up with my questions, or by contacting others likely to help, and this opportunity is taken to thank them all.

Ian Affleck	Australian War Memorial
Dorothy (Boyd) Ahern	Toowoomba
John Bisley	Sydney
Mr PA Boyd	Labrador, Queensland
Erhard Braune	West Germany; JG53
Real Brennan	Brisbane
Carolyn Brennan	Canberra
Brian Butler	Australian War Memorial
Fred Clewley	Melbourne
Steve Corvini	Australian War Memorial
Helen Creagh	Australian War Memorial
Betty Crombie (Mrs)	Brisbane
Brian Cull	aviation historian, Suffolk, UK
Mr & Mrs Darragh	Brisbane
T Dunn	Warwickshire, UK
Dave Ferraby	Yorkshire, UK
Richard Fisher	RAAF Historical Office, Canberra
Bill Fogarty	Australian War Memorial
Ron Gilchrist	Australian War Memorial
Kev Ginnane	Canberra
Doris Goldsmith (Mrs)	Cooma
Ken Gray	Dorset, UK
Ted Hall	RAAF 452 Squadron, Darwin; Junee, NSW
Mr LG Head	Bucks, UK; ASR unit, HS127, Malta
Andrew Jack	Australian War Memorial

Helen Johnston	Australian War Memorial
Dr Hugh Kennare AM	RAAF 79 Squadron; Adelaide SA
W Cdr Laddie Lucas	249 Squadron Malta; London UK
Eric Mahar	Bendigo, Vic
Keith Meggs	aviation historian, Melbourne
Ken Merrick	aviation historian, Adelaide, SA
Ken Mitchell	Brisbane
Paddy O'Brien	Melbourne
GC Pallisser	Melbourne
Colin Parkinson	Sydney
Ruth Pashen	Brisbane
Robert K Piper	RAAF Historical Office, Canberra
Norman Rankin	Sydney
GpCapt Alan Rawlinson	Adelaide; first CO RAAF 79 Squadron
Jan Reeves	Canberra
Len Reid	Cranbourne, Vic
Mrs June (Ulcoq) Robertson	Burleigh Heads, Qld
Frank Robins	aviation historian, Melbourne
John Ross	Sydney
Mervyn Shipard	Sydney
Graham Stoner	Brisbane
John Trouten	Australian War Memorial
Hugh Tweedale	Brisbane, Queensland
RH Ware	Melbourne
John Yarra	Canberra
Jim Yarra	Sydney

Much of the material on Tim Goldsmith came from his diaries and log-book, and Mrs Doris Goldsmith graciously allowed permission to quote from them; the diary entries in the text are identified as such.

Real Brennan also forwarded copies of the relevant pages of Paul Brennan's log-book, and Jim Yarra loaned me the log-book, diary and photo albums compiled by his brother Jack, known as Slim in RAAF service, with permission to quote from them as necessary.

Hugh Tweedale supplied letters, poems and photographs from Gordon Tweedale. Despite official letters at the time promising to forward Gordon Tweedale's belongings, nothing was received, and in fact the family received nothing from the date of his departure from the UK for Malta. Any such items held by anyone will be gratefully received by the family.

Shipping strike statistics and relevant detail of the actions over Malta were also extracted from RAF Coastal Command Summary No. 1, in the Australian War Memorial.

A special mention must be made of the normally unsung workers of the Australian War Memorial Research Centre, who tirelessly and with good humour go to and from the stacks, climbing ladders, carrying weighty tomes of bound reports back and forth, answering questions and assisting the hordes of visitors and researchers: my thanks to Tony Rudnicki, Ian Collier and Joyce Bradley.

*   *   *

Permission to quote from the publications below is gratefully acknowledged.

Thorsons Publishing Group Limited for *One Man's Window* by Denis Barnham (William Kimber, 1956), and for *Tattered Battlements* by Tim Johnston (William Kimber, 1985).

Chris Shores, Brian Cull and Nicola Malizia, co-authors of *Malta: The Hurricane Years* (Grub Street, London, 1987) and *Malta: The Spitfire Years* (Grub Street, London), kindly gave permission to quote from, and use material included in, both the above excellent works on the Malta campaigns. In particular, Brian Cull replied to my many questions and provided the details of Luftwaffe and Regia Aeronautica identifications in the combats in this book; my personal thanks.

Battle of Britain Prints International Ltd for 'After The Battle', No. 10, 1975.

Ernst Obermaier for material from his books on the Knight's Cross holders of the Luftwaffe fighter and dive bomber units (Verlag Dieter Hoffman, Mainz).

Notes

First Storm
1 'After the Battle' No. 10, 1975.
2 Letter to sister Dorothy, 25/1/41.
3 *Malta: the Hurricane Years*, Shores, Cull, Malizia.
4 *Ibid.*

Approaching Thunder
1 RAAF Historical Section 'Malta File'.
2 AP Goldsmith combat report via B Cull.
3 AP Goldsmith, expanded diary.

The Fury
1 Obermaier.
2 'Tattered Battlements'.
3 Obermaier.
4 'Tattered Battlements'.
5 Obermaier.
6 'Spitfires Over Malta'.
7 *Ibid.*
8 *Ibid.*
9 RAAF Historical Section 'Malta File':

The Tempest
1 Barnham.
2 Brennan.
3 Goldsmith.
4 Eric Mahar, letter to author 18/2/88.
5 Mahar, *ibid.*
6 Goldsmith.
7 Ken Mitchell, interview by author 14/5/88.
8 Mahar, *ibid.*

9 Mahar, *ibid.*
10 Maher, *ibid.*
11 Brennan.
12 Via Brian Cull.
13 Brennan.
14 Brennan.
15 Dave Ferraby, diary.
16 Barnham.
17 Brennan.
18 Brennan.
19 Brennan.
20 Yarra; Sydney *Daily Mirror*, 27/8/42, via Brian Cull.
21 Brennan.
22 AWM 54, file 423/4/103.
23 Colin Parkinson, diary.

Whirlwind
1 Fort Leavenworth (USA) C&GSC File N-13600.
1A Letter Reid-author 5 December 1988.
2 Ken Mitchell, interview 14/5/88.
3 *Ibid.*
4 Colin Parkinson, diary.
5 *Ibid.*
6 Obermaier.
7 Via Brian Cull.
8 Obermaier.
9 Via Brian Cull.
10 Colin Parkinson, diary.
11 *Ibid.*

The Storm Continues
1 Parkinson, diary.
2 *Ibid.*
3 *Ibid.*
4 *Ibid.*
5 DH Smith log-book, via Brian Cull.
6 Parkinson, diary.
7 Letter to author, 25/4/88.
8 *Spitfires Over Malta*, p. 92.
9 *Ibid.*

10 *Ibid.*
11 Brennan, log-book.
12 Tape interview May 1988.
13 Parkinson, diary.
14 *Ibid.*
15 DH Smith, log-book, via Brian Cull.
16 Parkinson, diary.
17 *Ibid.*
18 DH Smith, log-book, via Brian Cull.
19 Parkinson, diary.
20 DH Smith, log-book, via Brian Cull.
21 Pashen, diary and log-book.
22 Parkinson, diary.
23 Pashen, diary.
24 Mahar interview, 24/4/88.
25 Parkinson, diary.
26 Via Brian Cull.
27 Shipard, interview 26/3/88.
28 Parkinson, diary.
29 Reid, log-book.
30 Via Brian Cull.
31 Interview 26/3/88.
32 Len Reid.
33 Pashen, diary.
34 Len Reid.
35 Parkinson, diary and combat report.
36 Pashen, diary.
37 Parkinson, diary and combat report.

The Critical Week
1 Noel Pashen, diary.
2 Parkinson, diary.
3 229 Squadron combat report, via Brian Cull.
4 Letter, Ken Gray-author May 1988.
5 Pashen, diary.
6 Paddy O'Brien, diary.
7 Pashen, diary.
8 Parkinson, diary.
9 O'Brien, diary.
10 Pashen, diary.

11 Parkinson, diary.
12 Pashen, diary.
13 248 Squadron combat report, via Brian Cull.
14 Parkinson, diary.
15 Pashen, diary.
16 Interview, Shipard-author 25 March 1988.
17 John Ross, log-book.
18 Interview, Mitchell 15 May 1988.
19 Interview, Reid June 1988.
20 Parkinison, diary.
21 Mitchell, 15 May 1988.
22 Pashen, diary.

The Lull
1 Parkinson, diary.
2 Pashen, diary.
3 Parkinson, diary.
4 Reid, interview June 1988.
5 Pashen, diary.
6 *Ibid.*
7 Pashen, log-book and diary.
8 Via Brian Cull
9 Parkinson, diary.
10 Ross, log-book.
11 Oxby, tape August 1988.
12 Pashen, diary.

Last Lightnings
1 Parkinson, diary.
2 Pashen, diary.
3 Parkinson, diary.
4 *Ibid.*
5 *Ibid.*
6 *Ibid.*
7 Pashen, diary/log-book.
8 Mitchell, interview 15/5/88.
9 Parkinson, diary.
10 Gray, letter May 1988.
11 *Ibid.*
12 Parkinson, diary.

13 Gray.
14 Oxby, tape August 1988.
15 Gray.
16 Parkinson, diary.
17 Pashen, diary/log-book.
18 *Ibid.*
19 Reid, log-book.
20 Parkinson, diary/log-book.
21 *Ibid.*
22 Gray, letter/log-book.
23 Shipard, 26 March 1988.
24 Oxby.
25 Mahar, interview 24 April 1988.
26 Ross, letter 1988.
27 Reid, log-book.
28 Diaries, Parkinson and O'Brien.
29 Via Mrs Betty Crombie 1988.
30 Pashen, diary/log-book.
31 Mitchell.
32 Pashen, diary.
33 *Ibid.*
34 Parkinson, diary.
35 Reid, Mahar, Clewley, 24 April 1988.
36 Crombie, log-book.
37 Gray.
38 Pashen.
39 Parkinson.
40 *Ibid.*, log-book.
41 Gray.
42 *Ibid.*

Australia

Information on the squadrons came from combat reports, squadron record books and personal log-books of the participants. Japanese information came from interrogation reports at the Australian War Memorial (AWM 55 collection).

1 AWM 54 ATIS Interrogation Report (IR) 393.
2 *Ibid.*
3 *Ibid.*

4 ATIS IR 697.
5 ATIS IR 393.
6 ATIS IR 672.
7 ATIS IR 697.
8 ATIS IR 393 and 697.
9 ATIS IR393.
10 *Ibid.*
11 *Ibid.*

Index